WAYNESBURG COLLEGE LIBRARY
WAYNESBURG, PA.

D0845063

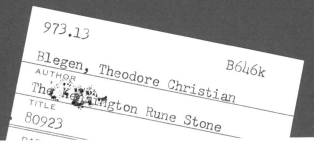

973.13

Blegen, Theodore Christian   B646k
AUTHOR
The Kensington Rune Stone
TITLE
80923

973.13   B646k
Blegen, Theodore Christian
The Kensington Rune Stone
80923
SEP 30 '88

Publications of the

Minnesota Historical Society

EDITOR AND DIRECTOR
Russell W. Fridley

MANAGING EDITOR
June Drenning Holmquist

the
Kensington Rune Stone
new Light on
an Old Riddle

By THEODORE C. BLEGEN

with a bibliography by MICHAEL BROOK

MINNESOTA HISTORICAL SOCIETY   St. Paul   1968

COPYRIGHT 1968 © by the MINNESOTA HISTORICAL SOCIETY
Library of Congress Catalog Card Number: 68-66739

a Word of thanks

My INDEBTEDNESS to individuals and institutions reaches out to many states and to Canada, Sweden, Denmark, Norway, Finland, and France. It is recorded throughout this book in the numerous citations of sources I have been privileged to use, but I should like here to extend a heartfelt thank-you, with my deep appreciation, to all the persons as well as libraries and other organizations that have come to my aid.

I must say a special word of thanks to the Louis W. and Maud Hill Family Foundation of St. Paul, which has provided funds for a research fellowship since 1963. I wish similarly to thank the Minnesota Historical Society for administering these funds, making available an office which I have used as my headquarters, and giving me through its staff — in the administrative, publications, library, newspaper, museum, manuscripts, and picture divisions and departments — most generous and efficient assistance at every stage of my work.

I need scarcely add that none of the individuals and institutions which have contributed to the progress of my research and writing is responsible in any way for my method, findings, and conclusions. They are solely my own. Though my book is published under the imprint of the Minnesota Historical Society, I do not write as its spokesman; the responsibility is entirely mine; and I have had complete freedom to find my own way in my search for the truth about the much disputed Kensington stone.

THEODORE C. BLEGEN

80923

Contents

Illustrations

Rasmus B. Anderson   Knut O. Hoegh
Gisle Bothne   Hjalmar R. Holand
Olaus J. Breda   Johan A. Holvik
George O. Curme   Julius E. Olson
George T. Flom   Frederick Jackson Turner
Andrew A. Fossum   Andrew A. Veblen
Ole E. Hagen   Warren Upham
Newton H. Winchell

SKETCHES FROM NEWTON H. WINCHELL'S FIELD BOOK

the kensington rune stone

Introduction

FEW QUESTIONS IN AMERICAN HISTORY have stirred so much curiosity or provoked such extended discussions as that of the authenticity of the runic inscription on a stone found near Kensington, Minnesota, in 1898.

The debates have centered on two major matters. One has to do with the circumstances of the discovery. The other relates to the origin, character, and dating of the runic symbols carved on two surfaces of the stone. The larger issue has been whether the symbols are a nineteenth-century hoax or a genuine record from the fourteenth century. The inscription bears the date 1362. A third aspect of the case has to do with a number of alleged "collateral finds," which defenders of the stone have used in support of the genuineness of the inscription.

Runologists of Sweden, Denmark, and Norway have declared the Kensington inscription to be a product of the nineteenth century — a hoax, a fraud, or, as Professor George T. Flom described it in 1910, a "modern inscription." The testimony of the runologists, based upon studies of the symbols and words carved in the stone, cannot be set aside by lay opinion. On the other hand, no one has confessed the hoax, if such it was — or if anyone wrote such a confession, it has not come to light. Nor have the discovery and the early history of the controversy received as critical a scrutiny as they should have long ago.

Despite the views of the runologists, many lay people refuse to accept a negative judgment. Questions are still raised about the circumstances of the stone's discovery and about additional finds which are purported to date from the fourteenth century. It is to

3

be hoped that a fresh study of the early years of discussion and investigation will disentangle some of the snarls and clarify some of the problems that have enveloped the Kensington story.

Such is the purpose of this volume. It is not a history of the entire controversy. Nor is it a study of the artifacts alleged to be related to the Kensington stone. Nor yet is it a linguistic essay. It is what I have indicated — an examination of various circumstances surrounding the discovery of the Kensington rune stone and the early history of the ensuing discussions and controversy. The story is restricted mainly to the interval from 1898 to 1915, with some exploration of episodes and persons in the period before 1898 and some consideration of happenings after 1915.

The collateral finds (halberds, axes, fire steels, "mooring stones," etc.) are being subjected to study by a competent Swedish archaeologist, Mrs. Birgitta L. Linderoth Wallace, who is doing her research under the auspices of the Carnegie Museum of Pittsburgh. The runological analyses have been handled by capable Scandinavian scholars, and their results have been published. (See Bibliography, p. 186–205.) Mrs. Wallace and I are working independently on related aspects of the same problem, but her research, I suspect, will have a wider range than appraisal of the Kensington stone.

My interest in the Kensington problem goes back many years. As long ago as the 1920s, I ventured to publish some corrections of misstatements by Hjalmar Rued Holand, outstanding champion of the claim for its authenticity.[1] These related to early Scandinavian settlement in Douglas County, Minnesota, where the Kensington stone was found. I wrote a brief article, and Holand promptly replied to it. I also took some interest in the lost La Vérendrye stone, which had been sent off to France in the eighteenth century, and I did what I could in the 1920s and 1930s to advance a search for this missing stone, which some people be-

---

[1] See Holand, "The Kensington Stone: Is It the Oldest Native Document of American History?" in *Wisconsin Magazine of History*, 3:174 (December, 1919); Blegen, "The Kensington Rune Stone Discussion and Early Settlement in Western Minnesota," in *Minnesota History*, 6:370–374 (December, 1925); Holand, "The Kensington Rune Stone: A Reply to Criticism," in *Minnesota History*, 7:65 (March, 1926).

lieve to have been runic. A summary of the story of the La Véren-drye stone is presented in the appendix.

My attention was again called to the Kensington riddle in the late 1950s by Professor Erik Wahlgren's enlightening and provoca-tive book entitled *The Kensington Stone: A Mystery Solved.*[2] The mystery did not seem to me to be wholly dissipated, and I therefore began a hunt for additional information. Other problems claimed most of my time, and after my retirement as dean of the Graduate School of the University of Minnesota in 1960, I at once began work on the preparation of *Minnesota: A History of the State,* which appeared in 1963. In that book I spoke of the Kensington stone as a "fascinating problem and a curiosity." The weight of scholarly authority, I said, was "against acceptance of it as an au-thentic record of a Scandinavian expedition into the American interior in the fourteenth century," and yet I thought that no one had proved it a hoax — nor had anyone proved its genuineness.

In this spirit I began to restudy the discovery of the Kensington stone and the early investigations and controversy. I did not set out to prove the inscription either genuine or a hoax. Naturally I entertained some hope that my research might yield new informa-tion pertinent to a conclusion, but my concern was for the truth only, whether it be for or against the authenticity of the inscrip-tion. It was not my intention to win readers over to one side or another. As my studies proceeded I began to realize that the Ken-sington stone was highly interesting as a problem in historical methodology.

Some runologists suggest that scholarship may never solve the problem of the precise genesis of the inscription. This is a possi-bility, for if the inscription is a hoax, it is unlikely that after seven or more decades an authenticated confession will turn up. On the other hand, this book is based in part on a few new sources modi-fying in certain ways the traditional story of the discovery.

[2] Wahlgren's book was published by the University of Wisconsin Press, Madison, in 1958. He concluded (p. 181) that the "planting of the Minnesota stone was a clever and understandable hoax." A summary of reviews and comments on Wahlgren's book is presented by Lawrence D. Steefel in *Min-nesota Archaeologist,* 27:97–115 (1965).

chapter 1

Cycles of Controversy

THE KENSINGTON STONE WAS FOUND IN MINNESOTA very probably in early November, 1898, by Olof Ohman, a forty-four-year-old Swedish-American farmer who was grubbing trees on a knoll above a surrounding area of swampy ground.[1] With him was his son Edward, a boy of ten. The farm was in Douglas County about three miles northeast of Kensington. This village in turn is a little more than twenty-three miles southwest of Alexandria, the county seat.

The stone was clasped by the roots of an aspen or poplar tree which stood over it. Ohman, who had pulled the tree over with a winch, did not at first notice that there were inscriptions on the stone. His son apparently poked at it with a stick or brushed it with his cap and then saw that some characters had been cut into one side, whereupon he asked his father to come and look. Disengaged from the roots, the stone proved to have a lengthier inscription on its downward face than on the narrow edge where incisions were first observed. In a recorded interview in 1949, Edward Ohman said that he sat on the stone after his father had "flopped" it up with his maddock or hoe. He did not mention a stick, but stated, "I started to dig in the dirt with my hands as kids usually do." He called his father's attention to the markings on the stone. Asked whether he had scraped "the dirt out of the scratches," he replied, "Well, we did the best we could." Edward said that after school he had brought lunch to his father and then helped him until he quit work. His memory placed the discovery

---

[1] Undoubtedly the correct original spelling of Ohman's name carried an umlaut on the first letter, but he himself dropped it, and in most writings about the Kensington stone the umlaut is omitted.

of the inscriptions late in the day, although other sources say that it was found near lunchtime.[2] The stone was an irregular rectangular slab of graywacke weighing about 202 pounds. About 2½ feet high, 3 to 6 inches thick, and 15 inches wide, it was shaped somewhat like a tombstone with the inscriptions placed on the part which presumably had been intended to stand above ground. According to the finder, it seems to have been embedded fairly near the surface in a slanting position with one end nearly protruding from the ground.[3]

Much has been written about the presumed age of the tree under which the stone was found, and only a few items need be noted here. No cross section of the tree was cut; many varying estimates of its age have been made through later years; and studies have been conducted on cross sections of trees thought to resemble the original. The resultant guesses — they have been nothing but guesses — have run from ten or fewer years to sixty-nine or seventy

[2] See chapter 2, below; Ohman to Warren Upham, December 9, 1909, in Minnesota Historical Society Archives (hereafter abbreviated MHS Archives) and Appendix 9, below; Hjalmar R. Holand, *Westward from Vinland: An Account of Norse Discoveries and Explorations in America, 982–1362*, chapter 11 (New York, 1940). Olaus Olson, in *Svenska Amerikanska Posten* (Minneapolis), May 23, 1899, p. 7 (Appendix 5, below), said that Edward Ohman poked at the inscribed characters with a stick; Holand, *The Kensington Stone: A Study in Pre-Columbian American History*, 1 (Ephraim, Wis., 1932) wrote that the boy dusted the stone with his cap. Wahlgren, *Kensington Stone*, 31, also had Edward using a cap. See also Edward Ohman, typewritten transcript of a tape-recorded interview conducted by Lucile M. Kane and others, December 28, 1949, in MHS. Unless otherwise indicated newspapers cited throughout this book are in the MHS.

[3] The irregularity of the stone accounts for some variations in measurements. The MHS museum submitted a sketch to the writer listing the maximum dimensions as 29½ by 14⅞ by 5½ inches. Birgitta L. Wallace gave them as 29½ by 15½ by 6 inches; see sketch and Mrs. Wallace to Blegen, June 3, 1968, in Kensington file, Theodore C. Blegen Papers, MHS. The weight, now established at about 202 pounds, was earlier thought to be 230 pounds; see William P. Holman to Blegen, June 27, 1968, Blegen Papers; MHS Museum Committee, *The Kensington Rune Stone: Preliminary Report*, 1 (St. Paul, 1910). This report was reprinted with the addition of only a brief "Note" in *Minnesota Historical Collections*, 15:221–286 (St. Paul, 1915), where it has been cited hereafter. See also Wahlgren, *Kensington Stone*, 3, 60, 191n. On the stone's position, see sketches in Newton H. Winchell Field Book, Winchell Papers, MHS, reproduced in Appendix 8, below, and Ohman to Upham, December 9, 1909, in Appendix 9.

or more. More than a decade after the discovery various affidavits were taken. These were signed by the finders, by a neighbor who saw the tree, and by others who had seen the root stump. They asserted that the tree was from eight to ten inches in diameter at its base. The discoverer of the stone told one investigator in 1910 that the tree "looked stunted."[4]

Later critics of the inscription as fraudulent have suggested that the stone was inserted under a growing tree by a hoaxer or hoaxers. One such writer believed the carving to have been done in the 1890s, even as late as 1898, the year of the discovery.[5] If such a hypothesis is entertained and if one notes that the runes are regarded by runologists as modern, the age of the tree would seem to have little or no relevance. Finding inscribed material under trees was no new thing in America when the Kensington stone was unearthed. For instance, in Wisconsin on September 14, 1845, some inscribed metallic plates purporting to be ancient were dug up from the roots of an "oak tree a foot in diameter." Four witnesses were present. The plates were the Voree tablets of James J. Strang, founder of the nineteenth-century "Kingdom of St. James," and the discovery of the tablets was a result, according to Strang, of divine revelations. In recounting this chapter in American religious history, the historian of the Kingdom of St. James does not precisely deny Strang's claim of divine guidance in the finding and translating of the tablets, but he says that the plates of metal had a "very material objective reality." If Strang fabricated and "planted" them, his career as a prophet was an "impudent imposture."[6] The present writer cannot escape the impression that the event was an imposture designed to convince Strang's followers that the plates were not of recent origin. With this and similar instances in mind, one wonders why the very presence of a tree over the Kensington stone has not stirred grave doubts in the minds of commentators instead of leading them to point to the tree

[4] The affidavits are reproduced in Appendix 7, below. See also chapter 6, note 3, below; the quotation is from George T. Flom, "The Kensington Rune Stone: A Modern Inscription from Douglas County, Minnesota," in Illinois State Historical Society, *Transactions*, 1910, p. 105 (Springfield, 1912).

[5] Wahlgren, *Kensington Stone*, 181.

[6] Milo M. Quaife, *The Kingdom of Saint James: A Narrative of the Mormons*, chapter 2 (New Haven, 1930).

as an argument to bolster the stone's authenticity. If the tree and its entwining roots were a planned obfuscation, they have surely proved successful in puzzling and confusing many observers through the years — though they have not influenced runologists. The Kensington slab, after its removal from the roots, was cleaned — brushed and washed. A Norwegian neighbor, Nils Flaten, was asked to look at it. He did so, but did not record his impressions until 1909, when he signed an affidavit. Ohman, he then said, showed him a tree about eight to ten inches in diameter under which the stone had been buried. The stone, "inscribed with ancient characters," was removed to a place near Ohman's house. After some time (the finder said "a few days," but the exact interval is not known), the slab was taken to Kensington and there placed in either a bank or a store — more likely a bank.[7]

No contemporary evidence relating to the Kensington stone is known from the time of its discovery in November, 1898, until January 1, 1899. No letter or diary record of it, written within a few days or weeks after the discovery, has come to light. The stone was unearthed by laymen, not archaeologists. The details of the find were not at the time recorded in a scholar's notebook. No report was sent to any newspaper in November or December, 1898, as far as is known, or to the Minnesota Historical Society. No one seems to have photographed the stone at the site where it was found or in the Ohman yard or at the bank or store in Kensington. The first known letter written about the stone bears the date January 1, 1899, and the first known mention of it in print is dated January 14, 1899.[8]

No one has offered a satisfactory explanation of this contemporary silence of two months, which is difficult to understand on any hypothesis. It may suggest the unfamiliarity of lay persons with channels of appropriate communication regarding an archaeologi-

[7] See Ohman and Flaten affidavits as well as Olaus Olson's statement translated from *Svenska Amerikanska Posten*, May 23, 1899, p. 7 — in Appendixes 5 and 7, below. Unless otherwise noted, translations for this book were made by the author.

[8] J. P. Hedberg to Swan J. Turnblad, January 1, 1899, in Archaeological Records, MHS Archives. This letter is discussed in detail in chapter 2. The article referred to was in the University of Minnesota's *Ariel*, 22:208 (January 14, 1899). It is reprinted in chapter 2.

OLOF OHMAN, *who found the rune stone on his farm near Kensington in 1898, was photographed with the stone in 1921. The picture was taken at Oscar Lake, near Kensington, at a carnival held to raise funds to establish a rune stone park. Photograph courtesy Park Region Echo (Alexandria).*

cal find. On the other hand, when it is recalled that the authenticity of the Kensington inscription has been challenged by runologists through all the years since 1899, one cannot ignore the possibility that the silence did not just happen, but was planned with some purpose. If the stone's inscription was a hoax, one might assume that the perpetrator or perpetrators gave thought to their strategy in making the find known to the world.

Some early hitherto unknown translations of the Kensington inscription are presented and discussed in a succeeding chapter, but it may be helpful to readers to quote here a standard English translation accepted by most modern scholars. Erik Wahlgren, a linguist and professor of Scandinavian languages in the University of California at Los Angeles, is responsible for the following version, published in 1958:

8 Swedes and 22 Norwegians on an exploration journey from Vinland westward. We had our camp by 2 rocky islets one day's journey north of this stone. We were out fishing one day. When we came home we found 10 men red with blood and dead. AVM save us from evil. We have 10 men by the sea to look after our ships, 14 days' journey from this island. Year 1362.[9]

The inscription was as startling as it was unexpected. The record, if genuine, was that of a Norse journey of exploration made to inland North America more than a century before Columbus sailed for the New World. The date was as surprising as was the concept of an inland journey 130 years before Columbus. And the reference to "14 days' journey from this island" was baffling. What sea was only fourteen days' journey from the finding place? Was the finding place the original site of the monument? Had the swampy ground surrounding the hill where the stone was found once been a lake bed? Did such immediately perplexing puzzles mean that the inscription was a palpable fake? Or did the improbabilities, so far outside the range of the readily explainable, suggest instead an authentic document? Was the language authentic for the period it purported to represent? If the symbols

[9] See chapter 2, below; Wahlgren, *Kensington Stone*, 3. Other commonly quoted translations say "skerries" instead of "rocky islets." Webster defines a "skerry" as a rocky isle or reef.

were a hoax, what led the hoaxer to choose the date 1362, more than three and a half centuries after Leif Ericson? If in the late nineteenth century someone buried the stone under a tree, why did he choose a Minnesota Scandinavian community as a finding place for it?

Interest in the Kensington rune stone seems to have developed in cycles through the decades since its discovery in 1898. The first cycle occurred in 1899, chiefly but not wholly in the early months of that year, when the find was announced and given newspaper publicity. It was soon ascertained that the symbols on the stone were runic, and the words were translated into Swedish, Norwegian, and English.[10]

Interest in the stone lapsed after the flurry of 1899 and did not revive until 1907. The second cycle then extended to 1915 and was marked by two interrelated phases. The first took its start in 1907 when a writer on Norwegian settlement in the United States went to Kensington. He was Hjalmar Rued Holand of Ephraim, Wisconsin. He visited the Olof Ohman farm, met the finder of the rune stone, and not only saw the engraved slab but acquired it from the owner and had it shipped — on the first of its many longer travels — to his home in Wisconsin. These events marked the beginning of Holand's lifelong interest in the stone. His advocacy of the genuineness of the inscription took the form of books and many articles in newspapers and magazines, as well as a debater's readiness to defend it orally and in print against all comers. Most of the major events in the rune-stone controversy from 1907 until Holand died on August 8, 1963, were related to him in one way or another. Some of them, particularly those of the earlier years, will be reviewed in later chapters.[11]

The other phase in the second cycle of public interest in the Kensington stone was of an investigative character. It began in 1909 with a special study by a committee of the Norwegian Society of Minneapolis, an organization interested in Norwegian culture and Norwegian-American history; and shortly after that

[10] *Minneapolis Journal*, February 22, 1899, p. 1; *Ariel*, 22:208. For the *Journal* article, see Appendix 1, below.
[11] For details and references, see chapters 2 and 3.

the Minnesota Historical Society's museum committee took the matter up. In both committees, which issued favorable verdicts, Holand played an active part.[12]

Holand was not involved, however, in the independent investigation undertaken by Professor George T. Flom, a linguist in the University of Illinois, who visited Kensington and personally examined the stone, which Holand had by then deposited at the Minnesota Historical Society in St. Paul. His report on the find, published in 1910, was condemnatory. He said that the inscription was "modern"; the stone had been "planted, later to be discovered."[13]

In the same year, 1910, a committee of seven scholars representing the Philological Society of the University of Illinois discussed Flom's report and also pronounced the inscription modern. Several other scholars took cognizance of the rune stone, including Frederick Jackson Turner, the noted American historian; Ole E. Hagen, Norwegian-American linguist; and Professor Julius E. Olson of the University of Wisconsin. Olson was a teacher of Scandinavian languages who thought the Kensington inscription a fake, and even believed that he knew who perpetrated it. The second cycle was one of widening interest in the stone, with sharp cleavages of views between those for and against authenticity. Holand gave the discussion a spectacular turn in 1911 when he took the stone to Europe, exhibited it in France and Norway, and debated its genuineness with Marius Hægstad, of the University of Oslo, who maintained that the inscription was fraudulent.[14]

The third cycle is not easy to date precisely. The discussions preceding 1915 had repercussions beyond that date, and a book published in 1914 about the voyages of Norsemen to America opened a new line of defense for Holand. This work by William Hovgaard gave defenders of the stone the concept of a "day's sail" as a medieval Norwegian nautical measure of about seventy-five miles. If applied to a trip from Hudson Bay southward, this measure fitted the stone's inscription, which spoke of fourteen days' journey from

[12] The reports of the Norwegian Society committee and the museum committee of the Minnesota Historical Society are discussed more fully in chapters 3 and 4, with citations of sources.
[13] Flom, in Illinois State Historical Society, *Transactions*, 1910, p. 124.
[14] See chapters 3, 4, and 5, below.

the sea. The change of concept from the ordinary meaning of a day's journey overland to a nautical measure made it imperative for Holand, who had already placed certain skerries or rocky islets mentioned in the runic inscription, to relocate them about seventy-five miles from the discovery site. This he soon did among the numerous lakes north of Kensington. Following a key article issued by Holand in 1919, many others wrote about the stone, and in 1932 and 1940 Holand published his first two books on the subject, *The Kensington Stone* and *Westward from Vinland*.[15]

Holand's writings fanned controversy, and several additional scholars entered the fray. Laurence M. Larson, professor of history in the University of Illinois, regarded the Kensington inscription as a hoax, and he gave short shrift to the application of a nautical measure of distance to overland travel. Milo M. Quaife, historian and editor of the respected *Mississippi Valley Historical Review*, rejected so-called "mooring stones" and other collateral finds and relegated the rune stone to the realm of myth. Martin B. Ruud, professor of English in the University of Minnesota, said in a review that such finds had no relevance if the inscription was a forgery, and their evidence was superfluous if it was genuine.[16]

The fourth cycle, extending roughly from about 1940 to the 1960s, included the publication of three additional books by Holand — *America, 1355–1364; Explorations in America Before Columbus;* and *A Pre-Columbian Crusade to America*. He also wrote an autobiography entitled *My First Eighty Years*.[17]

During this period Holand continued his efforts to prove a medieval origin for the Newport Tower in Rhode Island, and he reported the existence of various "mooring stones" and artifacts for which he claimed connections with the rune stone. He also introduced a new character into the drama, the Englishman Nicholas of Lynne, a fourteenth-century Carmelite friar known as "the

---

[15] Hovgaard, *The Voyages of the Norsemen to America*, 61–63 (New York, 1914); Holand, in *Wisconsin Magazine of History*, 3:153–183.

[16] Larson, "The Kensington Rune Stone," in *Minnesota History*, 17:20–37 (March, 1936); Quaife, "The Kensington Myth Once More," in *Michigan History*, 31:129–161 (June, 1947); Ruud, in *Minneapolis Journal*, August 7, 1932, editorial section, p. 4.

[17] These were published in New York in 1946, 1956, 1962, and 1957, respectively.

man of the astrolabe." Nicholas, believed by some to have been the author of a lost manuscript entitled *Inventio Fortunata,* was declared by Holand to have been a member of the group that he thought sailed from Norway under an authorization from Magnus Erikson, the king of Norway and Sweden.[18]

The fourth cycle also witnessed a temporary exhibit of the Kensington stone at the Smithsonian Institution in Washington, D.C., and the publication by that institution of an English translation of a monograph by William C. Thalbitzer, a Danish ethnologist who said that the inscription "may be authentic." The Smithsonian Institution did not endorse the Kensington rune stone as genuine, but its activities created a public impression that it favored the authenticity of the inscription. Meanwhile enthusiasts established a "Runestone Park" near Alexandria, and in it they erected a gigantic replica of the Kensington stone.[19]

This latest cycle was by no means a period of general acceptance of the Kensington inscription. In 1949 the leading runologist of Sweden, Sven B. F. Jansson, visited the United States under the auspices of the Swedish Academy of Sciences for the express purpose of making a study of the rune stone. In a published treatise

[18] Holand, "An English Scientist in America 130 Years before Columbus," in Wisconsin Academy of Sciences, Arts, and Letters, *Transactions,* 48:205–219 (Madison, 1959), and "Nicholas of Lynn: A Pre-Columbian Traveler in North America," in *American-Scandinavian Review,* 46:[19]–32 (March, 1958). See also *Dictionary of National Biography,* 40:418 (New York, 1894), for an article which, in condensed form, told much of the story that Holand reviewed, but stated that no evidence connected Nicholas with the book on the fortunate discovery. More recently Tryggvi J. Oleson wrote: "It may be stated conclusively that Nicholas of Lynn was not the author of the *Inventio fortunata,*" which was written by a Franciscan, whereas Nicholas was a Carmelite. Oleson advanced reasons to support his view that the author of the *Inventio* could not have visited the Canadian Arctic with the "mythical Norwegian expedition" of 1355–64. Oleson, *Early Voyages and Northern Approaches, 1000–1632,* 105–108 (quote on p. 106) (London and New York, 1964).

[19] Thalbitzer, *Two Runic Stones, from Greenland and Minnesota* (*Smithsonian Miscellaneous Collections,* vol. 116, no. 3, Publication no. 4021 — Washington, D.C., 1951). The essay by Thalbitzer appeared earlier in *Danske Studier* (Copenhagen), 43:[1]–40 (1946–47). On Runestone Park, see *Sons of Norway,* 57:209, 213 (November, 1960); *Minneapolis Sunday Tribune,* August 12, 1951, Picture Roto Magazine, p. 10; Alexandria Kiwanis Club, Runestone Replica Committee, *Souvenir Booklet of the Runestone Replica Dedication* ([Alexandria, 1951]).

he pronounced the inscription fraudulent — a hoax. Similarly a Danish runologist, Erik Moltke of Denmark's National Museum, studied the stone and found the inscription "suspect in every detail, in rune forms, grammar, syntax, vocabulary, in the weathering of the runes, in the history of the find." In conclusion he said, "Never has a spurious document stood on such feeble ground and given such striking proofs of its falsity." Meanwhile Professor Johan A. Holvik of Concordia College, Moorhead, Minnesota, had worked with a letter of John P. Hedberg written on January 1, 1899, from Kensington and a sketch of the runic inscription enclosed with it. Holvik found that the sketch, supposedly a copy of the inscription on the stone, differed from the chiseled inscription in so many ways that, in his judgment, it could not have been a copy but was, instead, a draft. If the document was in fact sent by Hedberg, it was evidence that the inscription was fraudulent. The sketch is reproduced below (p. 30).[20]

In 1958 Professor Wahlgren published his book on the Kensington stone. It was highly critical of Holand's methods and marshaled much linguistic and historical evidence to prove the inscription a hoax. The problem was stubborn, however. Holand and his supporters did not concede. In 1962, still firmly of the opinion that the inscription was of fourteenth-century origin, Holand published his final book on the Kensington problem, *A Pre-Columbian Crusade to America*. A year later the promoters of the stone had it transported to New York as part of Minnesota's exhibit at the World's Fair. The stone was returned to Alexandria, where it is now the central feature of the community's Rune Stone Museum.[21]

[20] Sven B. F. Jansson, " 'Runstenen' från Kensington i Minnesota," in *Nordisk Tidskrift* (new series), 25:[377]–405 (1949); Erik Moltke, "The Ghost of the Kensington Stone," in *Scandinavian Studies*, 25:1–14 (quotes on p. 13, 14) (February, 1953). The original Danish version was published in *Danske Studier*, 45:[37]–60 (1949–50). Holvik's ideas were reported in the *Concordian* (Moorhead), November 18, 1949, p. 1, a newspaper published by students of Concordia College. A copy of the issue cited is in Kensington file, Blegen Papers.

[21] Wahlgren, *Kensington Stone*, chapters 9 and 17. On the Kensington stone's trip to New York, see *Minneapolis Star*, May 31, 1965, p. 1; *St. Paul Dispatch*, January 8, 1965, section 1, p. 1. On the Alexandria museum, see *St. Paul Pioneer Press*, April 20, 1958, third section, p. 7; May 8, 1966, first section, p. 16.

Recent years have witnessed a lively interest in the voyages of the Norsemen to the New World, and there have been a few major discoveries. One is the excavation by the Norwegian scholars, Mr. and Mrs. Helge M. Ingstad, of a Norse village site in Newfoundland. The excavation, carried on for seven years from 1961 at L'Anse au Meadow, revealed evidence of Norse occupation somewhere around the year 1000—house sites, a smithy, traces of a great hall, and a soapstone spindle whorl of Norse origin. Inevitably these finds stirred interest in the old question of the location of Vinland, and they supported the view that the sagas were founded on fact. Some critics have withheld final judgment and suggested that the village may have been of Eskimo or possibly of early French origin, but the documented evidence presented by Mr. Ingstad leaves little, if any, room for such hypotheses.[22]

Even more dramatic was the announcement by Yale University of a newly discovered map dating from the pre-Columbian period (about 1440) with an inscription stating that Vinland had been discovered by "Bjarni and Leif in company"—a reference to Bjarni Herjulfson and Leif Ericson. The map was announced as the "earliest known and indisputable cartographic representation of any part of the Americas." It includes the Gulf of St. Lawrence and has a representation of the Hudson Strait and also of a body of water that may possibly be Hudson Bay. The Latin inscription tells of the arrival in Vinland of the bishop of Greenland (Eirik Gnupsson), who remained there "a long time in both summer and winter." The time was the final year of Pope Paschal II; that is, 1117.[23]

Some proponents of the Kensington stone thought that the Vinland map and the Newfoundland finds added support to the theory of a fourteenth-century expedition into mid-America. They could find no comfort, however, when the hundreds of runic inscriptions excavated under the Hanseatic structures in Bergen, Norway, were analyzed by that country's leading runologist, Pro-

[22] Helge Ingstad, "Vinland Ruins Prove Vikings Found the New World," in National Geographic, 126:708–734 (November, 1964).
[23] Raleigh A. Skelton, Thomas E. Marston, and George D. Painter, The Vinland Map and the Tartar Relation (New Haven, 1965); see especially p. v, 139, 140, 259n. On Herjulfson, see Einar I. Haugen, Voyages to Vinland: The First American Saga, 7–11, 17 (New York, 1942).

fessor Aslak Liestøl, in 1966. The runic symbols used, during a stretch of time from the mid-twelfth to the fifteenth centuries, including many from the fourteenth century, totaled more than 12,000 — the largest single group of such inscriptions ever found. They were of the kind "in continuous use by nearly all social groups" of that period, but among all 12,000 not a single one of seven unusual and "strange forms occurring in the Kensington alphabet" appears. Mr. Liestøl stated that if a runic inscription in America had actually been carved in the fourteenth century, it "would surely have been written with the runes which the people of those days were accustomed to using."[24]

Recently (1967) the Vatican is reported to have opened its archives to a search by Norwegian scholars for documents relating to Norse exploration and settlement in North America. It is hoped, and indeed expected, that new information about the Viking connections will be discovered.

[24] Aslak Liestøl, "The Runes of Bergen: Voices from the Middle Ages," in *Minnesota History*, 40:59 (Summer, 1966). In a book entitled *Norse Medieval Cryptography in Runic Carvings* (Glendale, Calif., 1967), Alf Mongé and O. G. Landsverk allege that medieval cryptograms are concealed within the texts of the Kensington inscription, the Heavener rock carvings in Oklahoma, some marks on the Newport Tower in Rhode Island, other alleged runes in New England, and the Latin lines on the Vinland map at Yale University. In the foreword it is stated that the supposed fourteenth-century runemaster made no fewer than *"sixty changes"* to achieve what is described as the "visible text" of the Kensington inscription. This seems to mean that the author of the cryptographic chapters of the new book made some sixty changes in the presently visible text of the Kensington inscription. These changes presumably were made as a means of accommodating or uncovering the supposed hidden message. The authors seem confident that the "mystery" of the Kensington stone is "gone," that there is "nothing more" to solve with respect to it. But Mr. Liestøl, after an analysis of the methods employed by the authors, writes that he has found in the book "not a single contribution to science or scholarship"; see Liestøl, "Crytograms in Runic Carvings: A Critical Analysis," in *Minnesota History*, 41:42 (Spring, 1968). David Kahn, author of *The Code Breakers: The Story of Secret Writing* (New York, 1967), writes that the Mongé-Landsverk book has "yielded no contribution to man's knowledge" and is "utterly without value"; see *American-Scandinavian Review*, 56:82 (Spring, 1968). The Mongé-Landsverk work, in the present writer's opinion, leaves the Kensington "mystery" in the same position it occupied before the book was written.

chapter 2

Documents and Puzzles

THE PRESENT CHAPTER TAKES A CLOSER LOOK at circumstances related to the discovery of the Kensington rune stone and the first
cycle of public interest in the inscription.

The earliest known record pertaining to the Kensington stone
is the letter telling of its discovery, written on January 1, 1899, by
John P. Hedberg, a Kensington businessman, to Swan J. Turnblad,
publisher of *Svenska Amerikanska Posten* in Minneapolis. This
letter was sent to the University of Minnesota and shortly thereafter reached the hands of Olaus J. Breda, professor of Scandinavian languages.[1]

I began my later studies of the Kensington stone with a search
for data about Breda, who in 1899 made an early translation of
the Kensington inscription from runic to English. This took me to
a file of a weekly publication of the University of Minnesota called
the *Ariel*. It was in part a news organ for students and faculty,
in part a magazine. In the issue for January 14, 1899, I found an
article about the Kensington stone, the first known notice of it
to appear in print.[2] Its text is as follows:

[1] Breda (1853–1916) held his Minnesota professorship from 1883 to 1899,
when he returned to Norway, his native land. After 1899 he was a respected
teacher in the Frogner Higher School in Christiania, a post he held until 1915.
See Henning Tønseth, in *Den Høiere Skole*, vol. 19, no. 2, p. 26–28 (Christiania, 1917); E. Bird Johnson, ed., *Forty Years of the University of Minnesota*, 310 (Minneapolis, 1910). Christiania became Oslo on January 1, 1925.
Breda explained in a letter to *Verdens Gang* (Christiania), April 24, 1899,
that a copy of the inscription reached him through a Swedish newspaper in
Minneapolis; photostat in Johan A. Holvik Papers, MHS.

[2] *Ariel*, 22:208. The only contemporary reference to the *Ariel* that I have
found is in *Northwestern* (Evanston, Ill.), March 9, 1899, p. 2. See Appendix

Runic Monument or "Mare's Nest?"

From Kensington, Douglas County, comes the report of a recent find, which, if genuine, is of some historical importance. While grubbing under a tree near Kensington Mr. Ohman found a stone bearing an inscription in Runic characters and brought it to town where Mr. Hedberg, a business man, copied the inscription and sent it for translation to the *Svenska Amerikanska Posten*. The editors could make nothing out of it and sent it to the University where it was handed to Professor Breda to be deciphered. Professor Breda says: "The language of the inscription presents a queer mixture of Swedish and Norwegian (Danish) and English words, the spelling of some words being such as to give the word a flavor of the old language." Some of the characters are not Runic and those indicating numbers are quite unintelligible thus making a complete translation impossible. Following is the English equivalent so far as Professor Breda was able to make it out: "Swedes and Norwegians on a journey of discovery from Vinland west — we camped ? ? one day's journey north from this stone — we fished one day — after we came home we found men red with blood and dead — save from evil. — Have men at the ocean to look after our ships. ? day's journey from this island. ? Year ?"

This transcription is literal. Until the stone itself be critically examined its value will remain doubtful. The probability of its being cut for the amusement of the *finder* is certainly not large when we consider how few Scandinavian farmers are learned in Runic characters, yet the strange mixup leads Professor Breda to set it down as probably spurious. Perhaps further development will decide whether this find is to be ranked with the Rosetta stone or with the "Cardiff Giant." [3]

2, below. I informed Professor Wahlgren of this report, and he mentioned it in "The Case of the Kensington Rune Stone," in *American Heritage*, April, 1959, p. 35. Most writers, including Holand, continued to give chronological priority to the *Minneapolis Journal* account of February 22, 1899. Ole G. Landsverk, *The Kensington Runestone: A Reappraisal of the Circumstances under which the Stone was Discovered*, 56 (Glendale, Calif., 1961), wrote incorrectly that Breda "made the first attempt" to translate the inscription in February, 1899. The "attempt" was made between January 1, 1899, when Hedberg wrote to Turnblad, and January 14, 1899, when the *Ariel* appeared.

[3] Dashes in the inscription were used by Breda to indicate characters he

This report antedated by more than a month the news stories previously supposed to be the earliest printed accounts of the rune stone. Articles about the stone appeared in Minneapolis and Chicago — in the *Minneapolis Journal,* for February 22, 1899; in *Svenska Amerikanska Posten,* for February 28, 1899; in *Skandinaven* (Chicago and Minneapolis), the *Chicago Tribune,* and the *Chicago Daily Inter Ocean* for several dates between February 20 and the early days of March, 1899.[4]

These papers announced the discovery of the rune stone and printed translations by Breda and by George O. Curme, a professor of German philology in Northwestern University. Curme had been sent a copy of the inscription, and a little later the stone itself was shipped to him. He was responsible for several successive translations, each an improvement on his earlier attempt. He finally concluded on linguistic grounds that the inscription was "ungenuine."[5]

An interview with Breda in the *Minneapolis Journal* for February 22, 1899, reported that the stone had been found "last November," that is, in November, 1898. The *Journal* interview said that Ohman came upon the stone "while grubbing under a tree of thirty or forty years' growth." The stone was "under the roots of the tree," and "copies" of the inscription "were forwarded to the department of Greek" at the university. There it was observed that the language was not Greek, and the copies were turned over to

could not make out. The Cardiff Giant, a notorious hoax, was the huge figure of a supposed prehistoric man unearthed on a farm near Cardiff, New York, in 1869. See James Taylor Dunn, *Cardiff Giant Hoax* (Cooperstown, N.Y., 1948).

[4] The Johan A. Holvik Papers include typewritten transcripts of articles in the *Chicago Daily Inter Ocean,* February 21, 1899, p. 5, and in the *Chicago Tribune,* February 20, p. 2, February 23, p. 7, February 26, p. 11, March 1, p. 3, and March 2, p. 12 — all in 1899. The transcripts were furnished by the Newberry Library, Chicago.

[5] Curme to Winchell, March 9, 1910 (quote), in Archaeological Records, MHS Archives. On Curme (1860–1948), a distinguished scholar who taught for many years in Northwestern University, see *Who Was Who in America,* 2:140 (Chicago, 1950). As early as February 18, 1899, he gave a talk about the Kensington stone to the German Society at Northwestern; see *Chicago Tribune,* February 20, 1899, p. 2; and *Skandinaven* (Chicago, St. Paul, Minneapolis), February 22, 1899, p. 4, microfilm copy in Luther College Library, Decorah, Ia. The MHS has an incomplete file of this newspaper.

Professor Breda. He came to the conclusion that "the whole thing was a hoax, or the result of an effort on the part of some one in part familiar with runic inscriptions to amuse himself." As a result, he made "no effort to secure the stone." Breda gave the *Journal* a translation that differed in a few details from the one in the *Ariel* but still omitted the numerals. It read:

> — Swedes and — Norsemen on a journey of discovery from Vinland west — We camped — one day's journey north from this stone. We fished one day. After we came home we found — man red with blood and dead. AVM save from — Have — men at the ocean to look after our ships — days journey from this island. Year —

The inscription in Breda's judgment was "a jumble of Swedish and Norwegian in late grammatical forms with here and there an English word, but all spelled in runic characters." A curious and startling item, virtually unnoticed by those who have written about the Kensington stone, appeared in the same *Journal* report. This was the statement that Breda's translation corresponded "exactly almost with a translation made shortly after the discovery of the stone and submitted by S. A. Siverts of Kensington." [6]

The *Journal* of February 22, 1899, also printed Curme's translation as well as a drawing of the Kensington inscription (see page 31, below), the source of which was not indicated although linguists say that it was not the Hedberg copy. Curme's first version was as follows:

> A company of Norsemen are out on expedition of discovery from the Vinland of the West. We had a camp along with two boats one day's journey from this stone. We go out daily and fish. One day after we came home we found a man red with blood and dead. Ave (good-bye). Rescue from fire. Has one ever had a comrade such as we have had. We are on our way to look after our ship, fourteen days' journey from this island.

Two days later on February 24, 1899, the *Journal* printed a revised translation by Curme:

[6] The *Minneapolis Journal*, February 22, 1899, also referred to a stone with "cuneiform inscriptions" which had been found "a few years ago in Wisconsin" and which told a story not unlike that on the Kensington stone, "though not of Norsemen." See Appendix 1, below.

Eight Goths (in Sweden) and twenty-two Norwegians are
out on an expedition of discovery from the Vineland of the
west. We had a camp along with two boats one day's journey
north of this stone. We were out fishing one day after we came
home we (literally "one") found a man red with blood and
dead good bye (or ave); rescue from evil has one any such
comrade (literally "man") as we have had. Move on our way
to look after our ships fourteen days' journey from this island;
year 1362 (on a second copy 1462).

In successive versions Curme worked his way toward the later
standard translations. As early as February 20, 1899, in the *Chicago Tribune* he gave the date as 1362. Later he was not certain
whether it should be 1362 or 1462. He translated the year as 1362
in *Minneapolis Tidende* of March 3, 1899, and again in the *Northwestern* (Evanston) of March 9, where he gave a new translation:

Eight Goths (from Sweden) and twenty-two Norwegians on
an expedition of discovery from the Vinland of the west. We
had a camp with two boats a day's journey from this stone.
We went out fishing one day. After we came home we found
a man red with blood and dead. Good-by, rescue from evil.
We have men at the ocean to look after our ships fourteen
days' journey from this island. Year 1362.

In the *Minneapolis Journal* interview, Breda had suggested that
copies of the inscription be submitted to Ludvig F. A. Wimmer of
Denmark and Sophus Bugge of Norway, runic experts who, he
believed, could quickly determine whether or not the inscription
was genuine. Both were asked for their views, and both later pronounced the inscription a fraud.[7]

The present discussion will be more understandable if further
reference is made to the Hedberg letter. As has been noted, it was
addressed to Swan J. Turnblad, publisher of *Svenska Amerikanska
Posten*. In 1925 the original of this letter was found in the files of
the president of the University of Minnesota and turned over to
the Minnesota Historical Society. Enclosed with the letter were

[7] See Moltke, in *Scandinavian Studies*, 25:3; Breda, "Rundt Kensington-
stenen," in *Symra*, 6:[65]-80 (1910), a Norwegian literary magazine published
in Decorah, Ia.

a copy (or a draft) of the Kensington inscription and a typewritten translation by O. J. Breda. The text of the letter follows: [8]

I Inclose you a copy of an inscription on a stone found about 2 miles from Kensington by a O. Ohman he found it under a tree when Grubbing — he wanted I should go out and look at it and I told him to haul it in when he came (not thinking much of it) he did so, and this is an exsect copy of it. the first part is of the flat side of stone the other was on flat edge. I thought I would send it to you as you perhaps have means to find out what it is — it appears to be old Greek letters please let me hear from you and oblige yours truly   J. P. HEDBERG

This letter, plus the evidence in the *Ariel* and in the *Journal*, makes it certain that Breda saw only a copy, or copies, of the inscription, not the rune stone itself. The stone was sent to Curme and arrived at Northwestern University on the last day of February, 1899. The *Chicago Tribune* for March 1, 1899, stated that the stone had reached Evanston on the preceding day, and the *Northwestern* for March 9, 1899, reported that "Last week the Runic stone, much heralded by the Chicago papers, came into the hands of Professor Curme of the German department."

At this point the story becomes more tangled. Note that Hedberg did not state in his letter that he had himself made the version he enclosed, though the *Ariel* article did say so. *Svenska Amerikanska Posten* of February 28, 1899, stated that Olof Ohman had made the copy Hedberg forwarded to Minneapolis on January 1, 1899. And the confusion is increased because Hedberg, writing in 1910, said that he himself made the copy that he sent in 1899 to *Svenska Amerikanska Posten*.[9]

By 1910 it is conceivable that Hedberg in eleven years had forgotten the details of what happened with respect to the document he enclosed with his letter. Undoubtedly he examined the stone when it was brought to him; he "took quite much interest" in it,

[8] The documents are in Archaeological Records, MHS Archives. A brief note about them appeared in *Minnesota History*, 6:399 (December, 1925). The next notice of them in print seems to have been an article by Milo M. Quaife, "The Myth of the Kensington Rune Stone: The Norse Discovery of Minnesota 1362," in *New England Quarterly*, 7:614n (December, 1934).

[9] Hedberg to Winchell, March 12, 1910, Archaeological Records, MHS Archives, in Appendix 12, below.

he said in 1910; perhaps he tried to make out the incised marks; he may even have copied them and later remembered that he had done so. He may a decade or more later have forgotten whether he or Ohman made the copy he mailed to Minneapolis.

If the hypothesis of hoax or fraud is entertained, however, one must probe beyond a possible lapse of memory. Wahlgren suggested that Hedberg was involved in a "runic hoaxing plot" and that what he wrote in 1910 was "devious." In such a context it becomes necessary to look at the assertion made by the late Johan A. Holvik of Concordia College that the Hedberg "copy" was not a copy but a draft — a draft prepared before the Kensington inscription was cut! Holvik announced his theory and findings in 1949, noting that the copy described by Hedberg as "exsect" proved to have seventeen divergences from the actual inscription, "three in punctuation, seven in spelling, and seven in forms."[10]

The burden of Holvik's charge is that the nature of the differences excludes the possibility that they were copying mistakes. Instead their character shows that the runic wording must have been composed by somebody who could read and understand runes, who could, in short, apply the runic principles to an inscription. The divergences are of a kind that a copyist could not make without knowing runes and having a purpose other than that of merely working out a copy. To Holvik, Wahlgren, and to some runic scholars abroad, including Erik Moltke, the Hedberg "copy" is a draft — a preliminary formulation antedating the stone's inscription.

If this interpretation of the Hedberg version of the inscription is sound and if that version was sent by Hedberg to *Svenska Amerikanska Posten*, the Kensington inscription is manifestly a fraud. The theory is plausible; it may be true. As a historian, I suggest that before full acceptance, the theory needs support on the provenience of the document, that is, of the runic text as found with the Hedberg letter. It will be recalled that the Minnesota Historical Society received the letter and sketch in 1925. The papers came

[10] Wahlgren, *Kensington Stone*, 139, 140, 143; Holvik, in *Concordian*, November 18, 1949, p. 1. Holvik's ideas were later expanded by George Rice in a series of articles in the *Minneapolis Star*; see especially April 11, 1955, p. 1.

from the archives of Cyrus Northrop, president of the University of Minnesota. No correspondence with Turnblad of *Svenska Amerikanska Posten* or with Breda of the Scandinavian department accompanied it. The fact that Breda's typed translation was included affords evidence that the papers were turned over to Northrop after Breda had studied the runic inscription.

We do not know how many copies of the runes were sent to the university and to Breda — the *Minneapolis Journal* used the plural word "copies." Did Breda and his students make copies (or variants) while he was studying the runes? Nor is it known how many copies were sent to Curme of Northwestern. The *Chicago Tribune* for February 21, 1899, carried a copy that resembled the Hedberg version. Copies perhaps were made by Turnblad or by others in his newspaper office. A Chicago news report stated that a letter was sent from Kensington to Curme several weeks before February 21, 1899, and one assumes that it contained a copy of the inscription.[11] These have not been found, since Curme's papers have never been located.

Thus we are left with a few unanswered questions. Was the "Hedberg version" actually his? Who wrote it — Hedberg, Ohman, or someone else? Was it a draft? Was it made after Hedberg's material reached Minneapolis? How many copies of the inscription were made in the Swedish newspaper office? At the university? Did Ohman and/or Hedberg knowingly send something as a copy which differed from the chiseled runes? If so, why?

In a taped interview in 1949, Edward Ohman was asked whether his father had attempted to copy the inscription. He replied, "I can't recollect for sure, but it seems to me they asked for a copy from St. Paul or wherever it was, and some way or another, I can't say for sure, they wanted another one, if it got lost, or how, I wouldn't know. So he tried to recopy another one." What Edward Ohman meant by saying "he tried to recopy another one" is obscure.[12]

Since Hedberg's name reoccurs in the Kensington story, some further information about him is desirable. He was born in Sweden in 1853, immigrating to America (and Minnesota) in 1869. Noth-

---

[11] *Chicago Daily Inter Ocean*, February 21, 1899, transcript, Holvik Papers.
[12] Edward Ohman interview, December 28, 1949.

ing has been learned about his activities from 1869 to 1882 except that he attended public schools in Minneapolis. It is not known how far he carried his education, what jobs he held, or what he read. In 1882 he went into the lumber business in Brandon, Douglas County, and he removed to Kensington in 1887. Since Olof Ohman built a house in Brandon in 1882 and Hedberg was then in business there, it is possible that the two men met as early as sixteen years before the Kensington stone was found. Hedberg's business at Kensington was first hardware and furniture, later loans and insurance. In the early 1900s he went to Warroad, Minnesota, where he was president of a bank and later head of a land investment company. He was prominent enough to be included in a *Book of Minnesotans* published in 1907. Later, with his family, he lived in Longview and Everett, Washington. I have corresponded widely in efforts to find Hedberg's personal papers, if they have been preserved, but thus far without success.[13]

Another name which turns up in the Kensington story is that of Samuel A. Siverts, who according to the *Minneapolis Journal* submitted a translation of the inscription which corresponded "exactly almost" with that prepared by Professor Breda. Siverts was cashier of the Kensington bank when the stone was found. He was born in Norway, the son of a sea captain. When he was seventeen he went to England, where he had a year of schooling. He seems to have come to the United States to work for Harald Thorson of Northfield, Minnesota, a businessman of extensive interests. Thorson controlled the Kensington bank where Siverts served as cashier in the late 1890s.[14]

Although the *Ariel* article indicated that Breda's translation was made from the copy sent by Hedberg, Breda later published an article in Norwegian in which he said that he had been informed from Kensington at New Year's time in 1899 that a rune-inscribed

[13] Minnesota Manuscript Census Schedules, 1905, Douglas County, p. 134, in Minnesota State Archives, St. Paul; Albert N. Marquis, ed., *The Book of Minnesotans*, 222 (Chicago, 1907). According to the state census, Hedberg and his family lived in Kensington in 1905, two years after he entered the banking business at Warroad.

[14] Ingvald T. Siverts, Sr., to Blegen, October 20, 1967, in Kensington file, Blegen Papers. Mr. Siverts added that his father worked under Thorson "almost his entire life," presumably also in the Citizens Bank at Morris.

stone had been found in November, 1898. In translation he then wrote: "After some correspondence Mr. S. A. Siverts, cashier of the Kensington bank, sent me a sketch of the inscription, which I read without great difficulty, basically in the same way it has later been read by men versed in runology, with the exception that I could not manage the numerals, since I did not understand the designation of numbers in the runic figures." Breda also said, in a letter to Warren Upham of the Minnesota Historical Society, that at his request Siverts had sent him a "rough draft of the inscription." He offered no explanation of the *Ariel* report which stated that he had made his translation from the version sent by Hedberg.[15]

The original of the "Siverts sketch" of the inscription is unknown, but Hjalmar R. Holand believed that the illustration appearing in *Svenska Amerikanska Posten* on February 28, 1899, was the work of Siverts. The same sketch was printed in the *Minneapolis Journal* of February 22, 1899. In both papers the sketches are without signatures. One thing is certain; these sketches did not present the Hedberg version of the inscription. (See illustration on p. 30–31.)[16]

Did Breda have in his hands any copy of the runic inscription other than the one sent to Minneapolis by Hedberg? No confirmation has been found for Breda's statement that Siverts sent him a sketch of the Kensington inscription. Nor do the earlier sources specifically support assertions that a sketch by Siverts was the

---

[15] See note 1, above. Breda, in *Symra*, 6:[65]–80; Breda to Upham, March 7, 1910, MHS Archives, in Appendix 11, below.

[16] Holand, *Pre-Columbian Crusade*, 30, 89, 91; *Explorations in America Before Columbus*, 163, 356n. In the first instance, Holand confused the Siverts copy with the Hedberg text; on p. 91 he stated that a translation made by Oluf Rygh in Christiania in 1899 was done from a copy "*like* Hedberg's." Rygh pronounced the inscription a fraud done by a Swedish American; photostat of Rygh's statement, signed "O. R.", in *Morgenbladet* (Christiania), March 12, 1899, in Kensington file, Blegen Papers. Holand (p. 163) had Siverts send either a copy of the inscription or the stone to Breda; he also had Breda "struggle" with the inscription for two months in translating it, whereas he did it in less than two weeks. The text Breda used was obviously the one sent by Hedberg or a version of it. Holvik attributed to Siverts the sketch in the *Minneapolis Journal*, February 22, 1899, p. 1; see *Concordian*, November 18, 1949, p. 1.

basis for drawings of the runic inscription that appeared in various newspapers in February, 1899.

Breda was a responsible scholar, a highly respected teacher who believed in 1910 not only that he had received a sketch of the inscription from Siverts, but that it was sent to him at his request. Moreover Breda recalled that he and Siverts had corresponded. There must have been some basis for this recollection. There is a further question: Did Siverts know that the inscription was runic, and if so, how soon after the discovery of the stone did he know this? Had he, as the *Minneapolis Journal* reported on February 22, 1899, "submitted" a translation of the inscription which he made "shortly after the discovery of the stone"? If he made such a translation, when did he make it? How soon after the discovery? What has become of it? It was not printed in the newspaper but was dismissed with the comment that it corresponded with Breda's translation and was "not far different" from Curme's. If Siverts made the translation soon after the discovery of the stone, why did Hedberg, a businessman in Kensington who must have known Siverts, suggest that the characters on the stone were "old Greek letters"? A broader question is whether or not — or how many — persons in the Kensington area knew that the inscription was runic?

In my hunt for information I made inquiries about where Siverts was living in the spring of 1899. As a result I received several interesting letters from Mr. Ingvald T. Siverts, Sr., of Morris. In one of them dated June 25, 1964, he wrote, "I am the son of Samuel A. Siverts, the cashier of the Kensington bank back in 1898 and 1899, and we moved to Morris in the summer of 1899. My father passed out some years back. I am about seventy nine years old now and at the time of the Rune stone find was about thirteen or fourteen." Mr. Siverts related that his father, with three companions, brought the stone to the bank in Kensington, where it was placed in a back room. "It was dark colored and even had some black dirt on it at the time." Mr. Siverts was under the impression that his father sent the stone to the University of Minnesota, where Professor Breda "considered it a hoax." Mr. Siverts, alas, had none of his father's papers and did not know of any that would shed light on the stone. In a second letter (June 29, 1964) replying to a ques-

WAYNESBURG COLLEGE LIBRARY
WAYNESBURG, PA.

REPRODUCED HERE *is a copy, or perhaps a draft, of the rune stone inscription that may have been enclosed in a letter written to Swan J. Turnblad of Minneapolis by Kensington businessman John P. Hedberg on January 1, 1899.*

THIS VERSION *of the rune stone inscription appeared in the* Minneapolis
Journal *on February 22, 1899, and in* Svenska Amerikanska Posten *on
February 28, 1899. Holand believed that the sketch was made by Samuel
A. Siverts of Kensington.*

tion, he wrote that the men who went to get the stone "drove out in a sleigh." He thought that the time was December.[17] Contemporary records do not support the statement that the elder Siverts sent the stone to Breda, but the family memory, Breda's recollection in 1910, and the item in *Svenska Amerikanska Posten* in 1899, indicate that Siverts did send something. It may have been a copy of the inscription, as Breda thought, or a translation, as the newspaper said. Records are conclusive that the stone itself was not sent, though even on this point there is a strange contradiction. Holand said that in 1935 he received a letter from Samuel Siverts in which the latter wrote, "I shipped the stone very carefully packed and by express to Prof. Breda . . . and the stone was returned to me at Kensington in a couple of months." According to Holand, it was then sent to Curme, but this involves a conflict in chronology. Holand also said that the Siverts' copy was on file at the Minnesota Historical Society, but no such copy is there, save in printed form in newspapers. As to the stone, the usual story is that it was sent to Curme by Samuel Olson of Kensington, not by Samuel Siverts.[18]

To return to statements made by the son of Samuel Siverts, his memory of a sleigh may offer further support for the presumption that the stone was unearthed in November, 1898. His letters also mention Sam Olson, John Wedum, and "Lillyquist," as having helped Samuel Siverts transport the stone to Kensington, thus in-

[17] The two letters from Mr. Siverts are in Kensington file, Blegen Papers, with others of January 7, 1965, and October 20, 1967, giving more detail on his father. That of January 7, 1965, spoke of Siverts as "a very fine penman." Siverts made copies of his letters in a letter book of the Kensington bank which later merged with the First State Bank of Kensington, but they have not been preserved. Palmer J. Score to Blegen, February 23, 1965, Kensington file, Blegen Papers. The *Alexandria Post News*, March 16, 1899, p. 4, stated that Siverts left Kensington "last week" for Morris, where he was to be a bank cashier. This means that Siverts left Kensington shortly after news of the stone had been made public. His name does not appear in the Douglas County census for 1895, but he is recorded for Morris in Stevens County for 1905 (p. 85). The manuscript census schedules indicate that his family moved to Morris, as his son stated, in 1899.

[18] Holand, *Pre-Columbian Crusade*, 31; *Explorations in America Before Columbus*, 356n. According to *Skandinaven*, February 24, 1899, p. 4, the stone had been sent by S. Olson of Kensington to Curme at Northwestern University.

troducing two names unfamiliar to the story. "Lillyquist" probably was Charles Lilyquist, a thirty-eight-year-old dry-goods merchant who lived in Kensington in 1895. Wedum was a "hardware merchant," twenty-seven in 1895, by which time he had lived in Kensington five years. Samuel Olson, jeweler, was thirty-nine in 1905 and had then lived in the state twenty-seven years and in Kensington ten. His name does not appear in the Douglas County state census returns for 1895.[19]

It is astonishing how many problems of evidence confront students seeking information about the finding of the Kensington stone. Even the date of the discovery is the subject of contradictory reports and theories. The near-contemporary records point decisively to November, 1898, and one source specifies November 8. But four affidavits, including one signed by the finder, state that the time of the discovery was August, 1898! These affidavits were recorded in 1909—more than ten years after the discovery—and they are so worded that it seems certain they were phrased in English by one or more persons who were not the signers.[20]

The first printed notice of the stone thus far discovered (in the *Ariel*) dated it, as already noted, as a "recent find." The *Minneapolis Journal* of February 22, 1899, recorded the date as "last November," and Breda confirmed this date in 1910. Other Minneapolis and Chicago newspapers of early 1899 placed the find in November, 1898, and the *Northwestern* (March 9, 1899) said "last November." George T. Flom, who interviewed Ohman in 1910, said that the find was made in "the fall of 1898." Newton H. Winchell, the Minnesota archaeologist who also talked with Ohman in 1909 and 1910, is the only person who recorded the date specifically—November 8, 1898—but he did not state his source of information. Holand used the August, 1898, date in his writings until the 1950s, when he adopted November, 1898.[21]

[19] Minnesota Manuscript Census Schedules, 1895, Douglas County, p. 259.
[20] Museum Committee, in *Minnesota Historical Collections*, 15:221. The affidavits are discussed in detail on p. 58–62, and Appendix 7, below.
[21] Breda to Upham, March 7, 1910, in MHS Archives, and Appendix 11, below; Flom, in Illinois State Historical Society, *Transactions*, 1910, p. 105;

Near-contemporary records agree that Olof Ohman uncovered the stone, but there is some dispute as to who was the first to notice the inscriptions on it and at what time of day the discovery was made. In a letter written in 1909 Ohman told Warren Upham of the Minnesota Historical Society that Edward was the first to notice the inscription, and that "The boys believed that they had found an Indian almanac." A Minneapolis physician, Knut O. Hoegh, who visited Ohman in 1909, wrote, almost certainly on the basis of a conversation with Ohman, that it was about lunchtime when Edward Ohman called his father's attention to the writing on the stone. During the noon period Ohman told his neighbor, Nils Flaten, about the stone, and later in the day Flaten went to see it, the tree and its roots, and the hole in the ground from which the stone and stump had been removed. Winchell reported a somewhat different set of circumstances when he wrote in 1909: "It is a fact, however, that the figures on the stone were not observed at first by the workman, Mr. Flatten [sic], who uncovered it, and the stone was for some time neglected." Just before making this statement, Winchell said that Ohman was clearing the land for plowing and was grubbing out roots. Another of Ohman's sons, Arthur, recalled in 1961 that Flaten was present and saw the stone excavated. Arthur said that Flaten was called back later in the day to see the inscription. As to the time of day, Arthur maintained that Edward went to the scene with an afternoon lunch for his father.[22]

The usual story of the finding of the stone is told by Olaus Olson in a little-known letter printed in *Svenska Amerikanska Posten* for

Winchell, in *Minnesota Historical Collections*, 15:221. See also Holand, *Kensington Stone*, 1; *Westward from Vinland*, 97; *Explorations in America Before Columbus*, 162; Winchell Field Book, December 2, 1909, March 4, 5, 17, 1910, Winchell Papers, and Appendix 8, below.

[22] Ohman and Flaten affidavits, Appendix 7, below; Ohman to Upham, December 9, 1909, Appendix 9, below, and Winchell's typewritten report to the MHS executive council, December 13, 1909, p. 5, Upham Papers, MHS Archives; Hoegh, "Kensington og Elbow Lake stenene," in *Symra*, 5:178–189 (1909); Arthur Ohman interview in Landsverk, *The Kensington Stone: A Reappraisal*, 63. Wahlgren asserted that, according to Winchell, Flaten uncovered the stone and "found no writing on it," but Winchell merely said that the writing on the stone was "not observed at first" — a very different matter. Wahlgren, again citing Winchell, said that the stone "lay neglected for a long time"; Winchell said it was "for some time neglected."

May 23, 1899. Ohman, wrote Olson, uprooted the tree and then left the place. One of his sons scraped dirt away from the stone with a stick, saw some inscriptions, and then "called his father to come and see that there was writing on the stone." The father came and, with a Norwegian helper (Flaten), pulled the stone out and discovered the writing on its flat underside. This account certainly does not suggest or imply any long lapse of time, but Professor Wahlgren, pondering the question of date and recalling the mention of August, 1898, in the several affidavits, suggested that the stone was actually found twice— once in August and again in November, 1898. He pointed to a letter written by E. E. Aaberg of Kensington on February 23, 1899, correcting a report that the stone had been found in a swamp. It was found, said Aaberg, not in a swamp, "but on a round hill surrounded by a slough." Wahlgren's theory is that the stone was found in the swamp in August, and then "reincarnated" for the November finding— that is, inscribed with runes and somehow placed under the roots of a growing tree. He does not explain how the stone could have been inserted under the tree without damaging the roots.[23]

One might have suspected a lapse of memory at the time the affidavits were written, and in fact Holand offered this very explanation in 1957. He suggested that perhaps the first man interviewed by Hoegh in 1909 made a mistake that was repeated in the other affidavits. No such solution can be accepted, for Holand himself, first in January, 1908, and then in October, 1908, gave the date of the find as August, 1898. This suggests that he got his information in 1907, when he first visited Kensington, talked with Ohman, and saw the stone— that is, two years before the affidavits were written.[24]

In the absence of Holand's contemporary notes, which presumably were lost when his house burned in 1934, we are left in

[23] For Olson's letter, see Appendix 5, below. See also Wahlgren, *Kensington Stone*, 42, 44. Wahlgren recognized that the "reincarnation" was a surmise and suggested as a possible alternative a substitution of stones. Aaberg's letter appeared in *Skandinaven*, March 1, 1899, p. 1; photostat obtained from Luther College Library, in Kensington file, Blegen Papers.

[24] Holand, in *Skandinaven*, January 11, 1908, p. 6, and *De norske settlementers historie*, 15 (Ephraim, Wis., 1908); Holand to F. Sanford Cutler, April 29, 1957, in Kensington Rune Stone Collection, MHS Archives.

ignorance as to just how the August date originated. Since we are dealing with an inscription that runologists say is fraudulent, the conflict in dates lends some weight to the hypothesis advanced by Professor Wahlgren. As will be noted later, however, his ingenious theory does not rule out all other possible explanations. It is not a Sherlockian solution, offered when only one possibility remains. There are some problems in relation to the flattening of the roots.

The question of dating suggests a query as to whether trees in Douglas County were being grubbed as late as November, 1898. Would the weather have permitted such work? The writer has searched regional Minnesota newspapers for weather reports, and nothing has been found to indicate that the tree could not have been grubbed on November 8, as Winchell said it was. At Moorhead, northwest of Kensington, the temperature went as high as 45 degrees Fahrenheit on November 7 and 26 degrees the next day. On November 24 a newspaper reported that a skater broke through thin ice on a lake near Kensington. It is doubtful that the ground was hard frozen by November 8, 1898.[25]

The discovery of the Kensington stone, as reported by the newspapers in February, 1899, had a number of interesting and important contemporary reverberations, some of which have never been mentioned in the long controversies.

The date 1362 was accepted in 1899. Holand in his first book about the stone wrote, "Nine years passed before the strange characters representing its numerals were correctly translated." The "correct" translation to which he referred was his own, published in 1908.[26] But this claim was completely without foundation. In the first place, Curme, though for a short time uncertain whether the date was 1362 or 1462, soon decided on the former. Breda was puzzled by the numerals, but others, besides Curme, read them correctly and quickly announced their versions.

F. Nosander of Taylors Falls, Minnesota, whose name has not hitherto appeared in articles and books on the rune stone, wrote a letter to *Svenska Amerikanska Posten* as early as March 1, 1899,

[25] *Alexandria Post News*, November 24, p. 8; *Moorhead Daily News*, November 7 and 8, p. 4 — all in 1898.
[26] Holand, *De norske settlementers historie*, 15.

and in it made a translation of the inscription which very nearly matches, word for word, the version later accepted as correct by specialized scholars. Nosander wrote "8 Goths and 22 Norwegians." He read the inscription as telling of 10 men red with blood and dead. His translation referred to 10 men by the sea, left there to look after the ships, 14 days' journey from "this island." And the date carved in the inscription he gave without question as 1362.[27]

We do not know who "F. Nosander" was, what books he had read, or where he gained his proficiency in reading runes. He was not a professor, he said in his letter to the newspaper, but had made himself able to translate runes by reading and study. He obviously worked from the facsimile that had appeared a few days earlier in the journal to which he sent his translation. At the end of his letter he used some unusual language. The translation that he offered was, he said, his own, and it would stand as his own even if fifty others should appear. His confidence was well founded, for his numerals and nearly all his words were correct. His version, in fact, was the best of any that appeared in 1899, including those done by linguists.

A few days earlier on February 24, 1899, the *Minneapolis Journal* printed a letter from H. M. Wagner of Starbuck (in Pope County, Minnesota, only a few miles from Kensington). He said that he had received a facsimile of the inscription and had been asked to decide on its "meaning and authenticity." Unfortunately he did not mention who made the request or what his own qualifications were, but obviously he had more than a casual familiarity with runes. He made an independent translation of the Kensington inscription which, the newspaper reported, differed somewhat from those of both Breda and Curme, but his text was not published with the letter.

Wagner wrote a sharp criticism of Breda, pointing out that in early times the values of runes were constantly changing—a fact, he said, that Breda had not taken into account. Wagner doubted that the stone had originally been placed where it was found. He thought it likely that it had been left somewhere to the east, perhaps on an island in the Great Lakes, and then transported west-

[27] Nosander, in *Svenska Amerikanska Posten*, March 14, 1899, p. 6, and Appendix 3, below.

ward by Indians. Unlike Nosander, Wagner had not solved the date of the inscription, for he assigned it to the eleventh century. One would like very much to know who sent Wagner a facsimile of the inscription, by whom the facsimile was made, and precisely how he translated it. But no clues to the man, except his printed letter, have as yet been found.[28]

Still another good translation was sent to *Svenska Amerikanska Posten* by J. K. Nordwall of Sebeka, Minnesota, in a letter dated March 7, 1899. He read the inscription's date as 1362, used the phrase "8 Goths and 22 Norwegians," and referred to the ships as being 14 days' journey "from this island." His translation agrees generally with those accepted by modern scholars except that he omitted the number of men found red with blood and dead and the number of those who remained at the sea to look after the ships. Nothing has been learned of the identity of Nordwall.[29]

These three men produced translations within a few days of the first appearance in newspapers of facsimiles of the Kensington inscription. They prove that there were persons in Minnesota, probably laymen, who found it relatively easy to translate runic inscriptions. Some have scoffed at the idea that in the 1890s everyday people in Minnesota could have known runes, but no writer on the rune-stone controversy has hitherto mentioned Nosander, Wagner, and Nordwall. The records show that there were yet others who had a knowledge of runic forms. And there is no question as to the general acceptance of 1362 as the date inscribed on the stone, notwithstanding Holand's claim that the right date did not appear until he translated the inscription in 1908.

The prompt appearance of translations of the Kensington inscription (two of them by persons living in parts of Minnesota not far from the county of discovery) suggests the need for further appraisal of the reading and independent study that existed among Scandinavian immigrants, and also of the transfer to America of schooling received in Sweden and Norway, especially in Sweden. Holand described the Kensington inscription as a "philological

[28] Wagner anticipated some parts of the argument later offered by Sivert N. Hagen, "The Kensington Runic Inscription," in *Speculum: A Journal of Mediaeval Studies*, 25:321–356 (July, 1950).

[29] Nordwall, in *Svenska Amerikanska Posten*, March 28, 1899, p. 14, and Appendix 4, below.

work of art." And then he asked, "Where could such erudition be found among the early pioneer Scandinavians of America?" The answer is in Minnesota, though modern linguists do not regard the inscription as a "philological work of art."[30]

Not too much has been learned about what books immigrants from the Scandinavian countries brought to America or bought in this country. It would be enlightening to know also just what books were printed in installments in early Scandinavian-American newspapers, and it would be useful if some bibliographer prepared, for the period 1870–1900, a list of American and Scandinavian-American articles, books, and reviews having to do with Norse discoveries, sagas, runes, and related subjects.[31] Evidence might show that there was more popular interest in runes than has been assumed. How does one explain, for instance, the publication of an illustrated essay on "Runes" by J. S. Gram in the Chicago magazine, Scandinavia, more than a decade before the Kensington stone came to light? Or the inclusion in a Minneapolis newspaper in 1892 of an article about runes (without illustrations)? Or the suggestion made by Skandinaven in the late 1890s that a rune stone should be erected in honor of Leif Ericson? Such questions and items of information do not prove that the Kensington inscription was fraudulent, but they indicate more knowledge of runes among the immigrants in America than some writers have realized.[32]

It is well known that in the late nineteenth century newspapers and magazines reflected the widespread interest in the Norsemen and their journeys. Professor Wahlgren took particular note of controversial articles that appeared after Gustav Storm in 1887 published his monographic study of the Vinland voyages. The

[30] Holand, Westward from Vinland, 256.
[31] For example, the North, a Minneapolis weekly, carried an article on "The Vinland Sagas and Their Critics" on December 24, 1890, p. 3. John B. and Marie A. Shipley, prolific writers about Norse exploration, proposed a historical exhibit on Norse colonization in America in the issue of January 28, 1891, p. 5; and Breda's suggestion that a model of the Gokstad ship be secured for Minneapolis was endorsed on November 13, 1889, p. 1, 4, and November 26, 1890, p. 4. As early as 1890 the North had at least one subscriber in Kensington.
[32] See Gram, in Scandinavia, 2:267–271 (November, 1885); North, January 20, 1892, p. 5; Holand, in Skandinaven, March 15, 1899, p. 9.

word *opdagelse,* for example, was used twenty-eight times in Storm's monograph either separately or as a compound *opdagelsesrejse;* that is, journey of discovery. The point was that the Kensington inscription included the word *opdagelsefard,* which linguists find to be an anachronism. Wahlgren suggested that the word as employed in the inscription originated from newspapers of the 1880s and 1890s. Storm accepted the theory that Norsemen got to the North American continent, but rejected the idea that Vinland was south of what is now the northeast border of the United States. His views provoked much dissent. Rasmus B. Anderson, one of the country's best known Norwegian Americans, was among those who took up the cudgels against the Norwegian scholar, and the controversy was "in full swing," according to Wahlgren, in 1890 and 1891.[33]

Popular interest was again stirred in 1893, when a replica of the Gokstad Viking ship was successfully sailed across the Atlantic and through the Great Lakes to Chicago for the Columbian Exposition of that year. This feat occasioned many articles in American newspapers, including the Scandinavian press of the Middle West; and it inspired a well-known Swedish-American writer, Johan A. Enander, to publish in 1893 a book entitled (in translation) "The Norsemen in America, or America's Discovery." The book was written in Swedish (*Nordmännen i Amerika, eller Amerikas upptäckt*) and issued at Rock Island, Illinois. It reviewed the story of the Vikings, Greenland, and the Norse voyages; and it closed with a chapter inquiring into the possibility that there might be remains testifying to the presence of Norsemen in America in Viking times.

The historical value of newspaper items roughly contemporary with the public announcement of the Kensington stone is reinforced by the interesting letter written on May 16, 1899, by Olaus Olson to *Svenska Amerikanska Posten.* Olson lived in Holmes City, a village not far from Kensington. He was one of a dozen men who

---

[33] Wahlgren, *Kensington Stone,* 122. Rasmus B. Anderson was professor of Scandinavian languages and literature in the University of Wisconsin, United States minister to Denmark, editor of *Amerika* (Madison), and the author of many books and articles. For a full biographical treatment of this Norwegian-American, see Lloyd Hustvedt, *Rasmus Bjørn Anderson, Pioneer Scholar* (Northfield, 1966).

visited the Ohman farm in the spring of 1899 to excavate the Kensington site in a search for relics having to do with the supposed expedition of 1362. The group was headed by Cleve W. Van Dyke of Alexandria, superintendent of the Douglas County schools. The date of the excavation (probably May 2, 1899) may have some bearing on the date of the discovery. If the inscribed stone was taken from the ground in August, 1898, the excavation of the site probably would not have been delayed until the following spring. This point, made by Ole G. Landsverk in a book on the Kensington stone, is pertinent, of course, only if the Wahlgren theory of a "reincarnation" is not sustained by facts.[34]

Olaus Olson, as has been noted, saw the roots, and he estimated the tree's age at from twenty-five to thirty years. He described Ohman as an honorable man who was no "humbugmaker." The stone, thought Olson, was genuine, and he accepted without question the date 1362. Speaking of the excavation, held "fourteen days ago" (that is, fourteen days before May 16, 1899), he said that the men found, about four feet deep on the north side of the area, some fragments four to five inches long which looked like limestone, but were thought to resemble moldered bones. He was of the opinion that the men reported to have been killed in 1362 were buried where the stone was uncovered, and he favored a more careful investigation of the site. As will be noted in chapter 4, Van Dyke also wrote about the excavation, but because the inscription was regarded as a hoax, he did not have a scientific analysis made of the pieces that seemed to resemble bones.

Van Dyke, it is of some interest to learn, must be added to the list of those in Minnesota in 1899 who had at least a little knowledge of Norwegian history and of runes, for he had attended "a course of lectures on Norse archaeology" at the University of Minnesota. This may well have been the course, announced in several university bulletins, in which Breda dealt with the history of the Scandinavian languages, Scandinavian archaeology, Norse mythology, and the Viking age.[35]

[34] Olson, in *Svenska Amerikanska Posten*, May 23, 1899, p. 7, and Appendix 5, below. See also Van Dyke to Winchell, April 19, 1910, Archaeological Records, MHS Archives, in Appendix 13, below.
[35] Van Dyke to Winchell, April 19, 1910, in Appendix 13, below. Breda's

One of the puzzles of history is that of determining what significance, if any, scholars should attach to silence — the absence of letters or diary records or reports in newspapers about happenings which presumably would have attracted contemporary attention, both public and individual.

One might suppose, for instance, that the people of Alexandria, Minnesota, would have been interested in the inscribed stone, especially after it became the subject of front-page newspaper stories in Minneapolis and Chicago. Alexandria was near Kensington; the finding of the rune stone was not ordinary news; and there was no newspaper in Kensington. Yet the *Alexandria Post News* gave the stone no attention beyond a formal reprinting of the first *Minneapolis Journal* story of the find and then, in the succeeding number, a reproduction of the *Journal's* sketch of the inscription.[36] It carried no firsthand story, no follow-up items; it expressed no curiosity; it did not even mention the expedition made by twelve men in the spring of 1899 to excavate the site of the discovery. There is no profit in scolding journalists of the past for sins of omission, but one cannot escape a feeling of regret that the Alexandria paper reported no interviews, made no drawings, took no pictures, and prepared no reports or editorials — a startling contrast to the community's promotional interest in the Kensington stone in later years.

Equally puzzling is the absence of references to the stone in the local news items and gossip sent every two or three weeks from Kensington to the Alexandria newspaper by one or more unnamed correspondents. Holand later said that the stone, while on exhibit in Kensington, was "inspected by thousands." But the Kensington correspondents of the Alexandria paper seemed totally unaware of any such inspection, though they occasionally looked at window displays. Kensington was a village of less than three hundred inhabitants. Where did the "thousands" come from — and if there were such numbers, why did the newspapers of the region totally ignore the matter? One may conjecture that the exhibition — if the stone was exhibited at all — took place be-

course is listed in the University of Minnesota *Bulletin*, 1898–99, and in some earlier catalogs.

[38] *Alexandria Post News*, February 23, p. 1, March 2, 1899, p. 1.

tween about January 1, 1899, when John P. Hedberg first reported
the discovery to the Swedish newspaper in Minneapolis, and a little after the middle of February, 1899, when it was shipped to
Northwestern University.[37]

Interest in the stone did not wholly evaporate after it was returned by Curme to Kensington. An illustration is a letter written
by John F. Steward of Chicago on October 15, 1899, to Ludvig
F. A. Wimmer of Denmark, one of the founders of modern runology. Steward, an amateur geologist and the author of a book entitled *Lost Maramech and Earliest Chicago*, sent to Wimmer, with
his letter, four clear photographs of the Kensington rune stone
which had been taken by or for Steward at the home of Professor
Curme. This probably means that the pictures were made soon
after March 1, 1899, and they rank as the earliest known photographs of the stone. As such they are reproduced below.[38]
What Steward wanted from Wimmer was his judgment as to
whether the Kensington inscription was genuine or fraudulent. He
told briefly of the finding of the stone, an "honest discovery," he
believed. He described the inscription as having been cut "as with
a 'diamond-pointed' tool," but, he said, the grooves showed "no
more newness than the natural surfaces of the rock."[39] Steward
said that he was "getting together all possible facts connected
with the matter with a view to sifting it to the bottom." He asserted that if the inscription should be a fraud, "the fact must be
known so that future historians shall not be deceived," and he
added, if "it proves to be a genuine record it is important."
To Steward the "record as found on the stone" seemed likely to
remain "the only evidence of fraud," for he regarded "the circumstances connected with its finding" as "all favorable to age and
genuineness." In the light of Steward's letter, every effort has been

---

[37] Holand, *Kensington Stone*, 2. The population of Kensington in 1895 was
264; Minnesota Manuscript Census Schedules, 1905, Douglas County, p. 257.
[38] Wahlgren, *Kensington Stone*, 68, 191n. Steward's letter is in "Collectio
Runologica Wimmeriana," item no. 556, Royal Library, Copenhagen, reproduced in Appendix 6, below.
[39] Wahlgren, *Kensington Stone*, 68, reported that the runic grooves, according to Steward, "were cut with a 'diamond-pointed' tool." But the word "as"
in Steward's statement conveys a different meaning.

THE ILLUSTRATION *above and the three which follow are copies of the earliest known photographs of the Kensington rune stone. The pictures were taken probably soon after March 1, 1899, by or for John F. Steward while the stone was at the home of George O. Curme in Chicago. The pictures were enclosed with Steward's letter to runologist L. F. A. Wimmer of Denmark. Photographs courtesy Royal Library, Copenhagen.*

44

made to discover his papers, if they have survived, so that modern scholars may know what "facts" he managed to collect and learn whether or not Wimmer replied to his inquiry. Thus far nothing has been found except the letter and photographs sent to Wimmer.

How long Curme kept the stone at Evanston before returning it to Kensington is not known precisely, though it probably was a month or more. Nor is it known when the stone was transported from Kensington back to the Ohman farm where it was unearthed. A letter written many years later indicated that it may have been returned to the Kensington bank and kept there for "about one year," but no confirmation of this statement has been found.[40] The usual story is that it was taken back to the farm, where it was used, face down, as a stepping stone to a granary. But here, as in many aspects of the rune-stone saga, it is difficult to separate legend from fact. Decades later, three of Ohman's sons denied that the stone had been used as a doorstep to their father's granary. Winchell, on his first trip to Kensington, noted in his field book, under date of November 30, 1909, that after the stone was returned from Illinois "it lay some years in the shed" at Ohman's. "Then Mr. Holand took it up." Curiously enough, in a published report, Winchell adopted the tale later denied by Ohman's sons — the story of the supposed stepping stone near the Ohman granary. This was told by Holand as early as 1908. Either Winchell had forgotten his own field book record or else for some reason he believed Holand's report to be well founded. The doorstep added a dramatic touch to Holand's rediscovery or rescue of the stone.[41]

One more item must be noticed before turning to the second cycle of Kensington interest. This is the fact that in 1906 the Swedish linguist, Adolf Noreen of the University of Uppsala, wrote about runic inscriptions and dealt with that from Kensington. The

[40] Andrew A. Davidson to J. A. Holvik, October 20, 1949, Holvik Papers.
[41] Wahlgren, *Kensington Stone*, 184n, 191n. John and Arthur Ohman were interviewed by Wahlgren on August 11, 1953. Edward said of the stone, "The story goes that it was used for a doorstep, but it never was"; Edward Ohman interview, December 28, 1949. See also Winchell Field Book, November 30, 1909, Appendix 8, below; *Minnesota Historical Collections*, 15:226.

inscription, Noreen said, was a mixture of Swedish, Danish, and English, and had been made up by a modern Swedish emigrant from Dalarna.[42]

[42] Noreen, "Runinskrifter från nyare tid," in *Föreningen Heimdals Populärvetenskapliga tidningsartiklar*, no. 6 (1906), clipping in Archaeological Records, MHS Archives. Copies of the inscription were sent to Noreen by Curme. Breda quoted Noreen at some length in *Symra*, 6:74. See also Wahlgren, *Kensington Stone*, 195n; Hagen, in *Speculum*, 25:324.

holanð Goes to kensington

THE SECOND CYCLE OF PUBLIC INTEREST in the Kensington riddle
may be dated from 1907 when Hjalmar R. Holand made his first
visit to the Olof Ohman farm. By 1910, only three years after he
"rediscovered" the stone, Holand had made himself the central
figure in its discussion. Professor Wahlgren has suggested that the
"Minnesota petroglyph would have died a natural death" if Holand had not "resuscitated" it. While it is conceivable that someone else might have brought the topic back to life, it is undeniable
that Holand, by his attacks, replies, speeches, books, articles, and
travels, was the chief defender and the central person in the controversy until his death in the 1960s. Much of the discussion re-
volved about him — his claims, his errors, his flair for debate, the
bulk and repetition of his writing.[1]

Because of Holand's large role in the drama, it is of interest
to inquire when he first learned about the Kensington rune stone.
The traditional story is that he chanced upon it in 1907 while
searching for information on Norwegian settlements in the United
States. A careful examination of Holand's own writings reveals no
clear or consistent picture of the circumstances of his introduction
to the stone. In one place he mentions that he went to Kensing-

---

[1] Holand, *Kensington Stone*, 4; Wahlgren, *Kensington Stone*, 9, 81 (quote).
Chester N. Gould, a distinguished linguist on the University of Chicago fac-
ulty who condemned the Kensington inscription as a fraud, also wrote that
Holand was the "main part of the Kensington stone." See Gould to Upham,
March 19, 1910, an unnumbered 24-page letter dealing with Holand's meth-
ods in Archaeological Records, MHS Archives. For the quotation, see p. [16].
On Gould's career, see *General Catalogue of the University of Minnesota,
1916*, 48 (Minneapolis, 1916).

ton in 1907 and there heard something about a stone "with some writing on it," and his assumption was that the "writing" was an Indian pictograph. Very different in tone is a statement in his first book. There he wrote that the Kensington people had a "vivid memory" of the stone, and he hunted up its owner "with eager expectancy." As to the first period of publicity in 1899, Holand was absorbed in writing a master's thesis on the Elder Edda and "knew nothing about the Kensington Stone." In a word, he suggested that chance led him to Kensington in 1907. But in one of his earliest articles, alluding to the 1899 period, Holand wrote, "At the time I had no faith in the alleged runestone; but having made a study of runes for many years, I finally found opportunity to visit the place of discovery." This conflict in recollection is psychologically curious. A review of the evidence indicates that Holand went to Kensington expressly to study the stone and that for some reason he twisted the facts when he said that he "accidentally came in contact with" it while on his visit to the village.[2]

Holand could scarcely have forgotten that in 1899, when he was a student at the University of Wisconsin, he was a reader of *Skandinaven*, the Chicago newspaper that gave publicity to the Kensington stone in late February and early March of that year. He was also a contributor to the paper in that very period. On March 15, 1899, he published a letter (in effect an article) in *Skandinaven* entitled (in translation from the Norwegian) "A Bauta for Leif." It was signed by the name he then used, "Hjalmar Rued," of Madison, Wisconsin. And it appeared only five days after *Skandinaven* had published a lengthy illustrated article on the Kensington rune stone by P. A. Conradi.[3]

Not only the name and address mark the article as an authentic

[2] Holand, *My First Eighty Years*, 185; *Kensington Stone*, 4; *Explorations in America Before Columbus*, 165; "First Authoritative Investigation of 'Oldest Native Document in America,'" in *Journal of American History*, 4:170 (Second Quarter, 1910). See also Wahlgren, *Kensington Stone*, 82; Holand, *De norske settlementers historie*, 15–21.

[3] Holand's article appeared on p. 9 of the second section of *Skandinaven*. Bauta, according to Webster, is a Scandinavian archaeological term meaning "an upright stone sometimes 20 feet high." Upham to Curme, February 25, 1910, MHS Letter Press Books, MHS Archives, mentioned that Holand used the name "Hjalmar Rued" in 1899. See also Conradi, in *Skandinaven*, March 10, 1899, p. 2.

Holand production, but also its style and matter. Certainly he had read earlier issues of the newspaper, for he took into account the point that *Skandinaven* had already advocated the erection of a rune stone in honor of "Leif and his people" to celebrate the nine-hundredth anniversary of Leif Ericson's arrival in America in 1000 A.D. The idea was excellent, thought Holand, but knowledge of runes was very rare. He believed it would be more appropriate, therefore, to raise an inscribed bauta stone fifty feet high on the Chicago lake front.

Holand did not then refer to the Kensington stone even though it had been discussed in *Skandinaven* in February and March, 1899. It is not unreasonable to surmise, however, that he had read about the stone. Apart from his interest in Leif Ericson, he had studied Old Norse and runes with Professor Julius E. Olson of the University of Wisconsin. Yet Holand later wrote that when the stone "was found and rejected," he knew nothing about it. Elsewhere, as has been mentioned above, he declared in a clear reference to 1899 that he had "no faith in the alleged runestone."[4]

Whatever the explanation of this strange muddle of testimony, his article of 1899 is of intrinsic interest, not only as one of the earliest known pieces from his pen, but also because his ideas of that year about the Norsemen are comparable with those he expounded from 1908 until the end of his life. Since the article from *Skandinaven* is virtually unknown — Holand made no reference to it in his autobiography or other writings — an English translation is here presented:

A BAUTA FOR LEIF

A Contributor Maintains That a Bauta Stone Would
Be the Worthiest Memorial

Mr. Editor: It is gratifying to see that *Skandinaven* is beginning to blow the trumpet for making preparations for the nine-hundredth anniversary celebration next year of the discovery of America. This will be the first celebration of this kind ever held here in America, and without doubt it will be the last in which any of us will take part. We ought, therefore, to take the matter in hand seriously.

[4] Holand, in *Journal of American History*, 4:170.

Skandinaven has voiced the idea that we ought to erect a great rune stone as a monument to Leif and his people. This, in general, is an excellent thought. Such a stone would be much preferable to one of those dreary statues of a man of whose appearance we have less knowledge than we have of the man in the moon. Let us, above all, keep ourselves free from such a figure of the imagination.

A rune stone, however, probably would not be altogether the best monument, for knowledge of runes is extremely rare. I therefore propose — and this will not cost anything — that we erect a gigantic bauta stone. On one side there might be written in plain English a concise passage surveying the discovery and colonization of America by the Norsemen so that it might become generally understood that the visit made by the Norsemen to America was not merely accidental, but an actual settlement that lasted for hundreds of years and was broken off only by the Black Death. On the other side one might find a place for a record of those who have raised the monument. The other two surfaces might be decorated with drawings showing the kinds of ships used, etc., as well as examples of runes.

If this bauta stone were creditably high — say fifty feet — and placed on a beautiful natural elevation, it would be a monument that could not easily be excelled in impressiveness. The best place might well be the lake front in Chicago.

This is a cause in which every Norwegian should [manifest an] [5] interest, and it is to be hoped that the newspapers will support it in such a manner that Norsemen in this country can carry the affair off with honor.

If, in addition, a day could be fixed on which there might be a general collection of money by ministers and others for this purpose, I am sure that we should get a rich contribution of funds. For such a cause our sturdy Norwegian farmers throughout the Northwest will take pleasure in giving their five-dollar bills.

Madison, Wis. March, '99

HJALMAR RUED

[5] The copy of the newspaper text that I consulted was slightly smudged and one or two words were illegible. Those supplied in brackets seem to fit the meaning and context.

If Holand stated correctly that at one time he had no faith in the Kensington stone, he experienced a conversion in 1907. When he visited Olof Ohman late in the summer of that year, he persuaded the finder to turn the stone over to him. In his own words in translation, he "procured the stone and made a minute and prolonged study of it." This study occurred in the months between August, 1907, and the following January. In an article in *Skandinaven* of January 11, 1908, Holand announced that the Kensington inscription was authentic.[6]

A possibly minor matter, though one that has figured in the controversy, illustrates a problem that needs clarification. This is the question of the ownership of the stone. Precisely how did Holand acquire it? Did he buy it? Was it given to him? Was it transferred to him with reservations? In most of his writings, Holand passed over the point without going into details. He "procured" the stone; he "persuaded the owner to let me take it home"; Ohman "gave it to me." When he wrote his autobiography in 1957, he remembered, or seemed to remember, his exact conversation with Ohman fifty years earlier. Holand asked, "What will you take for the stone?" Ohman replied, "How much will you give?" Holand offered five dollars; Ohman thought the stone worth ten. After some further conversation Ohman said, "I think you're just as poor as I am, so you can have the stone for nothing." In 1914 Holand told Milo M. Quaife that he had paid twenty-five dollars for the stone. And in an affidavit signed by Ohman in 1909, he stated that he "presented" the stone to Holand. Later Ohman said he "never gave the stone to Holand" as his personal property. This question of ownership will be the subject of further consideration in a later chapter.[7]

In 1908 Holand published his book on the Norwegian settlements and devoted a chapter to Vinland and the Kensington

[6] The article, "Runestenen fra Kensington," in *Skandinaven*, is usually referred to under the date January 17, 1908, but I found it in the issue for January 11, 1908, p. 6.

[7] Holand, in *Journal of American History*, 4:170; *Kensington Stone*, 6; *Westward from Vinland*, 100; *Explorations in America Before Columbus*, 166; *My First Eighty Years*, 187; Quaife, in *New England Quarterly*, 7:615n. See also p. 81, below.

stone. In it he declared that the Kensington runes were the most significant and interesting of all runic records, the "earliest American document," source material for a new chapter in the history of the Vinland expeditions, and of intrinsic interest as a record of plans daringly initiated and tragically ended. Nor was this all. The Kensington stone, he said, was the only rune stone found in America; chiseled on it was one of the longest runic inscriptions known, a record which would shed new light on the development of runic writing. Holand had no hesitation in pronouncing the inscription genuine. He included in his book a photograph of the stone, his own version of the inscription, and a translation of it into modern Norwegian. He summarized the reasons for his conclusions in several categories: the circumstances of the find, the appearance of the runes, the length of the inscription, the date, and the language, especially the presence of certain runes not previously known. The runemaster, Holand believed, was one of the Swedish Goths referred to in the inscription.[8]

Among the many frustrations that confront students of the history of the Kensington controversy is the absence of notebooks or other records kept by Holand in 1907 and later when he visited Ohman and others in the Kensington area. If he kept such contemporary records, they presumably were lost in a fire that destroyed his house at Ephraim, Wisconsin, in 1934.[9] For detail, therefore, one must turn to his articles and books and to letters of his in collections left by others.

In view of Holand's role in the Kensington drama, it is appropriate here to review briefly his line of defense of the inscription. Through more than five decades he upheld its genuineness, drawing upon linguistic, archaeological, and historical circumstances. In his first book devoted wholly to the subject (1932) he presented a general summary of his arguments. There was no "decisive evidence," he wrote, that the inscription was not authentic; the theory of forgery was "highly improbable"; in fact, external evidence proved such a theory "impossible"; and "Scandinavian arms and implements of the Middle Ages" found in western Min-

[8] Holand, *De norske settlementers historie*, chapter 2 (quote on p. 14).
[9] Holand, *Pre-Columbian Crusade*, 56.

nesota showed that the "region had been visited by Norse explorers several hundred years ago."[10]

Holand explained these conclusions in detail and amplified them in articles and books, adding new theories and reports of supplementary finds of artifacts.[11] Not a little of his writing consisted of replies to critics who believed the Kensington inscription was fraudulent. He often asserted that the reason philologists rejected the inscription in 1899 was their alleged inability to understand its numerical symbols, which, he insisted, were not read correctly until he himself did so in 1908. He engaged in rebuttals on many challenged words and forms of the inscription, and when runologists pronounced *opdagelsefard* (journey of discovery) anachronistic in a supposed fourteenth-century runic inscription, Holand suggested that oral usage may have preceded the appearance of a loan word in Scandinavian writing and that sailors might have used the spoken forms. He attempted to show that many other questioned words and usages in the inscription were acceptable in the fourteenth century.

In his first book Holand took the position that the inscription if genuine must necessarily be related to the supposed Paul Knutson expedition. A royal authorization had been made in 1354 for an expedition to Greenland under one of King Magnus' barons, Paul Knutson, for the purpose of restoring Christianity where it had fallen into decay. The only fourteenth-century reference to such an expedition seems to be the authorization itself. It is not known whether the ship allocated for Knutson's use sailed to Greenland.[12]

Holand believed that some members of the Knutson expedition returned to Norway in 1363 or 1364, and he argued that the chronology would fit the concept of a journey to the abandoned Western Settlements in Greenland, then a crossing to Vinland, thereafter a journey to Hudson Strait and Hudson Bay, and a trip by an expeditionary party southward to the Kensington region of the future state of Minnesota. Holand took into account the New-

[10] Holand, *Kensington Stone*, 190.
[11] For a summary of Holand's major writings on the Kensington problem, see Bibliography, p. 191, 196, 197, 203, below.
[12] Holand, *Kensington Stone*, 71–77.

port Tower in Rhode Island, to which he ascribed a Norse origin and which he defined as a central point in Vinland. He also gathered into the Knutson story the figure of Nicholas of Lynne, a fourteenth-century English friar who was supposedly the author of a lost manuscript dealing with the *Inventio Fortunata*.[13]

In meeting the objections of critics Holand necessarily had to devote much effort to linguistic defenses, but in his 1956 book he expressed the wish that critics would "lay aside their philological calipers" and look especially at three circumstances of the find that seemed to him clear proof of its authenticity. One was the age of the tree, which he then estimated at sixty-nine years. The second was the reference in the inscription to "this island." (He argued that five hundred years earlier the hill where the stone was found had stood above a surrounding lake and was therefore an island.) The third was the weathering of the inscription which, he contended, showed that the stone before falling face down had stood upright long enough for the inscription to have attained what he described as its "corroded appearance." Following these assertions about the age of the tree, the lake, and weathering, Holand touched on "the hunt for a forger" and sharply rejected the supposition that Olof Ohman, the finder, could have carved and planted the rune stone.[14]

Beyond the lines of defense mentioned, Holand gave emphasis to chiseled holes in rocks which he believed had once been made by Norsemen. These were called "mooring stones," that is, stones with bored holes in which ringbolts could be fastened and used for mooring boats. In his book of 1956 Holand offered maps locating ten such holes in rocks in western Minnesota, including the Kensington area. He believed that the holes were made by the visiting party of Norsemen in the fourteenth century. Throughout his books he also described various finds of axes, fire steels, halberds, and other artifacts to which he ascribed a medieval origin and which he believed were related to the Kensington expedition. Such discoveries were reported to him by persons in western Min-

[13] Holand, *America, 1355–1364*, 117–132, 204; *Pre-Columbian Crusade*, 103. See also Holand, in Wisconsin Academy of Sciences, Arts, and Letters, *Transactions*, 48:205–219. On Nicholas, see chapter 1, note 18, above.

[14] *Explorations in America Before Columbus*, 168–176 (quotes p. 168, 172, 174).

nesota and were duly recorded and described. He also believed that the La Vérendrye stone, found somewhere in the West in the 1740s (Holand said in 1738) and inscribed with characters resembling Tataric, was a rune stone.[15]

Thus the case for genuineness was to Holand one of multiple alleged proofs — the language, the appearance of the inscriptions, the idea of a trip from Hudson Bay southward, King Magnus' authorization of Paul Knutson to lead an expedition to Greenland in the fourteenth century, the theory that the Newport Tower was medieval, the various artifacts, the "mooring stones," and the Vérendrye stone from the eighteenth century.

As early as 1908 the Norwegian Society of Minneapolis took an interest in the Kensington stone. It also was curious about another stone reported to have been found at Elbow Lake, Minnesota, about twenty-three miles from the Ohman farm. The Minneapolis society, probably at the urging of Holand, decided to conduct an investigation of the Kensington stone. The organization believed that if a fraud had been perpetrated, it should be exposed. If the inscription proved authentic, it was of historical importance and should be studied in detail.

The society therefore appointed an investigating committee composed of three men: Knut O. Hoegh of Minneapolis, a well-known physician and surgeon; Gisle Bothne of the University of Minnesota, professor of Scandinavian languages and literature; and E. Kristian Johnsen of the United Norwegian Lutheran Church Seminary in St. Paul, a theologian. After the fashion of many committees, the job of this one was left largely to its chairman, Hoegh, who made several trips to Elbow Lake and Kensington in 1908 and 1909. He wrote a report that appeared in the Norwegian-American literary periodical Symra in 1909.[16]

Hoegh's report was brief and concise. If he made contemporaneous notes of his interviews with Ohman and others, they have

[15] Explorations in America Before Columbus, 139, 140, and chapters 16, 17, 23. On the Vérendrye stone, see Appendix 14, below.

[16] Hoegh, in Symra, 5:178–189. On Johnsen, see Dictionary of American Biography, 10:77 (New York, 1933). On Bothne and Hoegh, see Warren Upham and Rose B. Dunlap, comps., Minnesota Biographies, 1655–1912, 66, 335 (Minnesota Historical Collections, vol. 14, St. Paul, 1912).

not been found, nor indeed have any of his papers. Scholars searching for precise details of the investigation are therefore frustrated, as they are at so many other places in the story. The lack of detail in this instance is the more regrettable because Hoegh had a hand in the gathering of the affidavits about which there has been controversy, and his published report does not wholly clarify the points at issue.

In December, 1908, Hoegh saw a stone which had been found on a farm west of Elbow Lake. It had been used in a foundation for a mill built in 1890 at that village. It seemingly had an inscription of some 150 to 200 characters within a double circle eight and six inches in diameter. Hoegh did not know much about runes; most of the characters on the stone were difficult to make out; but he said that he saw some that reminded him of runes. What has become of this stone is not known. Supposedly it was secured by the Norwegian Society and conveyed to Minneapolis. Efforts to find records left by the Norwegian Society of Minneapolis, as in the case of Hoegh's papers, have thus far been fruitless.

In June, 1909, Hoegh, with Holand as a companion (the doctor explained that Holand chanced to be in Minneapolis at the time) journeyed to Kensington. Nils Flaten, whose house was about five hundred feet away, accompanied them to the place of the Kensington stone's discovery. Flaten pointed out a spot on the hill above the swamp about three-fourths of the way up. Hoegh remarked that Flaten had passed the site the day before the stone was found and had then seen no sign that the ground around the tree had been disturbed in any way. Hoegh then told of the tree, an aspen eight to ten inches in diameter, which had grown over the stone; and of the two flattened roots — one running down along the side of the stone, the other growing horizontally for about eighteen inches and then turning down over the side. He recounted that Ohman's son had first noticed inscriptions and called them to his father's attention about lunchtime, whereupon Olof Ohman summoned Flaten to come and see the stone. The doctor gave other information touching on the interest of neighbors, and he told of the stone being conveyed to Kensington without specifying just when that was done. He wrote that unfortunately someone had scraped the letters to make them more legible, and a couple of the marks were in fact probably made less clear. Then he gave the usual story of the sending of the rune stone to Evanston and of its condemnation as a fraud by Curme and Breda, after which it was returned to Ohman.

Hoegh declared himself incompetent to judge the inscription on the basis of the runes, the language, and the appearance of the stone. But he suggested that certain lines of external evidence should be studied, such as the place of discovery, the history of the find, the motives for a fraud, the skill to carry out one, and the trustworthiness of those who first saw the stone. He gave special attention to Ohman, whom he described as a trustworthy and understanding but unschooled farmer. Ohman, he said, had made no effort to turn his find into material gain. His behavior was precisely what might be expected if the stone were genuine. Hoegh thought there was not the least likelihood that Ohman had inscribed the runes, buried the slab, and then dug it up again. In general, Hoegh concluded that the stone was discovered at the spot reported; it was the slab then (1909) in the possession of Holand; none of those who took part in the discovery and the events immediately following could have had anything to do with the cutting of the runes; and the stone must have been in the ground long before the surrounding land was cultivated. On the hypothesis that the stone was genuine, Hoegh took into account the various improbabilities that had to be considered, but he thought that the theory of a southward approach by the Hudson Bay route obviated some of them. He undoubtedly believed the inscription authentic.

In view of the importance attached by Holand and others to the four affidavits presumably secured in the main by Hoegh during the summer of 1909, it is strange that his report did not give the texts of the documents in question. What Hoegh wrote concerning them (translated from his Norwegian text in *Symra*) was as follows:

All the neighbors were ready to believe in Olof Ohman, among them Roald Ben[t]son, an old settler well acquainted with the place, a faithful example of a trustworthy, wise Norwegian farmer. He is convinced of the truth of the story with respect to the discovery and the roots; also that there had been no earlier digging there — in all these matters he has given a solemn affidavit. Many others are willing and have testified to me the same as Ben[t]son. The goldsmith in Kensington, S. Olson, was one of those who helped to dig in the ground for relics. All these persons identify the stone with the illustration in Holand's book. All confirm the position and appearance of the roots and the size of the aspen. Some said that the aspen was thicker than a man's leg, and most of them thought the diameter was ten inches, some eight inches. One individual said it was "over five inches."[17]

Professor Wahlgren presented an interesting discussion of the affidavits of Ohman, Flaten, and others, and he printed four of them. The originals were never produced by Holand or Hoegh. The mystery of the documents caused Wahlgren to ask, "But are there, or have there ever been, any affidavits?[18]

Hoegh in his report stated that he went to Kensington with Holand in June, but the affidavits are all dated July 20, 1909. One gets the impression from Hoegh's account that the affidavits were secured on the June trip; the later date is unexplained. Possibly the report covered impressions received on more than one trip to Kensington despite the fact that Hoegh referred only to June; or conceivably the signing of the affidavits was not completed before a notary public until July 20. In any event, the language of Hoegh's report does not exactly sustain Wahlgren's view that "No fistful of affidavits is mentioned beyond one by Ben[t]son."[19] We have Hoegh's own assertion that "many others" were willing to testify and had done so for him. If he does not precisely claim a "fistful," he does indicate several.

Wahlgren, in discussing the possible whereabouts of the original affidavits and raising the question of whether they ever existed, does not mention a footnote that Holand included in his 1910 article on the rune stone. There, after quoting the Ohman affidavit, Holand wrote, "The facts in this affidavit are corroborated by five

---

[17] Hoegh, in *Symra*, 5:187.
[18] Wahlgren, *Kensington Stone*, 57 (quote), chapter 6. See also Appendix 7, below.
[19] Wahlgren, *Kensington Stone*, 56.

[*sic*] other affidavits now in the possession of Dr. Knut Hoegh, Minneapolis, Minnesota."[20]

This information may possibly illuminate Holand's later silence when he was asked to produce the affidavits. My own thought had been that the originals were destroyed when Holand's house burned, for in a publication of 1962 Holand said that he had "retained" the originals, but that his books and papers were destroyed in the fire of June, 1934. Although he did not specifically assert that the affidavits were then destroyed, he implied that they were.[21] Knowing how undependable Holand's memory was, I am now inclined to believe that he was correct in 1910 when he said that Hoegh had the affidavits. I suspect that Holand had copies and that the originals were retained by Hoegh. If they have survived, they probably are in Hoegh's papers.

The problems centering in the affidavits do not end, however, with the question of the whereabouts of the originals. The existing copies are phrased in formal legal language, and Professor Wahlgren was unquestionably right when he suggested that they were "the product of one and the same organizing intelligence." The language used by this "intelligence" was not that of the signers. In *Westward from Vinland,* Holand gave a somewhat confusing account of these documents. He referred to "five affidavits" and wrote that they "were personally obtained by Dr. Knut Hoegh." Subsequently he wrote that Edward Ohman, Bentson, and Samuel Olson, the jeweler, were "separately interviewed" by him and by Hoegh and that the latter "took down three of these statements in writing," after which they were read and signed. Then, he added, Olson "preferred to write his own," and his statement was also signed by Bentson.[22]

Perhaps Holand's reply to an inquiry from F. Sanford Cutler, curator of the Minnesota Historical Society's museum in 1957, comes as close as anything to revealing what really happened. Mr. Cutler was seeking an explanation of the conflict in dates given for the finding of the Kensington stone. The affidavits said

[20] Holand, in *Journal of American History,* 4:178n.

[21] Holand, *Pre-Columbian Crusade,* 56.

[22] Wahlgren, *Kensington Stone,* 54; Holand, *Westward from Vinland,* 110, 113.

August, 1898; near-contemporary and later evidence convincingly indicated November, 1898. Holand wrote Cutler that after "much investigation" he had been convinced that the correct date was in fact November. Referring to the time when the affidavits were recorded — that is in 1909 — he said: "It is understandable that after a lapse of eleven years there may have been some confusion about the date. If the first man interviewed by Dr. Hoegh and me said it was in July [*sic*], he or I or both of us may have accepted this date as correct and incorporated it in the other reports which then were read to the respective authors. After all, the main purpose of the affidavits was to report the circumstances of the discovery of the stone."[23]

This statement by Holand is remarkable in at least four respects. First, he wrote "July," whereas neither the affidavits nor any other known records fix the finding of the stone in that month. No explanation save a lapse of memory is conceivable. In the second place, Holand seemed to brush aside the date as not being one of "the circumstances of the discovery of the stone," whereas it was obviously a salient circumstance. But the most important revelation in Holand's letter is its implication that he or Hoegh or both of them wrote the affidavits and then read them aloud to their "respective authors." Thus these two men seem to have functioned as a kind of joint "organizing intelligence." The extent to which the signers were in fact "respective authors" is not clear. Nor is it clear that all the men whose names appeared as signers really understood what was read to them. Ohman, for example, referred to his affidavit as something he did not understand. The ultralegal tone of the documents makes it seem possible that the texts were revised by the notary public, R. J. Rasmusson, who also was one of two witnesses (the second was George H. Merhes). Such an explanation may also clarify the date, July 20, 1909, which does not coincide with the recorded visit of Hoegh and Holand. A fourth curious point in Holand's statement is his seeming assumption that the reference to the summer of 1898 originated at the time the affidavits were composed. But he himself had earlier placed the find in August, 1898, in two publications of 1908 — his

[23] Holand to Cutler, April 29, 1957, in Kensington Rune Stone Collection, MHS Archives.

article in *Skandinaven* and his chapter on Vinland and the Kensing-ton inscription in the book dealing with Norwegian settlements.[24]

While Hoegh seems to have been the most industrious member of the Norwegian Society's committee, the activities of his col-league Gisle Bothne resulted in the production of a little-known document penned by one of the leading historians of the day. Sometime before February 10, 1910, Bothne sought the advice of Frederick Jackson Turner of the University of Wisconsin with re-spect to the Kensington puzzle.

Turner in 1910 was at the height of his powers, an American historian of nation-wide fame. Seventeen years earlier he had writ-ten the essay on "The Significance of the Frontier in American History," which still ranks as one of the most thought-provoking studies in the interpretation of the nation's past. One can readily understand why Bothne turned to him for advice, though he surely was aware that Turner's fields of research interest did not include Norse history or runes.

Turner took Bothne's request so seriously that he wrote in his own hand a seven-page reply. His letter is important for the meth-odology it suggested and also as an illustration of the probing quality of Turner's mind, applied to a problem of evidence.[25]

Turner declined to offer a judgment on the authenticity of the Kensington inscription. He did not know runes, but he was skepti-cal about the stone. If the leading scholars of runology took a stand against the genuineness of the inscription and were able to sustain it, he believed their decision could be accepted in view of the "improbability of the whole matter." He emphasized "im-probability" because in the story itself he saw no "impossibility," predicating his view on a reading of the inscription as specifying 41 days' journey from the sea instead of 14 (actually the inscrip-tion did say 14).

If linguistic experts admitted that the text of the inscription "might have been the product of a man of the fourteenth century,"

[24] Holand, in *Skandinaven*, January 11, 1908, p. 6; *De norske settlementers historie*, 15.

[25] Turner's letter, written at Madison, Wis., on February 10, 1910, is printed with annotation by the present writer as "Frederick J. Turner and the Ken-sington Puzzle," in *Minnesota History*, 39:133–140 (Winter, 1964).

the question would turn to "matters of the physical evidence." Unless the case against the inscription was "decidedly clear," a careful testing was the more important, since the inscription itself might make necessary a "re-considering of the existing rules." In a characteristic Turnerian phrase, he wrote that rules "are formulated from inscriptions, as well as inscriptions tested by rules."

Turner's ingenuity as a scholar then found expression in the formulation of a series of systematic and practical steps that might be taken to clarify the puzzle. The "balance," he thought, was against the stone; there were suspicious circumstances about the time and place of the find, but the "puzzle should be worked out deliberately and not on the basis of assumptions one way or the other." What concerned Turner was the truth, whether it be for or against the authenticity of the inscription.

Among the numerous conundrums in the Kensington story is why Bothne seemingly made no use of Turner's letter either for the Norwegian Society or somewhat later for the investigation by the Minnesota Historical Society. Turner's name does not appear in the reports of either society, and his suggestions were not acted on. In fact, the letter itself was unmentioned in the Kensington discussions until 1964, when it was published. While Turner said that he was not writing for publication, he did not mark his letter "confidential," nor did he state that its ideas could not be communicated to persons investigating the Kensington stone. The very character of the document suggests that the historian was mapping out lines of inquiry which he hoped would be followed. But Bothne, a gentleman of the old school, may have felt that the letter was personal and private guidance to him on a problem of historical methodology. Or perhaps he believed that the only conclusive answer to the Kensington riddle would be runological. Whatever his reasons for keeping the letter under cover, it is indeed a pity that a hardheaded, unbiased investigation applying Turner's methods was not carried out in 1910.

chapter 4

Investigations and Repercussions

THE KENSINGTON DISCUSSIONS GAINED MOMENTUM in 1909 and 1910, not only because of the work of Hoegh and the Norwegian Society of Minneapolis, but also because of a study undertaken by the museum committee of the Minnesota Historical Society. News of this development — especially a report that the committee was about to declare the inscription authentic — stirred George T. Flom, the University of Illinois philologist, to make an independent investigation.

On February 3, 1910, Holand exhibited and defended the stone at the Chicago Historical Society. In a discussion of the inscription at that meeting, Flom took part on the negative side. Three months later he visited Kensington, interviewed Ohman and others, and made a transcription of the inscription from the stone itself, which Holand had returned to the Minnesota Historical Society in St. Paul. Flom said that only the "runological-philological questions involved" had scientific value with respect to the problem, but because of a "special request" he had investigated also the "general external evidence." On May 6, 1910, he presented the fruits of his studies at a meeting of the Illinois State Historical Society in Springfield, and his paper, described as "an address," was published by that organization in 1910.[1]

From Ohman, Flom learned that the aspen which stood over the stone "looked stunted" and that its age, therefore, "might be greater than its size would indicate." Like many others, Flom noted the

[1] For quotes here and in the next three paragraphs, see Flom, in Illinois State Historical Society, *Transactions*, 1910, p. 105, 107, 108, 116, 120, 122, 124. Flom's visit to Minnesota took place April 14–19, 1910. He took a witness with him to Kensington (p. 120).

smooth surface of the stone. He had the impression that it had been "shaped and chiseled in recent times." He emphasized the "thoroughly modern character of the narrative" in the inscription— its circumstantial account of various details, including the finding of comrades "red with blood and dead." He spoke, too, of the uncharacteristic "preciseness" of the numbers given in the runic account, and he regarded as preposterous the assumption that the group could "cooly sit down and remain" while one of them carved on stone a record of their experience.

But Flom's main argumentation was based upon internal evidence— "the vocabulary and the linguistic forms" of the inscription. After making an analysis of the inflections, spellings, and meanings, Flom concluded that the inscription was modern, "the work of one who was familiar with the Dalecarlian runes." Dalecarlia (The Dales) is a west-central region of Sweden extending from the Norwegian border almost to the Baltic, an area rich in historical associations and lore with its own dialect and customs. With respect to the use of *opdagelsefard* (journey of discovery) in the inscription, Flom asserted that neither the word nor its concept existed in the Scandinavian North in 1362. The modern author of the inscription not only came from the Dalecarlian region, Flom believed, but was an immigrant from somewhere between Orsa (where Ohman originally came from) and Mora in North Helsingland, Sweden.

Toward the end of his article Flom told of the visits he had paid to St. Paul and Kensington in April, 1910; of his conversations with Ohman, who spoke a Swedish dialect and said he had immigrated to America in 1879. Ohman had seen the famous Forsa Ring runic inscription in his own Swedish community, but "disclaimed emphatically any ability at cutting runes." Flom conceded that the author of the inscription not only must have known runes but also must have been skilled at chiseling in stone. He set aside, however, the assumption made by some supporters of the inscription that no early settler could have had the "requisite knowledge of runes." He cited Ohman and Sven Fogelblad, a former Swedish minister and an itinerant schoolteacher who was a familiar figure in the Kensington community in the 1880s and early 1890s, as persons who knew something about runes. As we have seen, if Flom

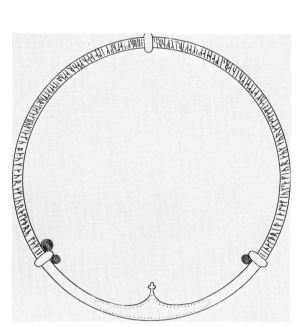

OHMAN *saw the Forsa Ring in his native Helsingland, Sweden. This copy of the runic inscriptions on the one side of the ring, "after Carl Säve," was sent to Johan A. Holvik at Concordia College, Moorhead, in 1950, and is in the Holvik Papers.*

had explored the press of 1899 he would have found others who translated the Kensington inscription quickly and with seeming ease soon after it was made public. In any event, Flom did not feel that he had to produce a forger. To him "the lateness of the runes and the modern character of the language" proved that someone had chiseled the stone "in recent times." As a subtitle for his address, which actually was a short monograph, Flom used the words "A Modern Inscription from Douglas County, Minnesota." The only interest that the stone would have for scholars in the future, he thought, was that it added "one more chapter to the already long list of fraudulent inscriptions in modern times."

Flom's study, as has been noted in chapter 1, was subjected to the scrutiny of a committee of the Philological Society of the University of Illinois. This group, composed of seven scholars selected because of their "philological knowledge of Old Norse," discussed the report and authorized Flom (who was a member) "to announce and publish . . . the verdict of the committee . . . that the Kensington inscription can not be from 1362." The reasons advanced were "the absence of the inflexions of the language as spoken at the time"; the failure of the inscription to "exhibit the runic series of the time"; and the identification of its language with a modern Swedish dialect. In short, the committee said that the inscription was a forgery of recent manufacture. Some members thought that its origin lay in the discussions of the Vinland voyages which took place in the 1870s and early 1880s. Their failure to include the 1890s may perhaps be ascribed to the circumstantial evidence of the tree's roots having embraced the stone.[2]

There can be little doubt that it was Holand who persuaded the museum committee of the Minnesota Historical Society to investigate the Kensington stone. He presented his views on its inscription to the executive council of the society as early as December 13, 1909. At the same meeting Newton H. Winchell discussed geological aspects of the stone, Dr. Knut Hoegh told of his interviews with Ohman and others in the Kensington area, and Professor Andrew A. Fossum of St. Olaf College presented the theory that the alleged explorers of 1362 had come into the Minnesota region southward from Hudson Bay.[3]

Olof Ohman had also been invited to attend the December 13 meeting. In the invitation, Warren Upham, the society's secretary and librarian, had asked Ohman (if he could not be present) to write "about the discovery of the Rune Stone on your farm." In reply Upham received a four-page letter in Swedish — the only known

[2] For the report of the Philological Society's committee, see appendix to Flom, in Illinois State Historical Society, *Transactions*, 1910, p. 124. The members, in addition to Flom, were Julius Goebel, chairman of the society and professor of German in the University of Illinois; Laurence M. Larson, biographer of Canute the Great and a distinguished historian; Harry S. V. Jones, Daniel K. Dodge, and Chester N. Greenough, professors of English; and Josef Wiehr, instructor in German. Not until many years later did Wahlgren suggest that the inscription might have been carved as late as 1898; *Kensington Stone*, 181.

[3] MHS, Executive Council Minutes, December 13, 1909, in the office of the society's director; *St. Paul Pioneer Press*, December 14, 1909, p. 1. On Fossum's idea, see *Norwegian-American* (Northfield), October 22, 1909, p. 1. Holand communicated with Winchell as early as 1908; see Holand to Winchell, August 3, 1908, in Archaeological Records, MHS Archives.

record by the stone's finder in his own handwriting describing the circumstances of his discovery.[4]

In acknowledging Upham's invitation, Ohman said that his assets did not permit him to be present; moreover he did not think it necessary. The rune stone was found under a poplar, and it was in between the roots with the larger inscribed surface facing downward and the side runes facing toward the taproot. The tree fell, said Ohman, when he cut the roots. In his letter he sketched the roots and the tree, showing the slanting position of the stone and the points at which he cut the roots.

Ohman said he noticed that the stone was thin. He turned it over with his grubbing hoe, and his son Edward "was the first to see that there was something inscribed on the stone." Ohman himself "saw that there was something written," but, he added, "to read was a mystery to me." He then wrote, "I am Swedish, born in Helsingland, but I have never seen any rune stone before." He closed by saying that the stone "lay 44 feet above the present water level" and that the poplar "was about 8 inches in diameter."

With this document already on hand, the museum committee soon began its work. Some two months later, after a few preliminary meetings, Winchell offered the following motion: "*Resolved,* That this Committee investigate, during the next month, before the Council Meeting of March 14, the conditions of discovery, and the runic and linguistic character of the inscriptions, of the Kensington Rune Stone." The motion was carried, and plans were worked out for assignments to the various members.[5]

The governing body of the Minnesota Historical Society never endorsed the report of the museum committee, but the latter's favorable findings have received much attention from Holand and others. The nominal chairman was Edward C. Mitchell, a Swedenborgian clergyman who had made a hobby of archaeology and had written books on such subjects as scriptural symbolism and

[4] Upham to Ohman, December 6, 18, 1909, and Ohman to Upham, December 9, 1909, in MHS Archives. An incomplete and inaccurate English translation of Ohman's letter is in Archaeological Records, MHS Archives. For the complete letter in Swedish with a translation by Professor Erik Wahlgren, see Appendix 9, below.

[5] Museum Committee Minutes, February 15, 1910, in Archaeological Records, MHS Archives.

the parables of the Bible. The actual leader was Winchell, geologist and archaeologist. Warren Upham, secretary and librarian of of the society who also served as secretary of the committee, had taken part in various geological surveys and written numerous reports and studies, including a monograph on Glacial Lake Agassiz. A fourth member was Olin D. Wheeler, a railroad advertising man who in the early 1870s had served as topographer for Major John W. Powell's survey of the Colorado River and had written a two-volume work on Lewis and Clark. The fifth member was Father Francis J. Schaefer, professor of New Testament Greek and church history in the St. Paul Seminary. He had been educated in Rome and at the Catholic University in Paris.[6]

These committee members were able and enlightened men, well versed in their chosen fields of competence. With respect to runology and the history of the Scandinavian languages and dialects, however, they were laymen. Not a single member seems to have known runic symbols, runic literature, or any modern Scandinavian language. The committee sought the opinions of a number of competent linguists, but made little use of the analyses and arguments received from scholars who were critical of the inscription. Thus an extensive and scholarly letter submitted by Chester N. Gould of the University of Chicago was put aside and not used at all, though he was listed among "eminent and critical scholars" who aided the committee. Gould noted that the occurrence of the word *opdagelse*, which he found to be anachronistic for the year 1362, was in itself sufficient to make "Holand's house of cards" tumble. He wrote critically about Holand's methods and gave linguistic reasons for considering the inscription a fabrication. Otto von Friesen, the leading runic scholar of Sweden, also submitted a sharply negative view, but his name did not appear in the committee's report.[7]

[6] On the members, see Upham and Dunlap, comps., *Minnesota Biographies*, 514, 673, 800, 844, 870. The title of Wheeler's work was *The Trail of Lewis and Clark, 1804–1904* (New York, 1904). Schaefer later became rector of the St. Paul Seminary.

[7] Gould to Upham, March 19, 1910, Archaeological Records, MHS Archives. Filed with Gould's paper is an English translation of a March 28, 1910, statement by Magnus Olsen, the Norwegian scholar, which declared the Kensington inscription "entirely worthless" from a philological point of view. See

Winchell seems, by reason of his energy and interest, to have guided the deliberations of the committee. He visited Kensington three times and gathered considerable information that he recorded in a handwritten notebook or field book. Much of the data used in the committee's report reflected his knowledge of geology and information on the Kensington find that he gathered during his visits. On the other hand, correspondence in the Minnesota Historical Society's files shows that he relied heavily on Holand for analysis of the language of the inscription, both in the main text and in attempts to refute linguistic criticisms.[8]

Winchell was neither a historian nor a linguist. When he drafted the museum committee's report (or most of it), he spoke as an expert geologist in dealing with the stone and its weathering. The slab was then in the Minnesota Historical Society's quarters in the basement of the Capitol in St. Paul, where Winchell had ample opportunity to examine it. He wrote that the "first impression derived from the inscription is that it is of recent date, and not 548 years old." The "edges and angle" of the chiseling were sharp, showing "no apparent alteration by weathering." On the other hand, the incisions on the front side revealed none of the crushed white powder of the stone. The runes on the narrower side showed some powder, but, the report said, they had been scraped with a nail in the cleaning process; in some of the incisions Winchell detected, while using a magnifier, traces of fresh metallic iron.[9]

Early in the report Winchell suggested that the stone, if erected by explorers in 1362, "was set upon end," and that the lower end, uninscribed, "was buried in the ground." Because of the beveling on one side, the stone should have been facing upward if it had fallen as a result of gravitation. Since the face was down, he as-

also Von Friesen to Upham, April 4, 1910, MHS Archives; Museum Committee, in *Minnesota Historical Collections,* 15:254–256, 283.

[8] See Winchell Field Book in Appendix 8, below; Wahlgren, *Kensington Stone,* 103; Museum Committee, *Minnesota Historical Collections,* 15:220–286; Holand to Winchell, June 15, 1910, January 28, March 15, 24, 1911, and "Notes on Minn. Hist. So.'s Report," with a letter from Holand to Winchell, May 19, 1910 — all in Archaeological Records, MHS Archives.

[9] For quotes here and in the next two paragraphs, see *Minnesota Historical Collections,* 15:233, 234, 236, 237. A typewritten copy of Winchell's address, signed by him, is in the Upham Papers, MHS Archives.

sumed that it was knocked over by some external force — a storm, a buffalo, or Indians.

In an address to the executive council of the society on December 13, 1909, Winchell told of the topography of the find. He had recently visited Kensington and the site of the discovery. He said that "the stone was found on an elevation surrounded on practically all sides by a marsh. The elevation has an extreme hight [sic] above the surface of the marsh of fifty-five feet. It is divided into two hills, one being about fifty feet above the marsh. The lower ground intervening between the hills is about forty feet above the marsh. The stone was found on the southern slope of the larger of the hills, at an elevation of about forty-four feet above the marsh."

The condition of the incisions made it certain, Winchell believed, that if the inscription were genuine, the slab had lain face downward during most of the long period. "If it were not thus buried and still is intact," he said, "it must have been exposed and

THE SUPPOSED site of the rune stone discovery, shown about 1910, was visited by investigators from the Norwegian Society of Minneapolis, the Minnesota Historical Society, and the Philological Society of the University of Illinois in 1909 and 1910. The men in the photograph are thought to be (left to right) Edwin Bjerklund, Nils Flaten, and Olof Ohman.

the inscription must have been made less than a hundred years ago, and probably less than thirty years ago." He added, "The composition of the stone makes it one of the most durable in nature, equalling granite, and almost equalling the dense quartzyte [sic] of the pipestone quarry in the southwestern part of Minnesota." Despite his first impression, he concluded that the inscriptions were indeed old; the state geologist of Wisconsin, William O. Hotchkiss, estimated their age as "at least 50 to 100 years."

Winchell also gave some thought to the stone itself, searching the land where it was found for boulders resembling the Kensington slab. He recorded in his field book on November 30, 1909, that he found one "exactly like it." He also commented that some five in a hundred of the stones in the area he searched were comparable. In the light of this testimony from a trained geologist, it seems certain that the stone was of local origin. That Winchell found a rock "exactly like" the engraved slab is an interesting and possibly significant circumstance. He did not see fit to include this fact in the published report.

Winchell was inclined to regard the inscription as genuine, but he did not overlook the possibility of a fraud or hoax. He referred in his field book to a long talk he had with Ohman, noting that he was impressed by the "evident candor and truthfulness of all his statements." Winchell echoed this view in the printed report, where he spoke of the "honesty and candor" of the man. He described the finders of the stone as "simple farmers, working hard to derive a subsistence for themselves and families from their land." He spoke of Ohman's statement that he had had only six terms of schooling in Sweden, each of six weeks, the school having been conducted by an itinerant teacher who spent a term at each place he visited. Ohman told him, he said, that "Every school boy, and every Swede and Norwegian, knows something about runes, but not so as to use them." Ohman, Winchell recorded, did not speak English readily but seemed to understand it "in common conversation." Commenting on Ohman, Winchell added, "I find he is a more intellectual man than I had supposed."[10]

A somewhat surprising find is an entry in the field book made

[10] Winchell Field Book, March 5, 1910; *Minnesota Historical Collections,* 15:225, 242.

on March 18, 1910, at Kensington. Winchell had met Samuel Olson, a jeweler, who spoke of Ohman, of a neighboring farmer Andrew Anderson, and of Sven Fogelblad (an itinerant schoolteacher usually called "Flugelblad" by Winchell) as "queer characters" who had "lived (chummed) together." After reporting the interview with Olson, the field book recorded in an independent paragraph the fact that the three men were Swedes. Then, referring to the Kensington inscription, it said: "if there be any fraud in it it lies with one or all of them." This appears to be a comment by Winchell, but with his mind still on his talk with Olson, he may possibly have been paraphrasing the jeweler. In either case he recorded the idea that one or all of the men mentioned were involved in the fraud if there had been one. In the museum report (p. 249) Winchell turned the statement completely around. He said that if there had been fraud, Ohman and Fogelblad should be exonerated "from the imposition." The doubt, whether emanating from Winchell or from Samuel Olson, is in either case a matter of record in Winchell's handwriting.

In the published report Winchell did not mention two interviews he conducted with men who knew Ohman well. The first — on March 5, 1910 — was with Joseph Hotvedt, who had had a farm adjoining Ohman's and in fact was there before the latter began farming his land. Hotvedt regarded Ohman as "quite a mechanic when he wants to be." He also said that Ohman "talked about runes" and "had some old books, telling about runes." In Hotvedt's opinion, "Ohman may have made the inscription." Perhaps Winchell did not mention Hotvedt in the published report because his driver scoffed at Hotvedt's trustworthiness, saying "You cant go much on what he says."[11]

The second interview of interest was conducted by Winchell with a certain O. F. Olson of Brandon. O. G. Juul, secretary of the school board at Elbow Lake, had told Winchell that Olson was the only man who could get Ohman to tell the facts about the finding of the Kensington stone. Olson had known Ohman for twenty-six or twenty-seven years. He described him as a "queer genius"

[11] Winchell Field Book, March 5, 1910; *Minnesota Historical Collections*, 15:249. The Reverend Torbjørn A. Sattre also questioned the reliability of Hotvedt; see Field Book, March 17, 1910.

who "talked but little, thought much." Olson asserted that Ohman "used to make rune characters about Brandon." As to the Kensington inscription, he would not "say that Ohman made or could not make the stone," but he "always had an impression that he may have made it."[12]

Ohman in talking with Winchell evidently made no mention of a worn whetstone found near the site of the rune stone (and later lost). Or, if it was mentioned, Winchell did not regard it as significant enough to record. Ohman told of the incident to E. E. Løbeck, who had grown up not far from where the rune stone was found, and he in turn reported it to J. J. Skørdalsvold, a Minneapolis journalist. The story obviously had been told by Ohman in the context of the rune stone. The exact spot where the tool was found was not stated. The whetstone seems to have been a surface find, and it could not have been from the fourteenth century. It is a small incident, but it invites the question: Why did Ohman mention it at all? Could he have been trying to convey a hint of a hoax? Skørdalsvold thought it strange that Ohman had not told the story to the museum committee or to Holand.[13]

It may appropriately be recalled here that Cleve Van Dyke, the county school superintendent from Alexandria who was the leader of the excavators of the Kensington site in the spring of 1899, later (1910) remembered Ohman as a man "underestimated by his neighbors." In Van Dyke's opinion, Ohman "had more literary knowledge" than the community credited him with. The schoolman described him as "an interesting character" who had traveled much and seemed to know about "runestones and other remains." He recalled that Ohman had told him of a visit to an English museum where he had seen rune stones, and that a teacher in Ohman's district once showed him some excuses written in rhyme by Ohman for his children.[14]

If there should be any doubt as to the intellectual quality, historical interest, and curiosity of Ohman, certain printed materials

[12] Winchell Field Book, March 17, 18, 1910.
[13] Skørdalsvold, "Kensingtonstenen og 'de lærde'" in Kvartalskrift, 9:78 (July, 1913), a quarterly magazine published at Eau Claire, Wis.
[14] Van Dyke to Winchell, April 19, 1910, Archaeological Records, MHS Archives, in Appendix 13, below.

present in his farmhouse and owned by him should dispel it. One item is a scrapbook that evidently belonged first to the school-master Sven Fogelblad and later to Ohman, who continued it. This document was discovered by Professor Holvik and borrowed by him from the Ohman home. Wahlgren gave much attention to the book and listed various pieces pasted into it on such subjects as Buddhism, ancient religion, and Atlantis. He called special attention to the syllable AUM at the end of a note on Buddha and pointed out its resemblance to the AVM on the rune stone. It is not known when or under what precise circumstances Ohman acquired the scrapbook, but both he and Fogelblad seem to have taken an interest in occult matters.[15]

A second object of interest in the Ohman household was a bound series of items clipped from *Svenska Amerikanska Posten* in 1897–98. It comprised a history of Sweden, volume 1, by Oskar Montelius, reprinted as a newspaper supplement from the original 1877 Swedish edition of his book, with page sizes and numbers duplicating those of the original. The immigrant newspapers often ran entire books as feuilletons of this kind, encouraging readers to clip and bind them. The Montelius volume included some information about the runic alphabet and the use of runes which was analyzed by Wahlgren, who also reproduced two pages of the work as illustrations in his book. Only two points need to be underlined here. One is that Ohman was a reader of the Minneapolis Swedish newspaper. The other is that he took a lively interest in Swedish history, clipped the Montelius study, and had it bound in book form.[16]

A third and possibly even more interesting find made by Holvik

[15] Wahlgren, *Kensington Stone*, 164. The MHS has a microfilm of the Fogelblad-Ohman scrapbook, which Holvik sent to it for filming. The original is in the possession of Arthur Ohman, Kensington. Holvik believed that the rune stone's letters were actually AUM, a symbol pertaining to the "Supreme God of the mystery religions of the East"; see Wahlgren, *Kensington Stone*, 139.

[16] The Montelius history began in *Svenska Amerikanska Posten* on November 16, 1897, and volume 1 was completed in the issue of February 15, 1898. The work also discussed runes in Greenland and included Latin. Ohman, it is reported, had the clippings bound in leather by a shoemaker. The name of J. P. Hedberg is written on the back of the volume. See Wahlgren, *Kensington Stone*, fig. 4 following 82, 129, 130. See also George Rice, in *Minneapolis Star*, April 12, p. 1, April 14, p. 1, 1955.

is a book that Ohman owned called *Den kunskapsrike skolemäs-taren* (usually translated "The Well-Informed Schoolmaster"). The compiler was Carl Rosander, and Ohman's copy was of a Stockholm edition of 1882. The book bears his signature, with the date, March 2, 1891, and the place, Kensington. It was a comprehensive single-volume reference work for general use, a compact encyclopedia, and its special interest, as Holvik and Wahlgren demonstrated, was its inclusion of an account of the Swedish language, with a detailed section on runes. According to Wahlgren this runic information was so inclusive that "Very little" beyond it "is required to penetrate the orthographic rationale of the Kensington inscription." [17]

The present writer must leave to linguists the runic significance of the Rosander book. To him that volume, the scrapbook, and the Montelius clippings are convincing testimony to the alert and active intelligence of Olof Ohman. They make a mockery of assertions that he was ill-informed or dull-witted, as legend in part tends to portray him. This farmer who said "but little, thought much" evidently read and studied more than his detractors supposed. His native reticence, plus his halting English, may have contributed to an underestimation by some persons of his true qualities. Actually, as we have seen, not a few people understood that Ohman was very intelligent, and Holvik quoted a dentist who described Ohman "as one of the keenest and best informed men" he had ever met. [18]

Another description of Ohman was recorded by Rasmus B. Anderson, the editor of *Amerika*. He told of meeting Andrew Anderson — at whose house Fogelblad died in 1897 — in the western North Dakota village of Stanley. This Anderson described Ohman as "a great reader," and said that he spoke of himself and of Fogelblad as "well versed" in runes. Andrew did not admit that the three men were involved in the origin of the inscription, but when

---

[17] Wahlgren, *Kensington Stone*, 132. He also called attention to an illustration in the Montelius work of a Swedish rune stone standing on "the sloping surface" of a mound not unlike the hillside on which the Kensington stone was found; see p. 130.

[18] Quote from mimeographed form letter by Holvik, November 22, 1949, Holvik Papers.

OLAUS J. BREDA
From E. Bird Johnson, ed., Forty Years of the University of Minnesota *(Minneapolis, 1910)*

GEORGE O. CURME
Courtesy University Library, Northwestern University, Evanston, Illinois

HJALMAR R. HOLAND
In the Minnesota Historical Society collections

KNUT O. HOEGH   WARREN UPHAM

NEWTON H. WINCHELL
*The three photographs on this page are in the
collections in the Minnesota Historical Society*

ANDREW A. FOSSUM
From Olaf M. Norlie, History of
the Norwegian People in America
(Minneapolis, 1925)

GEORGE T. FLOM
From Johannes B. Wist, ed., Norsk-
Amerikanernes Festskrift 1914
(Decorah, Iowa, [1914])

GISLE BOTHNE
*In the Minnesota Historical Soci-
ety collections*

FREDERICK JACKSON TURNER
*Courtesy State Historical Society
of Wisconsin, Madison*

RASMUS B. ANDERSON
From Rasmus B. Anderson, The
First Chapter of Norwegian Immigration *(Madison, Wisconsin, 1895)*

ANDREW A. VEBLEN
From Norlie, History of the
Norwegian People in America

JULIUS E. OLSON
From Wist, Norsk-Amerikaner-
nes Festskrift 1914

OLE E. HAGEN
From Skandinaven *(Chicago),*
March 23, 1927

JOHAN A. HOLVIK
Courtesy Concordia College, Moor-
head

he and R. B. Anderson parted, the latter wrote that Andrew "gave me some significant winks."[19]

Holvik picked up a hint as to a possible motive for Ohman to have played a part in the hoax. The information was obtained from Henry H. Hendrickson, former postmaster at Hoffman and a man whose reliability Holvik described as "assured." He told Holvik that in 1890 he heard Ohman say that "he Would like to Figure out Something that Would Bother the Brains of the Learned." Hendrickson said that he had a long conversation with Ohman, and he even recalled the Swedish words Ohman used: "Min Högsta Önskan är at uppfinna nogot Som ville Bråka Hjarnan Po de Lärde." The postmaster also remembered Fogelblad and said that he furnished the brains, Ohman the work. Both men, he said, liked to invent jokes. Why Ohman wished to crack the brains of the learned, if he did, is a matter for speculation. His mind had a quality of dissent and reached out to ideas beyond the pale of the accepted. And he may have been influenced by Fogelblad, who sharply challenged authority.[20]

As to the Kensington relevance of the materials turned up by Holvik, it may be noted, first, that if the Montelius history published in 1897–98 played a major role in the making of the inscription, the runic words were composed and chiseled after Fogelblad's death in 1897. But if the Rosander book was a principal source and the Montelius history did not contribute to it, possibly the hoax had an earlier origin and Fogelblad took part in it. As to the scrapbook, the fact that Ohman carried on what Fogelblad began suggests a bond of shared interest between the two men, whatever the circumstances of the transfer.

If Fogelblad had any part in the hoax (if hoax it was), he necessarily played that part before the summer of 1897. Therefore, those who believe that the inscription was chiseled in 1898 must interrelate Fogelblad's part, if any, to something done, said, or written before 1897. He might conceivably have suggested the hoax, de-

[19] Anderson, "The Kensington Rune Stone Once More," in *Amerika*, May 27, 1910, p. 1, reprinted in *Minneapolis Journal*, June 2, 1910, p. 7, and Holand, *Kensington Stone*, 280.
[20] Hendrickson to Holvik, undated 1949 (quotes), and Holvik form letter, November 22, 1949 (quote), Holvik Papers; George Rice, in *Minneapolis Star*, April 11, 1955, p. 1, and four successive issues.

vised its ideas, or composed the inscription in runic symbols. If the inscription is a hoax, many possibilities have to be looked at. One is that the carving of the inscription might have taken place earlier than 1898, at some time when Fogelblad was at the Ohman or the Anderson farm.

A farmer in the Elbow Lake area, Victor Setterlund, in an affidavit signed on May 9, 1965, asserted that Fogelblad was a friend of his father, and that the teacher told his father that he had made and buried a rune stone. More, that its discovery would cause a furor. Through runes Fogelblad was going to make it known that people were here before Columbus. Mr. Setterlund also said that a certain Nils Underdahl told him that he once went to the Ohman farm and saw Fogelblad in the granary chiseling on stone.[21]

Amid such curious reports and rumors, there is one that has received almost no attention. This was brought to light by F. Sanford Cutler, curator of the Minnesota Historical Society's museum in the 1950s. Mrs. Arthur Nelson of Seattle called at the museum on July 13, 1955, and told Mr. Cutler a story often repeated, she said, by her grandfather, Moses D. Fredenberg, who operated a tool shop in Alexandria. Fredenberg, so ran the story, often laughed and joked about the Kensington stone because "two Swedes" from out of town — that is, from outside Alexandria — had come to him to get tools with which to carve the Kensington inscription. After Mrs. Nelson's visit, Mr. Cutler wrote to her requesting a written statement; in reply, she referred him to her cousin, Mrs. W. W. Christopherson of Kenyon, Minnesota, who supplied some details. The grandfather, who visited Mrs. Christopherson's family each spring when that family lived at Detroit Lakes, Minnesota, had told about two young men who asked him to make chisels for use on stone. The two men said that they were "going to have some fun." They were Scandinavian; Mrs. Christopherson could not recall their names; her grandfather's description of them indicated that "they would go to any length to play a joke on anyone they desired." Mrs. Christopherson's father, Alfred E. Fredenberg, also knew the story but had done nothing about it because "no one had asked him."[22]

[21] Setterlund affidavit, Kensington file, Blegen Papers.
[22] For the Fredenberg story, see Mrs. Arthur Nelson to Cutler, July 14,

What weight one should attach to such reports, or even to affidavits, is a puzzling question. The statements lack precision, and the episodes to which they refer took place long ago. The principals are dead. It is a striking circumstance that the Winchell field book should contain an item — antedating the charge made by Rasmus B. Anderson — suggesting a possible collaboration in the origination of the Kensington inscription by the same three men Anderson mentioned. The Fredenberg story also points to (1) a scheme involving at least two persons, and (2) something conceived as a practical joke.

It must be emphasized that Winchell, though the idea of fraud crossed his mind, championed the authenticity of the inscription and did this despite the negative items in his field book. In reply to Professor Anderson, he published letters from both Andrew Anderson and Ohman. Andrew Anderson maintained that he had not told Professor Anderson "half of what he got into his paper." He admitted, however, that he had said Fogelblad "could possibly have written the inscription on paper" and that Ohman "could have chiseled the runes on the stone." But he did not believe that either had had anything to do with the inscription. Ohman ridiculed an assertion that Andrew Anderson had once been a student at Uppsala. He had "never seen" Uppsala; he might if drunk quote Swedish poetry, but if he knew Greek and Latin, as Professor Anderson alleged, he must have acquired his knowledge very recently. That Fogelblad had written long sentences in runic on paper was, said Ohman, a "barefaced untruth." Nor was Andrew Anderson his brother-in-law (his wife and Anderson's wife were cousins).[23]

On behalf of the museum committee, Winchell also looked into the question of how Holand "obtained" the Kensington stone. This sorry matter has already been touched upon but it calls for further scrutiny. Ohman told Winchell that he had never heard of Holand until the latter called on him about the rune stone. Another source

1955; Cutler to Holvik, July 14, 1955; Mrs. W. W. Christopherson to Cutler, November 17, 1955, in Kensington Rune Stone Collection, MHS Archives.
[23] "Letters from Rune Suspects," in *Norwegian-American*, June 10, 1910, p. 1, 8.

confirmed the fact that Holand had never before visited the community, that he was a stranger in the Kensington area, and that he had no relatives there. Ohman also told Winchell that he "never gave the stone to Holand" as his personal property. It was for the "Norwegian Historical Society," by which he surely meant the Norwegian Society of Minneapolis, which had sponsored Holand's history of Norwegian settlements. Ohman's sons said that Holand got the stone on the condition that it should be deposited "in some public museum." Ohman asked Winchell not to let the stone go from St. Paul even as a loan to Holand for exhibition in Chicago.[24]

Winchell noted in his field book on December 2, 1909, and March 5, 1910, that he talked with two witnesses to the agreement between Holand and Ohman. They were Samuel Olson and Ole Stenberg. Olson confirmed Ohman's statement; the stone was to go to the museum of the Norwegian Historical Society; Ohman "was paid nothing for it." Olson was reported as asserting that the Kensington stone belonged either to Ohman or to the Norwegian Society. Stenberg supported Ohman's statement but added that Holand had promised Ohman a book, and if Ohman actually got the book, Stenberg thought that the stone was Holand's.

As has been mentioned, an affidavit dated July 20, 1909, and signed by Ohman stated that he "presented the stone to H. R. Holand." Ohman must have been referring to this affidavit when on March 5, 1910, he said, according to Winchell's record, that "he never gave the stone to Holand, & if he signed such a statement he did not know it." To this Winchell added, "He did not read it all, & never gave the stone to Holand." The field book strongly supports doubts that the Ohman affidavit was understood by its signer. A small detail is the affidavit's use of the word "presented," not "gave." "Presented" could mean "gave" but, when he talked with Winchell a year later, Ohman said that he "never gave the stone." With his inadequate English, he possibly did not under-

<hr>

[24] Winchell Field Book, November 30, December 2, 1909; March 5, 18, 1910. Edward Ohman said that his father received "No money whatsoever" from Holand for the stone, but that Holand gave Ohman a copy of his book on Norwegian settlements. When asked whether his father turned over the stone to Holand "to look into it," Edward replied affirmatively. Edward Ohman interview, December 28, 1949.

stand the word "presented" to mean that the stone became Holand's personal property.

As we have seen, Holand's own references to the transfer varied. He offered $5; he got the stone for nothing; he "procured" it; he persuaded the finder; he told Quaife he paid $25; fifty years after the event he wrote as if he recalled his conversation with Ohman. But he never referred to Ohman's understanding that Holand obtained the stone not as a personal gift (or sale) but on the condition that it was to go the Norwegian Society. Ohman wanted the stone "preserved and deposited at a suitable place in Minnesota." He apparently intended that it was to be kept by the society "till found to be genuine." Ohman himself said he "had no use for it."[25]

In the museum report Winchell did not give any particular attention to the question of the ownership of the stone. What he wrote (p. 226) was that Holand "obtained" it from Ohman, and it is significant that he used this vague word. It seems apparent that Ohman did not intend to give or sell the stone to be Holand's personal property. Therefore, Holand did not own the Kensington rune stone unless some further unknown agreement was made with Ohman at or after the 1907 transaction. Holand's writings do not make any allusion to such an agreement. His claim to ownership apparently stood on his own assertions, his attempts to sell the stone, and an affidavit of somewhat dubious value.

In 1910 Holand offered the stone to the Minnesota Historical Society for $5,000. He felt that this price should be considered compensation to him for his "contribution to American history." Further detail on the financial side was given by Wahlgren, who mentioned a $25,000 value set for a bond in an abortive later lawsuit. In January, 1910, Holand wanted $3,000 from the Minnesota Historical Society as a stipend and $2,000 for the stone. He became impatient with Winchell, Upham, and the museum committee because they delayed action on the purchase. A month's option, given by Holand to the society on December 17, 1909, was renewed again and again. In February, 1910, Winchell wanted further delay to ascertain and acquire any rights that Ohman might have. In the light of his field book, one can understand why he must have entertained serious doubts about Holand's claim

[25] Winchell Field Book, December 2, 1909.

to ownership of the stone. By April 11 Holand's patience was wearing thin, but no stipend was forthcoming.[26]

If Winchell entertained doubts about Holand's claim, they must have been deepened by an event of 1911. This was nothing less than the sale of the stone by the finder, Olof Ohman, to the Minnesota Historical Society. The negotiations were handled through an intermediary, Andrew A. Fossum, who was then a teacher at Park Region College in Fergus Falls. Fossum held a doctorate from Johns Hopkins University, was a professor of Greek and French, and had taught for many years at St. Olaf College. He was interested in the Kensington stone and more generally in Norse exploration. In 1918 he published a book on the Norse journeys to America, which omitted any mention of the Kensington rune stone.[27]

Fossum had talked with Upham at the Minnesota Historical Society. Acting upon a suggestion by Fossum, Upham on April 15, 1911, authorized him to see Ohman and buy his right of ownership in the stone "so far as not already transferred by him to Mr. Holand." Upham promised to pay expenses and specified that the purchase price was not to exceed $200. On the same date Upham wrote to Holand asking him to clarify the "legal status of the stone as a piece of personal property," but he did not mention a plan to buy the stone from Ohman.[28]

On April 19, 1911, Fossum, with Torbjørn A. Sattre, a local minister, paid a visit to Olof Ohman at his farm. Fossum wrote Upham in detail about this meeting. Ohman "denied explicitly and emphatically that he had sold the stone nor had he given it to Mr. Holand." He remembered an affidavit and another paper (handwritten) "which he signed for Mr. Holand in the presence of Dr. Hoegh. What the papers contained Mr. Ohman knows very little about, as they were presented to him for signature and he did [not] know English well enough to understand them. If he

[26] See, for example, Holand to Winchell, January 11, 1910; to Upham, January 30, February 14, 1910, in MHS Archives. See also Wahlgren, Kensington Stone, 97.

[27] The Norse Discovery of America (Minneapolis, 1918). On Fossum (1860–1943), see Minneapolis Star Journal, October 21, 1943, p. 19.

[28] Upham to Fossum, and to Holand, both dated April 15, 1911, in MHS Letter Press Books, MHS Archives.

has signed away the stone, he says he must have done so unknowingly." He repeated that he "had not to his knowledge sold or given the stone to Mr. Holand." Earlier, in 1910, Ohman had referred to the "Norwegian Historical Society." Now, in 1911, he seemingly meant the Minnesota Historical Society when he spoke of "the Society," for, according to Fossum, he wanted the rune stone kept where it then was, at the Capitol. He was "much wrought up" because Holand had not "turned it over to the Society as its property." How "wrought up" Ohman was, Fossum illustrated by saying that when he and Sattre asked if Ohman had given or sold the stone, he struck a horseshoe against the wheel of the visitors' carriage and said "*Nei*." Reverting again to Holand, Ohman suggested that there must have been "false representations, making him sign what was represented to be something else." He wanted the stone to be at "the Society where it could remain forever."[29]

Fossum purchased the stone from Ohman on payment of $10. A bill of sale dated April 19, 1911, was drawn up, signed by Ohman, witnessed by Sattre and O. W. Johnson, and duly attested by a notary public, R. J. Rasmusson.[30] The specific language of the legal paper is interesting because of its detail in describing the stone. In the bill of sale Ohman conveys to the Minnesota Historical Society:

> All the right title interest and ownership that I am seized of in and to the socalled Runesten found by me on my farm of Ninety eight acres in section fourteen in the town of Solem in the county of Douglas and state of Minnesota. In the year Eighteen Hundred Ninety eight (1898)
> A more and particular description of said stone being: —

[29] Fossum to Upham, April 19, 20, 1911; Samuel Olson to Upham, March 7, 1910; Upham to Ohman and Olson (2 letters), March 8, 1910, in MHS Letter Press Books — all in MHS Archives. In the Olson letter (written for Ohman and presumably put into English for him) Ohman said that Holand got the stone for the "Norwegian Historical Society," and it was to be "retained" in a safe place.

[30] The original bill of sale is in Archaeological Records, MHS Archives. Wahlgren, *Kensington Stone*, 97, discussing Holand's efforts to sell the stone, remarked that Ohman's claim to ownership was not "a definite matter of record." But Wahlgren had not had an opportunity to read the Winchell Field Book, which put it on record.

Said stone being a Greywacke about twenty eight inches long, fifteen inches wide and five and one half inches thick, weighing two hundred and thirty pounds, containing the following inscription in runes: 8 göter ok 22 Norrmen po opdagelsefard fro vinland of vest vi hadhe läger vedh 2 skjar en dags rise norr fro dheno sten vi var ok fiske en dagh äptir vi kom hem fan 10 man rödhe af blod og dhedh AVM fräelse af ily har 10 mans vi havet at se äptir vore skip 14 dagh rise from dheno öh ahr 1362

It was this sale that Fossum described in two letters to Upham on April 19 and 20, 1911. He reported a verbal promise to Ohman to pay him "ninety dollars more" if he "proves to have title and right and ownership of stone." In transmitting the bill of sale, Fossum advised Upham not to let Holand remove the stone from the Minnesota Historical Society unless he first proved his legal right to take it away. He also said that Ohman would be "willing to be witness and give evidence."

Upham promptly acknowledged the receipt of the bill of sale and Fossum's letters. The outcome had been, he said, "to the great satisfaction of Professor Winchell and myself." They thought that no one "could have carried this business through" so well as Fossum and Sattre. "It is a very important result, as I am convinced, for this Society and for our State history." The ten dollars and expenses would be paid to Fossum after a meeting of the executive council on May 8, 1911, and Upham also anticipated authorization at that time for payment of the additional ninety dollars.[31]

The minutes of the council meeting held on May 8, 1911, make no reference whatever to the bill of sale, but there can be no doubt that it was reviewed in a long discussion of the Kensington stone. The council decided by a vote of six to five to return the stone to Holand, "by whom it was deposited in this Society's Museum." It also authorized the museum committee to continue its researches, "but without expenditure for sending the stone to Europe." The committee had recommended that Holand and Winchell be sent on the European mission.[32]

[31] Upham to Fossum, April 21, 1911, in MHS Letter Press Books, MHS Archives.
[32] MHS Executive Council Minutes, May 8, 1911.

Upham wrote Fossum that the council, to his "great regret," had voted to return the stone to Holand because it wished "to avoid any legal controversy" (an explanation that did not appear in the minutes). Fossum was disappointed by the council's negative action, and he wrote an indignant reply to Upham: "If we had known that the Minn. Hist. Society would not make any use of the right to the stone, we should not have boug[h]t it." The Kensington rune stone, he said, "*is* or *is not* a genuine historical record." To wait a hundred or more years for a definite decision on genuineness before buying could mean that after such a long time there might "be no stone left for the H. Soc. to take care of."[33]

Fossum returned to a more basic matter when he said that the society did not have a "correct view" of its problem. He granted that it was the society's "duty and business" to take charge of records, but not to decide in every case whether a record or monument was genuine. That, he said, was "not primarily the function" of the institution. He thought that some student "who has the facilities for that study will decide," but that the vote of a large body of people on such a question "is worthless, not to say ridiculous." He added his opinion that the papers should be returned to Ohman.

On May 10, 1911, Upham wrote to Ohman, explaining the action taken by the executive council and stating again his "great regret." He expressed appreciation of the favor Ohman had done the society, but for some unexplained reason he chose to retain the bill of sale. It has been in the society's possession through all the years since 1911. Upham informed Ohman that he could not "expect . . . the further payment" of ninety dollars. To this letter Ohman made no reply.

Holand, busy with his plans to take the stone to Europe, had written to Winchell on April 27, 1911, renewing his offer of it for $5,000. This sum was not a payment for the stone, he said, but compensation for three and a half years of work on "exploiting of early Minnesota History." He also said that he would expect

---

[33] For quotes here and in the two paragraphs below, see Upham to Fossum, and to Ohman, both dated May 10, 1911, in MHS Letter Press Books; Fossum to Upham, May 15, 1911, MHS Archives.

the society to pay "a small amount" to Ohman, though the latter had "no legal claims on the stone."[34]

Thus this drama-within-a-drama was played out. What the handwritten paper was that Holand persuaded Ohman to sign at the time of the affidavits in 1909 is not known. Holand seems never to have made it public, and it may have been lost when his house was destroyed by fire. About three weeks after the May, 1911, meeting of the executive council, Holand withdrew the rune stone and took it with him to Europe.[35] The story of the sale is one of frustrated hopes and melancholy interest. It is brightened by the good sense of Professor Fossum, evidenced in his thoughts about ways of appraising the genuineness of historical records.

In yet another phase of its investigation of the rune stone, the society's museum committee took some account of the adverse opinions of various linguists both in Scandinavia and the United States, on the genuineness of the stone. As the committee's secretary, Upham corresponded in 1910 with two such scholars who had been concerned with the inscription in 1899 — Olaus Breda and George Curme.

In February, 1910, Upham wrote to Breda, who was then living in Christiania, Norway, asking his opinion on the genuineness of the Kensington inscription. In his reply, Breda referred to an article on the Kensington problem which he had written for *Symra* and suggested that someone might translate it. He then summed up his views.[36]

Referring to a "rough draft" of the inscription which he said he had received from Samuel Siverts of Kensington early in 1899, Breda commented that he thought it suspicious that an inscription exposed to the Minnesota climate for five hundred years was

[34] In addition to Holand's letter of April 27, 1911, see his "Items of Agreement between H. R. Holand and the Minnesota Historical Society," May 8, 1911, both in correspondence files, MHS Archives.

[35] See memorandum by Upham following MHS Executive Council Minutes, May 8, 1911. The stone now rests in the Rune Stone Museum at Alexandria. The MHS has a replica.

[36] Upham to Breda, February 19, 1910, in MHS Letter Press Books; Breda to Upham, March 7, 1910, in MHS Archives, and Appendix 11, below. No translation of the published article by Breda has been found. The italics indicated below are Breda's.

so excellently preserved "that a man absolutely ignorant of Runic characters" should have been able to make a copy "that could be easily read and deciphered." He described the story told in the inscription as one of "*utter absurdity.*" The trip inland, the fishing excursion, the calm carving of "an elaborate account," including a reference to ten men not merely "'dead,' but even 'red with blood'"—such details led him to say that the "annals of discovery contain nothing like it" save Frederick A. Cook's expedition to the North Pole.

Breda then turned to the language of the inscription, which to him "appeared to be a peculiar jumble of ancient forms, old-fashioned spellings and entire modern Swedish words intermixed with occasional English forms." It "could not possibly represent any genuine Northern language of the period indicated." He reviewed the later history of the stone and reported the adverse findings of such scholars as Sophus Bugge, Gustav Storm, Oluf Rygh, Magnus Olsen, and Adolf Noreen. Runic specialists in Norway and Sweden, he said, had "*unanimously pronounced the Kensington inscription a fraud and a forgery of recent date.*" Breda then speculated on how the inscription could have been made and spoke of the possibility that in frontier times someone from an Indian agency, a member of a hunting party, or a soldier of Swedish origins, who had a hammer, a chisel, and a knowledge of runic characters, might have carved it. He assumed that the stone had been buried before Ohman arrived on the scene. He conceded that other possible explanations might emerge, but he insisted that the inscription was not genuine.

Upham turned also to George Curme, the second linguist who had played a role in the Kensington story. It will be recalled that he had studied the stone for a month or more in 1899 and had concluded that the inscription was modern. In 1910 he wrote several letters to Winchell and Upham. The solution of the Kensington problem, he believed, lay solely in the hands of linguists; and he urged that the matter be referred to Scandinavian, primarily Swedish, runologists. In one letter he suggested Adolf Noreen as the top authority, and he also recommended one of Noreen's students, A. Louis Elmquist of Northwestern University. Curme wrote that he had found the inscription's umlauts too "modern." Several scholars in Christiania, he added, agreed with him, and he therefore "lost all interest in the stone." This statement presumably means that Curme corresponded with Norwegian scholars in 1899, a fact which increases one's regret that Curme's papers, if he preserved them, have not come to light.[37]

As early as March 2, 1910, just before Winchell was to leave St. Paul on a trip to Kensington, Upham wrote to him, pointing out that "Nearly all the expert linguists to whom the Kensington Rune Stone or copies of its inscriptions have been submitted declare it almost surely a modern forgery." He named ten scholars: Magnus Olsen and Helge Gjessing of Christiania, Norway; O. J. Breda, formerly of the University of Minnesota, and his successor Gisle Bothne; George Curme of Northwestern University; Starr W. Cutting and Chester N. Gould of the University of Chicago; George T. Flom of the University of Illinois; and Rasmus B. Anderson and Julius E. Olson of the University of Wisconsin. "Their emphatic objections," wrote Upham, "based on the language and runes of the inscriptions, which they consider too modern in word forms, inflections, order and usage in sentences, etc., indicate that very probably a fraud has been attempted." If so, he suggested, "the account of a poplar tree clasping the Rune Stone under its roots may be a part of the deception." He mentioned ill will between Ohman and Holand, and advised Winchell to gather as much information as possible about the honesty or dishonesty of the two men. He even suggested that Holand might have been sufficiently competent in 1898, the year of his graduation from the University of Wisconsin, to devise and cut the inscription.[38]

Although much has been written about the report of the Minnesota Historical Society's museum committee, little has been said about its indecision in the light of Flom's monograph on the Ken-

[37] See Upham to Curme, February 19, 1910, in MHS Letter Press Books; Curme to Winchell, March 9, 1910, and to Upham, February 21, 28, 1910, in Archaeological Records, MHS Archives, and Appendix 10, below.

[38] Upham sent photographs of the Kensington inscription to Magnus Olsen, Wimmer, Noreen, and Von Friesen; see his letters of March 8, 10, 11, 1910, in MHS Letter Press Books. See also Von Friesen to Upham, April 4, 1910; Elmquist to Winchell, April 19, 1910; Upham to Winchell, March 2, 1910 — in Archaeological Records, MHS Archives. Winchell believed that the poplar was older than Ohman's residence on the farm; Winchell Field Book, March 5, 1910.

sington inscription as a fraud. The doubts that assailed Upham in March were shared by some other members of the committee after Flom's study appeared in June—three months after Upham told Winchell that Flom's analysis was one of the most formidable attacks on the inscription's genuineness. The museum committee was shaken. At a meeting on July 23, 1910, more than two months after it had submitted a favorable report to the society's executive council, the committee with all members present very nearly reversed its earlier action. To quote from Upham's minutes:

It is proposed and generally approved to adopt the following resolution, but on further discussion it is not adopted, not to appear in the Committee's printed Report:

Resolved, That this Committee regards the genuineness of the supposed Kensington Rune Stone as not established, but that they deem the preponderance of evidence to be in favor of the Stone.

Upham recorded that the "suggested resolution and discussion of it proceed partly from consideration of objections urged by Prof. George T. Flom in his recent paper of 43 pages, issued in June by the Illinois State Historical Society." [39]

One of the committee members, Olin D. Wheeler, spoke of the earlier idea of having "a competent Scandinavian philologist" verify references and quotations in the report and concur in the committee's findings. Upham noted that the committee saw "increasing reasons for obtaining the aid and indorsement of some prominent and able Scandinavian authority." A question was raised whether Winchell should accompany Holand and "go with the Rune Stone to Norway." Wheeler remarked that the committee "should reckon on a probable or possible final verdict in Norway and Sweden adverse to the Stone." The committee voted to print a preliminary report after some revision, and it expressed the wish that the document be sent to Norway "for judgment by the Scandinavian linguists and runologists."

Flom received a copy of the committee's report and wrote Upham that he did not consider it worthy of a detailed refutation.

[39] Material here and below is from Museum Committee Minutes, July 23, 1910, Archaeological Records, MHS Archives.

Sections of it, he said, contained "errors too numerous to men-tion." The science of semasiology proved the inscription to be later than the date it bore. (Holand commented on Flom's use of the word "semasiology" and said scornfully and ignorantly "whatever that may be.") One part of the report seemed to Flom "a con-glomerate of misprints or misquotations." Another part was dis-missed as "crudely ignorant of the simplest facts of linguistic history and runic chronology." He said that his earlier condemna-tion of the inscription as modern was correct, and he suggested that the committee consult Frederick F. Klaeber, the University of Minnesota's renowned philologist. But this was never done.[40]

Perhaps the most revealing and appalling view voiced in the committee was that of the chairman, Edward C. Mitchell. Up-ham's minutes recorded that Mitchell "regards this Committee as a jury, or as a judge, before whom all evidence and arguments on both sides should be brought, to be duly weighed and decided."[41] Questions of history are not settled by juries or the votes of com-mittees. They are not disposed of by resolutions of historical in-stitutions. Sometimes they are not solved at all and continue to puzzle generation after generation. It may happen that new evi-dence or new discoveries on some disputed problems can add sources of knowledge not previously used. And it is possible that fresh analyses of old sources, made by newer scholarship with the aid of new evidence or altered perspectives, or both, may help to clarify questions that have defeated scholars in the past.

By one action after another, coupled with failures to pursue certain lines of inquiry, the museum committee invalidated much of its work. The group might have sent an experienced lawyer to Kensington, as both Andrew Fossum and Frederick Turner recom-mended. It might have denied Holand a share in the report, since he obviously was partisan. It might have enlisted the services of

---

[40] Holand to Winchell, January 28, 1911; Flom to Upham, January 22, 1911, MHS Archives. As late as October 23, 1912, the committee once more considered its report, discussed whether or not to prepare a "final report," and decided to "continue further the getting of evidence, pro and con." Minutes of the October 23 meeting are in a handwritten notebook bearing on its cover the words "Collection. J. V. Brower 1897, 1898, 1899, 1900. Catalogue, By paper boxes," Archaeological Records, MHS Archives.
[41] Museum Committee Minutes, July 23, 1910.

one or more of the world's most competent runologists. And it might have rejected the view of its chairman that it must act as a judge. Instead, it might have been content to present all the evidence, pro and con, that it was able to find, leaving to later scholarship the search for further evidence, other documents, and new analyses of the problems involved.

Mitchell and his colleagues attempted an impossible task. Their investigation, as Wahlgren convincingly demonstrated, lacked controls. Its direction was influenced by what he called "private, promotional interests"—in a word, by Holand with his uncritical enthusiasm and persuasiveness. Wahlgren proved beyond question that Holand was part author of the report. Though he was listed among the "eminent and critical scholars" who aided the committee, Holand was not a runologist, and the report ignored the comments of the qualified runologists who condemned the inscription. The resolution that was nearly, but not quite, adopted bespoke a realization by the committee that its report had not nailed down, beyond doubt, the genuineness of the inscription. No one would have quarreled with the committee for believing, as its members did, that the preponderance of its evidence (as they understood it) favored the inscription. But the committee lacked the sagacity to suspend final judgment. The society's executive council was wiser when it refused to endorse the committee's judgment that the inscription was a "true historic record."[42]

[42] Andrew Fossum to Upham, March 7, 1910, MHS Archives; Wahlgren, *Kensington Stone,* 179; Museum Committee, in *Minnesota Historical Collections,* 15:256, 286. The May 9, 1910, motion of the society's executive council used the words: "The Council and Society reserve their conclusion until more light may be received on this subject." The minutes recorded a discussion in which "several of the speakers" deemed it "inexpedient for the Council and this Society to give a formal verdict concerning the Rune Stone, preferring rather to wait for more agreement of opinions for or against it." The committee's published report said "the Council and Society reserve their conclusion until more agreement of opinions for or against the runic inscription may be attained." See *Minnesota Historical Collections,* 15:268. Why the original motion, obviously broader than the substitute, was not published has not been learned.

chapter 5

An Itinerant Schoolmaster and a Retired Professor

SVEN FOGELBLAD, THE ITINERANT SCHOOLMASTER, was a familiar figure in the Kensington region in the 1880s and 1890s until his death in 1897. His name recurs again and again throughout the Kensington controversy. Little has been known about him, however, except a smattering of information gathered more than fifty years ago by Holand, Flom, and Winchell. Flom noted a rumor connecting Fogelblad and Ohman with the "manufacture" of the rune stone that almost took "the form of conviction in the country east of Elbow Lake." In reply to Flom Holand published in 1910 a newspaper article about Fogelblad ridiculing the idea that he could have written the inscription. Many years later Wahlgren suggested that Fogelblad, because of his university education and "reportorial abilities," may have been "more important to the genesis of the Kensington inscription" than Holand cared to admit. Yet none of the commentators explored Fogelblad's background, and it is only bit by bit that a fuller portrait of the man has emerged. As Fogelblad can now be interpreted, with the use of newly found sources, it is clear that Wahlgren was right. The wandering teacher may indeed have been "more important" in connection with the Kensington problem than Holand wanted to concede.[1]

Holand pictured Fogelblad as a "jolly curate," a lazy man and

[1] Flom, in Illinois State Historical Society, *Transactions*, 1910, p. 122; Holand, quoted here and below, in *Minneapolis Journal*, August 9, 1910, p. 4, reprinted in *Minnesota Historical Collections*, 15:277–280; Wahlgren, *Kensington Stone*, 175.

a drinker, who went to America about 1870 after having resigned his post as an assistant pastor in a Swedish parish. He became an itinerant schoolteacher in Minnesota, working out from Litchfield, going from community to community and holding classes in farmhouses. Holand depicted him as a man who had to contend with his "old enemy, drink" but was welcomed by farmers because of his skill in purveying local news. His "literary efforts" were chiefly "humble doggerels," but Holand mentioned a report that the teacher once had an article published in Sweden. He was kindhearted but lacked ambition and "never studied." To Holand he was a man who could not possibly have devised the Kensington inscription because of "the limitations of his early training and later opportunities."

Without specifying the date he was discussing, Holand said that Fogelblad was "about seventy years" of age. In fact, he was born on December 10, 1829, in the parish of Fåglum in the province of Västergötland in Sweden, and died on July 12, 1897, at the home of Andrew Anderson not far from Kensington. He thus was in his sixty-eighth year at the time of his death. Holand at first said that the teacher died in 1895 but later corrected the date to 1897. His portrait of Fogelblad contains a few grains of truth, but important revisions are needed. Holand's account, moreover, was far from objective, since his purpose was to refute Flom and convince readers that the schoolmaster could have had nothing to do with the rune stone.[2]

Fogelblad was the son of a farmer, Anders Andersson.[3] After his elementary education, he enrolled in 1849 in the Skara Gymnasium, a famous Swedish secondary school. His scholastic record there was ordinary, but nevertheless he was accepted by the Uni-

[2] Professor O. Fritiof Ander explored many sources for me in Sweden in 1966 and wrote me fully. "Matrikel från Vest göta (Nation) Landskapsförening öfver indskrifna medlemmar, V.T. 1838–1856," in the manuscripts division, University of Uppsala Library, confirms the date of Fogelblad's birth; Ander to Blegen, April 28, 1966, Kensington file, Blegen Papers. The death of "Sven Fugelblad" on July 12, 1897, is recorded in Douglas County Death Record, 8:54, in Douglas County Courthouse, Alexandria. His age is listed as "67–8–2." He died in Solem Township, Douglas County, near Kensington.

[3] Ander to Blegen, April 31, 1966, Kensington file, Blegen Papers, cites L. A. Cederblom and C. O. Friborg, eds., Skara stifts herdaminne 1850–1930 (Stockholm, 1930).

versity of Uppsala in 1854 as a theological student, and his matriculation certificate was signed by Christopher J. Boström, who was known as the "Plato of Sweden." Fogelblad's grades on his entrance examinations were mostly "acceptable" as, for example, in Latin translation and "Latin language," but he was somewhat better in history and geography ("commendable"); and in "living languages" he was "defendable." In his studies at Uppsala he received mainly passable standings, though he was better in church history than in other subjects.[4]

Fogelblad was ordained in 1857 and at some later time became an assistant minister (*adjunkt*) at Bredared. He served for a while concurrently at Kyrkefalla and at other parishes as well. Little information is available about his career from 1857 to 1865, but church records show that he was greatly discontented at Bredared. He wished to be transferred to a more friendly parish environment, and his troubles came to a head in November, 1865.[5]

Two forces seem to have brought on the crisis. One was an allegation that Fogelblad was guilty of conduct unbecoming to a clergyman. The other was the fact that Fogelblad, who had studied with Boström — the Enlightenment philosopher and a disciple of Kant — found himself at odds with church doctrines. He said he had no *sinne* (mindedness) for the church, and he wanted to withdraw. It is clear from the records, however, that his colleagues and parishioners also wanted to get rid of him. Charges were preferred against him, but they are vaguely phrased in the documents. Conduct unbecoming to a clergyman could have meant drinking, but in Sweden at that time many clergymen were said to be extremely fond of liquor without being disciplined for their addiction. The

[4] Ander to Blegen, April 28, 1966, Kensington file, Blegen Papers, refers to printed catalogs of the University of Uppsala for fall, 1855, spring and fall, 1856, and to a report of Fogelblad's admission as a student signed by Christopher J. Boström, September 11, 1854, in the university's records. His Skara grades are given.

[5] Material here and in the next two paragraphs is based on documents of the Skara Cathedral Chapter reported in Ander to Blegen, May 14, 1966, Kensington file, Blegen Papers. A petition of November 7, 1865, from Rektor P. G. Landahl of Bredared requested Fogelblad's removal and the appointment of a new assistant pastor. In Bredared, Fogelblad alleged, he was surrounded by "hypocrites." In a letter of November 24, 1865, he asked for his own dismissal. His resignation was accepted and he escaped official hearings.

charges (an "irregular life") could have meant other matters than drinking, but if so they are not detailed.

In any event, Fogelblad resigned and asked for dismissal. He was averse to having the charges aired and was contrite. In his request, however humble he was about the aspersions against his conduct, he was emphatic that the ministry was no longer a calling to his taste. He had thought for a long time of resigning. Moreover, he felt that if the charges against him were made public they would be harmful both to him and to the church. In any case, he no longer accepted the dogmas he had promised to preach when he was ordained. As judged by the documents, his behavior had been unsavory, but in justice to him it should be added that a number of young Swedish clergymen, influenced by the Enlightenment as expounded by Boström, got into trouble with the church about the same time on allegations of heresy.

It is of extraordinary interest to know that a Swedish writer on the popular interpretation of runes was closely associated with the region in Västergötland where Fogelblad grew up and went to school, and that this runic enthusiast was in fact a cominister from 1855 to 1859 at Bredared — the very church in which Fogelblad served. He was Claes J. Ljungström (1819–82), an Uppsala-educated man with a deep interest in Swedish history and runes. He was not a professional runologist, but he founded an antiquities society for Västergötland in 1863, and three years later he published a book entitled *Rúna-list eller Konsten att läsa runor* (Runic Skill or the Art of Reading Runes — Lund, Sweden, 1866). A second edition appeared in 1875, and the Swedish government distributed copies to teachers. The work was designed for school use and for reading by lay people. It included the runic alphabet, a clear explanation of runic writing, and four illustrations of rune stones, with their symbols transcribed and translated into Swedish.[6]

It is almost a certainty that Fogelblad knew Ljungström. When one adds that Fogelblad through the first four decades of his life

[6] On Ljungström, see Ander to Blegen, May 18, June 26, 1966, Kensington file, Blegen Papers. A copy of the 1875 edition of Ljungström's book is in the University of Minnesota Library. O. E. Hagen took note of the work in "Ad Utrumque Parati Simus," in *Amerika*, April 1, 1910, p. 1, as did Wahlgren, *Kensington Stone*, 129.

WAYNESBURG COLLEGE LIBRARY
WAYNESBURG, PA.

was familiar with those areas in Sweden which were especially rich in runic monuments, it is safe to assume that he knew something about runes. The romantic interest of Esaias Tegnér and the "Gothic school" in the Viking age was still strong in Sweden.[7]

It is a plausible conjecture that Fogelblad knew at least as much about runes as did the several Minnesota laymen who were able quickly to translate the Kensington inscription in 1899 and, as a Swedish-educated man from the runic region, he may well have known much more than they did. Moreover, as has been noted in chapter 4, some persons well acquainted with him in his later years stated that he did know runes and that he was capable of having written the Kensington inscription.

Little is actually known about Fogelblad's life from 1865 to the early 1880s. The happenings in Sweden in 1865 were undoubtedly tantamount to an unfrocking, but there is no evidence that anything similar took place in America. Holand wrote that Fogelblad "was almost persuaded to re-enter the ministry" at Litchfield, but no evidence has been found to support this. Many decades after Fogelblad's death there was a rumor that in Litchfield in the 1870s at a Christmas celebration held above a saloon, he preached a sermon while under the influence of alcohol. No confirmation of this story has been found. And it is known that Fogelblad no longer accepted the doctrines of the church; for this reason alone he probably would not have re-entered the ministry.[8]

One of the interesting and important aspects revealed about Fogelblad since Holand wrote the sketch in which he spoke of him as a writer of mere doggerel is that Fogelblad was the author of several thoughtful essays. It has been supposed by some that these were published in a bilingual paper issued irregularly from Litchfield; it bore two names — Rothuggaren (The Root Chopper) and the Radical. It was edited by Frans H. Widstrand, a Utopian who had dreams of reforming society and who, like Fogelblad, had studied at Uppsala. Widstrand was an Icarian socialist, a vegetarian, advocate of a world language, believer in universal

[7] Esaias Tegnér (1782–1846) was a romantic poet, a member of the so-called Gothic League. His best-known work was Frithjofs Saga (1825). See Encyclopaedia Brittanica, 21:877 (London, New York, 1929).

[8] Holand, quoted in Minnesota Historical Collections, 15:278; Karl Holvik to his father, August 25, 1949, Holvik Papers.

education, and exponent of a score of reforms looking toward a government and society of "the good."[9]

Some of the Fogelblad articles were included as clippings in the scrapbook that once belonged to him and later was owned and continued by Olof Ohman. Unfortunately neither the dates nor the sources of these clippings are indicated. The finding of an additional Fogelblad article by Professor O. Fritiof Ander, of Augustana College, in the Royal Library at Stockholm indicates (by the character of the type) that the articles were not published in the bilingual *Rothuggaren*, but in a magazine or paper bearing the title *Upplysningens Tidehvarf* (Age of Enlightenment). This was an independent, anticlerical publication described in its subtitle as "A Philosophical-Religious Journal for the Swedish People in America." It was issued successively at Hutchinson, Glencoe, and Grove City, Minnesota, and it ran from 1877 to 1881. Widstrand seems to have edited the journal for a brief period (1880–81), but its chief backer was a Grove City druggist, C. J. Erickson.[10]

Fogelblad contributed at least five well-written essays in Swedish, presumably all during the period 1877–81. One appeared in 1877 in *Upplysningens Tidehvarf* under the title "The Clergy and Religious Instruction." In it Fogelblad contrasted progress, especially emancipation from prejudice and increasing understanding of nature, with what he regarded as lay ignorance and immaturity. For the latter he placed the blame on the clergy and on the inadequacy of religious instruction. In all religions, he wrote, the priests had been a class apart, committed to keeping people igno-

[9] On Widstrand, see Ander to Blegen, May 6, 8, 1966, Kensington file, Blegen Papers; Ernst Beckman, *Amerikanska studier*, 1:118–121 (Stockholm, 1883); Alfred Söderström, *Blixtar på tidnings-horisonten*, 303–306 ([Warroad, 1910]); Ernst Skarstedt, "En misskänd samhällsdanare: Biografiskt utkast," in *Präireblomman Kalender för 1908*, 8:124–137 (Rock Island, Ill., 1907).

[10] The Fogelblad articles, commented on here and below, with one exception are mounted in the Fogelblad-Ohman scrapbook. The exception (and the only one for which a date is known) — "Presterna och religions-undervisningen" (The Clergy and Religious Instruction) — was located by Professor Ander in *Upplysningens Tidehvarf* (Glencoe), December, 1877, p. [4], in the Royal Library. A microfilm copy of the Royal Library's file was secured by the MHS, but unfortunately there are some large gaps in the early years. Holand reported that Fogelblad once published an article in Sweden, but efforts to find it have been unsuccessful; *Kensington Stone*, 285.

rant and to upholding their own hierarchy. Church people, he said, had been instructed by the clergy to distrust their own thinking and to accept the dogmas of the priests. And ignorant folk could be easily led. Fogelblad dealt not only with religions of past centuries, but also with the contemporary church in Sweden and America. He scoffed at the practice of memorizing the catechism; he advised people to throw away dogmatic short explanations (the reference is to Luther's "Short Explanation"), and to insist upon methods of instruction whereby they could find release from old prejudices and a new appreciation of what was true, good, and beautiful.

In an article on the nature of truth, Fogelblad made it even clearer that he dissented fundamentally from the central tenet of the Christian church. Jesus, he contended, was not what the Christian church assumed or what evangelical accounts reported him to be, since he either would not or could not answer Pilate's question, "What is truth?" Toward the end of this article Fogelblad ventured to define truth for himself. Truth, he wrote, was (in part) every idea that finds its full validation in reality.

In an essay on the American public schools, Fogelblad criticized what he regarded as their superficiality, but he applauded the religious freedom and the separation of state and church which they typified. A fourth article about the honoring of great men is an interesting one. He decried the human tendency to wait a hundred years before recognizing greatness and spoke of the need for memorials honoring such men as Theodore Parker, Ralph Waldo Emerson, Samuel F. B. Morse, and John Ericsson.

Evidence that Fogelblad knew about Widstrand, the Icarian idealist, is furnished by a fifth article, an ironical essay entitled in translation "War in Minnesota 1881." In it Fogelblad told of a controversy between two men in Buffalo, Wright County, Minnesota, one called "W," the other "E." There can be no doubt that "W" was Widstrand, who tried to establish a Utopian colony near Buffalo. The identity of "E" has not been ascertained, but Fogelblad described him as jeering at Widstrand's theories, especially his alleged socialism and communism. The colony itself proved a failure, and Widstrand's house was taken over by two settlers who threatened to shoot him if he tried to force them out. Fogelblad wrote with sharp humor, relating the controversy to a comet that came and disappeared. He closed by assuring the contestants that the world was "still altogether the best world we have." The essay is of interest both as an illustration of Fogelblad's irony and humor and as clear evidence of his acquaintance with Widstrand's ideas. It is highly probable that the two men knew each other. Widstrand moved to Litchfield, where Fogelblad lived.

Such essays — and there may have been more — do not betoken a lazy mind and they confute Holand's statement that Fogelblad "never studied." They bear witness to the fact that he read and thought about large problems, and that he was a man of independent mind, ready to take a position in public opposition to the clergy.

The scholarly tone of the articles makes one wonder how much of a library Fogelblad owned. Some of his books, left after his death with Andrew Anderson, and later given by Anderson to a minister, were reported to be German philosophical works. He also owned a Swedish grammar by Carl J. L. Almquist which is of interest for three reasons. (1) It contained a runic alphabet. (2) The book was found in Ohman's house in 1910. Evidence indicates that Andrew Anderson gave it to Ohman after Fogelblad's death and some time after the rune stone was discovered. (3) Fogelblad wrote his name on its flyleaf and dated it Stockholm, 1868. Certain sources suggest that Fogelblad may have emigrated to America in 1865, others that the time was "about 1870." The signature in the book is conclusive evidence that he remained in Sweden until after the date he then recorded, November 16, 1868. It is not known precisely when he did leave, but the time obviously was between 1868 and 1870.[11]

While experts have written much about the Almquist grammar, two points have usually been overlooked. One is the date of Fogelblad's signature. Why did he acquire the grammar in 1868, long

---

[11] *Minnesota Historical Collections,* 15:237–240, 280; C. J. L. Almquist, *Svensk språklära* (Stockholm, 1840). Ohman's copy was secured by Winchell and is preserved by the MHS. That two books on philosophy were in German is mentioned by the minister who remembered them, Magnus A. Nordström, in a letter to the MHS, September 20, 1910, in Archaeological Records, MHS Archives. Knowing that Fogelblad's teacher was a disciple of Kant, it seems possible that these books were by Kant.

after he had finished his university education? Did the acquisition signify a special interest in the Swedish language? The second point is that those who have suspected Fogelblad of playing a role in the origination of the Kensington inscription have no reason to suppose that his knowledge of runic characters was based merely on the elementary runic information set forth in the Almquist grammar.

When Holand wrote that Fogelblad was "entirely ignorant of the fine runological and linguistic points" (later he added the word "paleographic") involved in the Kensington inscription, he did not give any weight to the fact that Fogelblad had had considerable training in languages.[12] To enter the University of Uppsala, he had to prove competence in "Latin translation" and "Latin language" as well as "living languages." That he treasured German books of philosophy must mean that he read German. And Holand never knew that Fogelblad probably was acquainted with the runic enthusiast, Ljungström.

If Fogelblad seems enigmatic, the answer may in part lie in the fact that certain stretches of his life are nearly blanks because contemporary records are few. The newly found items, however, have helped to fill out the picture. A man who could write understandingly of both Emerson, poet and philosopher, and of Parker, the Unitarian theologian, obviously was familiar with the writings of these men. When Fogelblad wrote about them and when he probed the nature of truth, he was composing not doggerel but thoughtful articles. These writings show that he was more of a scholar than his student grades may have indicated. And he was not quite so unstable as the emphasis on his "old enemy, drink" might imply.

It is clear that Fogelblad was a drinker, but assertions that he was a drunkard are open to some question. Holand reported that nobody in the Kensington and Hoffman communities "ever saw

[12] Holand wrote "the fine runological and linguistic points" in *Minnesota Historical Collections*, 15:280. In 1932 (*Kensington Stone*, 286) and 1956 (*Explorations in America Before Columbus*, 349) he wrote "the fine runological, paleographic and linguistic points." In *Pre-Columbian Crusade* (p. 38), Holand dismissed Fogelblad as a "gentleman tramp" who "was not interested in history and read very little." This was long after Holvik had disclosed the existence of the Fogelblad-Ohman scrapbook, with its articles by Fogelblad.

him drink or under the influence of drink." If he had been a ha-
bitual drunkard, it is doubtful that he would have been received
year after year in farmers' homes, where he taught the neighborhood children. Andrew Anderson, who knew him very well, said
flatly that he was not a drunkard. Perhaps the truth is to be found
in a remark made by Ohman, who said that Fogelblad, though a
gentleman in manners, was "intemperate, drinking when ever he
had any money." Certainly he earned very little money from his
teaching. It is only fair to add that any rumor of drinking on the
part of a preacher or former preacher was likely to excite comment, and perhaps exaggeration, in church circles. For example,
a local minister reported that Fogelblad had been jailed for drunk-
enness in Fergus Falls (the minister placed such episodes in the
early 1870s). Fogelblad did not appear in that area until later,
and in any event the case was clearly one of mistaken identity.[13]

Fogelblad's alleged laziness has no pertinence to his possible
role in the Kensington story. He may indeed have been physically
lazy, but the criticism or comment seems to have come from farmers who noted that Fogelblad took no part in their hard work.
Obviously he did not wish to. He was a teacher with Swedish university traditions, and probably few of the farmers realized that
teaching is work. It is interesting that Holand, who gathered up
gossip, commented that Fogelblad did "repair old pipes, bind
books, make kitchen knick-knacks, etc."[14] Such hobbies indicate
that he had manual dexterity, and this, plus his other talents, may
have more significance than any alleged "laziness" or liking for
drink.

Holand wrote that the "only possible reason" for associating the
"poor old man" with the "supposed forgery" was that he was dead
and could not deny accusations.[15] In view of what is now known
about Fogelblad, this is rhetorical nonsense. What is to be re-

[13] Holand, quoted by Museum Committee, in *Minnesota Historical Collections*, 15:278; Winchell Field Book, March 17, 19, 1910. The local minister was Olaus A. Normann of Ashby, who served there for many years from
1879; see Olaf M. Norlie, ed., *Norsk lutherske prester i Amerika, 1843–1913*,
122 (Minneapolis, 1914). It turned out that Normann's "preacher" was not
Fogelblad but a man of quite another name.
[14] *Minnesota Historical Collections*, 15:279.
[15] *Explorations in America Before Columbus*, 349.

gretted is that he did not live long enough to be asked about his part, if any, in the origination of the Kensington inscription. In recent times expert runologists analyzing the inscription have declared it to be "modern," as did Breda and Curme in 1899 and Flom in 1910. If so, one or more "modern" persons must have devised the wording and chiseled the symbols. In the light of the information available, one can no longer brush Fogelblad aside as a "poor old man" who could not possibly have had anything to do with the Kensington rune stone. He was capable of composing it and perhaps even of carving the letters.

There has been speculation about how long it may have taken a hoaxer to chisel the characters, but no one has ventured a theory as to how much time was needed to devise the words and their symbols or how much thought went into the entire conception of the inscription on the stone. Wahlgren shrewdly assumed that whoever did the job, with or without the collusion of others, was intelligent, "a ponderer and a seeker."[16] On the hypothesis that the inscription was a hoax, someone may have "pondered" the matter for a considerable time, and there may have been more than one "ponderer." In the light of the new information, surely no one can doubt that Fogelblad would qualify as a "ponderer."

There is one additional piece of evidence that has received little attention — a letter about Fogelblad written by Johan Schröder of Souris, North Dakota, and published in *Minneapolis Tidende* in March, 1928. Schröder said that he had known Fogelblad in the 1880s, in fact had spent much time with him. He wrote that Fogelblad was an "expert in runes" and also that he was a great joker. After the letter appeared, Andrew A. Veblen of San Diego, California, a former professor of physics in the University of Iowa and a brother of the famous Thorstein Veblen, wrote several probing letters to Schröder, asking precisely where and when Schröder had known Fogelblad. In two replies written in Norwegian, Schröder gave further details. He had gone to Grant County in 1881, he said, and not only knew Fogelblad but lived under the same roof with him in three places near Barrett, Minnesota, in 1882–84. He named three of his relatives with whom they had stayed. He

[16] Wahlgren, *Kensington Stone*, 181.

reported that everybody knew that Fogelblad could write runes, and he repeated his statement that Fogelblad was a joker.[17] Schröder said that he did not really believe that Fogelblad had written the runes on the Kensington stone, but at the end of his letter he mentioned reports that people were raising money for a monument in celebration of the rune stone. Earlier he had suggested that Fogelblad made the runic inscription "for fun"— as a joke. As to the monument, Schröder said, if it should turn out that it was "an old dismissed preacher who had carved the runes," the monument would be a joke to make even the wildest Indians roar with laughter. George Flom, to whom Veblen also wrote, said that such a monument would be "an everlasting mockery"— a monument to false claims, credulity, and dilettantism.[18]

For Veblen's information Schröder enclosed a letter written to him from Chicago on April 26, 1928, by A. Frithiof Malmquist, a Swedish-American journalist and poet. Malmquist had received his information about Fogelblad from Oliver A. Linder, the managing editor of the Chicago newspaper *Svenska Amerikanaren,* who was well informed about the Kensington stone. Reflecting Linder's opinion, Malmquist wrote that "Fogelblad was sufficiently at home in runic writing to have composed the inscription." Linder believed that Fogelblad had written it secretly and that after his death someone who knew about runes used the Fogelblad text to carve the inscription. Schröder interpreted the information to mean that Fogelblad had written the runic text as a joke.[19]

Assar G. Janzén of the University of California also regarded the Kensington inscription "as a hoax or a joke, and a pretty good

[17] Holand read the Schröder letter in *Minneapolis Tidende* and wrote a reply to it that was splattered with mistakes; *Tidende,* March 29, 1928, p. 10. Holand never mentioned Schröder in his books. The Schröder letters of April 9, May 1, 1928, and copies of Veblen's letters of March 26, April 14, May 7, 1928, are in the A. A. Veblen Papers, MHS. Schröder corrected some of Holand's errors in incisive fashion in his letter of May 1.
[18] George T. Flom to Veblen, December 3, 1928, Veblen Papers. A photograph of the enormous Kensington monument built at Alexandria is the frontispiece in Holand's *Explorations in America Before Columbus.*
[19] See Veblen Papers. On Malmquist and Linder, see Ernst W. Olson and Martin J. Engberg, eds., *History of the Swedes of Illinois,* 2:364 (Chicago, 1908); *Who Was Who in America,* 1:731 (Chicago, 1942).

one"; and Wahlgren thought of the "planting of such a mock runic monument" as "a clever and understandable hoax." But no one in the early period of the Kensington controversy save Linder (as reported by Malmquist and interpreted by Schröder) seems to have entertained the idea that the joke, if such it was, may have been composed on paper by someone who had nothing to do with the carving of the stone. Although the suggestion is ingenious, the inscription seems palpably designed for a monument. Wahlgren's theory was that it may have been chiseled as late as 1898, but if Fogelblad wrote the text and if it was carved before 1897, one might also consider the possibility that he both wrote and cut the inscription.[20]

A second teacher, who like Fogelblad has been accused of authoring the Kensington stone, was Ole Eriksson Hagen (1854–1927), a linguist who specialized for four years (1886–90) in Oriental languages for the Ph.D. degree at the University of Leipzig. He had taken undergraduate work at the University of Wisconsin, where his studies included Old Norse and where he assisted R. B. Anderson in listing the books in the university's Norwegian collection. Before going to Germany he had taught Greek and Latin at an academy — or college — in Galesville, Wisconsin.[21]

Hagen had a special interest in unlocking difficult linguistic problems. On his way to Germany he visited Dighton Rock in

[20] Janzén, in *Swedish Pioneer Historical Quarterly*, 8:31 (January, 1957); Wahlgren, *Kensington Stone*, 181. For further discussion of this point, see chapter 6, below.

Some note should be taken of a remark made by Mrs. Olof Ohman to Professor Holvik. Holvik had mentioned Fogelblad, and Mrs. Ohman then made the following "spontaneous comment": "Inte hade Fogelblad något at gjöra med stenen, inte." (Fogelblad had nothing to do with the stone, nothing.) Holvik remarked, "The Swedish intonation of the statement makes the implication clear." He does not amplify this comment, but a fair conjecture is that to him the implication was that Mrs. Ohman *did know* who had something to do with the stone — that is, who carved the inscription. See Holvik form letter, November 22, 1949, Holvik Papers.

[21] John A. Hofstead, *American Educators of Norwegian Origin*, 75 (Minneapolis, 1931). On Hagen, see Lars M. Gimmestad, in *Skandinaven*, March 23, 1927, p. 3; Blegen, "O. E. Hagen, A Pioneer Norwegian-American Scholar," in J. Iverne Dowie and J. Thomas Tredway, eds., *The Immigration of Ideas: Studies in the North Atlantic Community*, 43–65 (Rock Island, Ill., 1968).

Massachusetts, which was thought by some to have runic markings. He went equipped with records of all known forms of runes and other alphabets and even syllabaries; on his return from Germany four years later, this time fortified by paleographic knowledge gained during his German studies, he again inspected the markings on the much discussed rock. He found the inscription, in general, without form or system, an "epigraphic impossibility."[22]

In 1891 Hagen, with his Leipzig doctorate, went to the young University of South Dakota at Vermillion, where he served on its faculty for a decade (with an intermission of one year). He taught many languages, including Old Norse, gave courses in German and French literature, and held classes in German and Scandinavian philology, and in modern Norwegian. The South Dakota period was marked by severe dissension, controversy, and cleavage in the faculty, and Hagen's intermission (1896–97) was really a dismissal followed by reappointment. All in all, the decade was an unhappy one for him, climaxed by a requested resignation in 1901. He retired to a Wisconsin farm and never taught again, though he published not a few articles, poems, and books. The experience at Vermillion — its details were never clarified — left deep scars on him, but neither Hagen nor anyone else ever explained why he thereafter chose to abandon academic life.[23]

Among Hagen's various later publications was an essay on the Vinland problem. Hagen was sharply critical of the Norwegian scholar Gustav Storm, whose excessive caution in dealing with the sagas seemed, in Hagen's opinion, to border on hostility. To Hagen these sources were basically trustworthy, and he believed that

[22] See Hagen, "Nogle ord om Vinlandsforskningen" (Some Words on Vinland Research), which first appeared in *Amerika*, June 26, 1908, p. 10, and was thereafter reprinted as a pamphlet; a copy is in the library of the State Historical Society of Wisconsin, Madison.

[23] Gimmestad, in *Skandinaven*, March 23, 1927, p. 3; *Volante*, 5:75 (November 5, 1891), 8:21 (October 8, 1894), 9:30 (October 28, 1895), and numerous other issues of the university paper; Cedric Cummins to Blegen, May 6, 1965; Herbert S. Schell to Blegen, April 2, 1965; and numerous letters and notes from Donald N. Meeks, especially May 10, 21, 1965 — all in Kensington file, Blegen Papers. Mr. Meeks also supplied me with notes on many of the items in *Volante* and excerpts from catalogs of the University of South Dakota. For detailed references, see Blegen, in Dowie and Tredway, eds., *The Immigration of Ideas*, 43–65.

evidence of the Norse discovery of Vinland would be ultimately found in European cloisters or other depositories — an interesting forecast. In his essay Hagen told of his studies of Dighton Rock; he touched on the Newport Tower; and he discussed runes at length, commenting on their beauty, compactness, and adaptability to epigraphic combinations. He made no allusion to the Kensington inscription.[24]

In 1910, however, he entered the Kensington discussion with an article entitled "Ad Utrumque Parati Simus," by which he obviously meant that the inscription might or might not prove to be genuine. He knew about the hoax of a "petrified man" dug up near Argyle in northwestern Minnesota in 1896; and it was this episode that caused him to break his silence on the Kensington problem. He scoffed at the idea that popular approval had any significance with respect to the validity of the inscription. "The stone," he said, "bears its own evidence — its own vindication or condemnation" — and he underlined the sentence for emphasis. He found the "vocables all within a thoroughly surveyed dialectal range," but some words were suspicious "as to form and use." On the geographic side, he did not think it improbable that exploration had taken place west and south of Baffin Bay, and he cited the Kingigtorssauq cairn inscription in Greenland. He closed by pointing out that knowledge of runes persisted in Sweden into modern times and he spoke of Ljungström's *Rúna-list* of 1866.[25]

Hagen published a second article in 1910 entitled "The Kensington Stone."[26] It was centrally a linguistic discussion, but is of special interest because after writing his first article he visited

[24] Hagen, in *Amerika*, June 26, 1908, p. 10.
[25] Hagen, in *Amerika*, April 1, 1910, p. 1 (quotes). Olson to Upham, May 8, 1910, MHS Archives, criticized the Hagen article as a "gigantic 'bluff.'" The article was occasioned by two reports written by Rasmus B. Anderson in the same newspaper for February 25, 1910, p. 1, and March 11, 1910, p. 1. Anderson, after writing about the "petrified man," touched on the rune stone and remarked that the "woods and prairies" of Minnesota were full of men "able and shrewd enough" to have concocted the inscription. The Kingigtorssauq or Kingiktorsooak inscription was discovered near Upernavik, Greenland, in 1824. For a brief account, see Gwyn Jones, *The Norse Atlantic Saga: Being the Norse Voyages of Discovery and Settlement to Iceland, Greenland, America*, 49 (London, 1964).
[26] *Amerika*, January 6, 1911, p. 9, reprinted from *Skandinaven*. Hagen dated his essay December 20, 1910, and it appeared in *Skandinaven*, De-

St. Paul, examined the rune stone, copied the inscription for himself, and studied some words that had occasioned disagreement. He advised scholars to keep their eyes open for dialect words and ways of speech. He denounced as charlatanism any attempt to draw upon nationalistic feelings in trying to get at the authenticity of the document; and he closed with the warning that archaeology, from ancient times on, had witnessed many impostures. He would not offer a judgment on the Kensington inscription, but he suggested that all possibilities of fraud be taken into account.

Hagen next commented on the Kensington stone in a somewhat casual note accompanying a ballad from the time of the Black Death in Norway. He had heard it in Wisconsin in 1873; it had been printed in 1909; and he reprinted it in 1911. Its possible pertinence to the Kensington problem lay in a line similar to one in the inscription:

Hjelpe os Gud å Maria møy. [Help us, God and Virgin Mary,]
Å frels os alle av illi! [And save us all from evil!]

The lines closely resemble the controversial Kensington "AVM fräelse af illy." Hagen suggested that their occurrence in the old ballad made it unnecessary to reject the phrase as invalid in the Kensington text.[27]

Hagen continued to study the Kensington problem through more than a decade after 1911 and in that period he wrote an article or monograph on it. At a celebration in his honor held in 1924, he said that he intended soon to publish his findings on the Kensington rune stone. In 1926, however, a fire destroyed his house near Meridean, Wisconsin, and most of his books and papers were lost, including those relating to the Kensington inscription.

cember 24, 1910, p. 3, under the title "Kensington-stenen: Lidt og [sic] ordet 'From' og andre sider af spørsmaalet."

[27] Hagen, "Førnesbronen: En mærkelig vise fra den sorte døds tid," in Samband, October, 1911, p. 363–369, a monthly magazine published in Minneapolis. Wahlgren, Kensington Stone, 163, suggested that if Hagen heard the ballad in 1873, it might well have been known twenty years or more later when, as he believed, the Kensington inscription was carved by a hoaxer. Wahlgren quoted Holand as saying that the ballad was recorded in Minnesota in 1873 by "E. Hagen." However, it was heard in Wisconsin near Eau Claire by O. E. Hagen that year. The text as printed came from an old man named Tortvei, who gave it to Torkel Oftelie, a ballad collector in Fergus Falls, Minnesota.

He died the next year, but meanwhile he had written a letter in which he again dealt with the Kensington puzzle. He said he had not been able to find epigraphic evidence that the inscription was not what it purported to be. On the linguistic side, he wrote, there were some peculiarities, perhaps graphical errors, but he had not found "actual philological proof" that the inscription was fraudulent. It was an "intelligible document," and evidence of forgery had not been forthcoming. Nearly everything that Hagen said in this "categorical" statement carried a qualification or carefully phrased reservation, and he avoided making a flat claim that the runic inscription was from the fourteenth century.[28]

Apart from Hagen's own writings about the Kensington problem, there is a somewhat special reason for giving space to his role in the discussion. This is the fact that Professor Julius E. Olson of the University of Wisconsin believed that Hagen himself had devised the Kensington inscription. He did it, according to Olson, after completing his Leipzig studies. He had the "requisite knowledge for the forgery" and he carried off the prank (Olson asserted) in 1891 before he went to South Dakota. The motive, Olson intimated to some of his later students, was jealousy, presumably a desire to humiliate Olson himself, who had been chosen instead of Hagen to succeed R. B. Anderson at Wisconsin. The suggested motive seems tenuous. No connection of Hagen with the Kensington region has ever been discovered. In 1891 he was fresh from his success in winning his degree in Germany and was about to start on his South Dakota professorship.[29]

It is an unhappy circumstance that Hagen's Kensington monograph and records were lost, including the copy he made of the inscription. Undoubtedly he was well informed on the Kensington problem as the result of his studies and linguistic skills.

[28] *Reform* (Eau Claire, Wis.), October 2, 1924, p. 8; April 29, 1926, p. 3.
[29] See Warren Upham Notebook, April 29, 1910, in MHS Archives; Flom to Veblen, December 3, 1928, Veblen Papers. In an interview in *Minneapolis Tidende*, August 24, 1911, p. 7, Olson described how a hoax might have been perpetrated, but he did not mention Hagen. On Olson's possible motive, see Einar Haugen to Blegen, November 19, 1966, Kensington file, Blegen Papers.

chapter 6

By Way of Summary

Even if the runologists had declared the Kensington inscription authentic, the circumstances and apparent coincidences surrounding the discovery and early history of the stone would have puzzled historians.[1] When it is realized, however, that authoritative runologists, with no dissenting voices, have pronounced the inscription modern, these items have a possible significance that calls for most careful consideration.

The circumstances that envelop the Kensington story begin with the striking fact, hitherto little appreciated, that among the Scandinavian pioneers in Minnesota in the 1890s and earlier there were not a few persons, including laymen, who well understood runes. They could read and translate them, and the ease and quickness with which some of them did so constitute strong evidence that they also could have devised runic inscriptions. The truth contradicts Holand's implication that runic erudition could not be found among the Scandinavian pioneers. It was precisely among such settlers in the state where the Kensington stone was found that three persons independently translated the inscription within a few days after it was reproduced in newspapers in 1899. More than a possibility exists that Samuel A. Siverts, the Kensington banker, also made an early translation. And there were yet others in Minnesota who knew something about runes. Rasmus Anderson drew a long bow when in 1910, looking back two or more decades,

[1] Since this is for the most part a summarizing chapter, footnote citations given earlier in the text are not repeated. Where new material is added, it is supported by references.

109

he said that the "woods and prairies" of Minnesota were then full
of men "able and shrewd enough" to have produced the Kensington inscription. His exaggeration is not as far afield as Holand's
incredulity at the idea that any Scandinavian pioneer had the
"erudition" needed to devise the inscription.

A second circumstance, not much labored in this volume since
others have dealt effectively with it, is that the Kensington stone
was dug up on the land of a Swedish-American farmer, in a
Scandinavian community, in a state with a large Scandinavian
population. These facts defy easy explanation. Professor Turner regarded the finding of the stone in a Scandinavian community as a
suspicious circumstance, and he recorded the thought long before
either defenders or critics of the inscription learned about the
knowledge of runes prevalent in the Minnesota of the 1890s. Most
of those who interpret the Kensington evidence as pointing to a
hoax do not ascribe the origin to a time earlier than the 1880s or
1890s. During these years, the population of Douglas County and
of the Kensington region was strongly marked by Swedish and
Norwegian elements, and it was this basic fact of scene and setting
that made Turner skeptical.

American interest in the sagas and Norse voyages to North
America was no new thing in the late nineteenth century, but it
deepened from the 1870s to the 1890s. Many books and articles
were published on the Norsemen, especially on the Vinland question, in the late decades of the nineteenth century. Here it is sufficient to recall only a few items, including the provocative if not
original book by R. B. Anderson issued in 1874 under the title
America Not Discovered by Columbus, with a third edition published by 1883. One may note also the interest in runes that found
expression in an illustrated article about them in a Chicago magazine in 1885, and the burst of public excitement that followed Gustav Storm's challenge in the late 1880s of the claim that Vinland
was in the area that later became the United States.

The *North* of Minneapolis, as has been mentioned, supported a
proposal in 1889 to get a model of the Gokstad Viking ship for
that city, and the proposal materialized a year later. The same
publication carried articles on the sagas and promoted an ambi-
tious plan for an exhibit on Norse colonization for the period

1000–1347. The *North* had subscribers in Kensington as early as 1890.

The discussions of the 1880s and early 1890s reached the attention of Scandinavians in Minnesota. Interest rose to a high level when the Columbian Exposition was held in Chicago in 1893 and a replica of the Gokstad ship sailed across the Atlantic and through the Great Lakes to Chicago. This feat occasioned many articles in the Scandinavian press of the Middle West; and it inspired Johan A. Enander to publish in Swedish in 1893 a book in which he inquired about the possibility that there might be remains testifying to the presence of Norsemen in North America in Viking times. Enander's suggestion that evidence might yet be found to confirm the sagas may conceivably have stirred someone to try his hand at creating such "evidence" as a fraud or a joke. In 1910 Turner thought it a "suspicious" circumstance that the Kensington stone was found "just about the right time after a general and heated discussion of whether the Scandinavians were within the limits of the United States prior to Columbus."

No revisions of earlier ideas about Kensington persons and backgrounds are more significant than those relating to Sven Fogelblad. The traditional picture of him, repeated again and again, is that of a drunkard, a man too lazy to execute a practical joke, a writer of mere doggerel, a person ignorant of the fine points involved in the Kensington inscription, a man who never studied — a "poor old man" who was implicated in the "supposed forgery" only because he was dead and could not defend himself.

This denigrating characterization of Fogelblad is largely unfounded. Fogelblad was a man of intellectual ability. He was handy at practical jobs. His alleged laziness, as has been suggested, was surely the reaction of an intellectual who did not take to heavy farm work. He was a man who liked jokes. Those who knew him well believed he could read and write runes, and he had grown up in a Swedish area rich in runic inscriptions. He very probably was acquainted with C. J. Ljungström, the author of a popular book on the art of reading runes. He was a writer of thoughtful essays which are proof that he "studied." In Douglas County, where he was well known, not a few persons suspected him of being involved in the Kensington hoax. Add to these items the facts that he was a friend of Olof Ohman, had stayed at his house, and that the two men were united in a bond of iconoclasm, and one has a picture that sharply upsets traditional views. Holvik and Wahlgren established that Fogelblad had both linguistic and historical interests, and their findings are now strengthened by records found in Sweden as well as in this country.

All this cannot be brushed aside as coincidence in considering the origin of an inscription said by runologists to be fraudulent. A half-legendary figure is now replaced by the image of a real man who is nothing less than a major suspect in a hoax that required such knowledge and skills as he possessed.

Inevitably one recalls the shrewd question asked by Turner in 1910 — whether or not there had been in the neighborhood of the Kensington find a professional man "who had the general training needed to frame the text." He mentioned a schoolteacher or minister or lawyer; Fogelblad was a schoolteacher who had been a minister. When Andrew Anderson denied parts of Rasmus Anderson's story, he admitted that he *had* said that Fogelblad "could possibly have written the inscription on paper" and that Ohman could have chiseled it on stone. He did not believe they had done so, he said, but the thought had come to him that each might have played a part. Perhaps he knew more than he acknowledged in words to R. B. Anderson.

A similar thought occurred to the Swedish-American editor, Oliver A. Linder, who suggested that Fogelblad might have created the runic text on paper as a joke, and that someone else might have carved it on the stone after Fogelblad's death. These ideas are nothing but conjectures, but they are not conjectures of the present writer. They were made long ago.

It is always puzzling to know what degree of intelligence is hidden by the outward aspects of one who says little. Olof Ohman was taciturn. He was better at understanding English than at speaking it. He was a man who did not talk much, but thought much — one whose abilities might easily have been underestimated. He was called a "queer genius." Even Winchell, who did not understand Swedish, came to realize that Ohman was "a more intellectual man" than he had at first supposed him to be. Less restrained was the view of a professional man (a dentist) who told Holvik that Ohman was "one of the keenest and best informed men" he had ever met.

Ohman was a thoughtful, well-informed, inquiring, well-traveled man.[2] His letter of December 9, 1909, to Warren Upham, printed in the appendix, is obviously not the work of an educated man, but it is clear, to the point, and vigorous in tone. Ohman said flatly that he had never before seen a rune stone, but he did not say he had never seen a runic inscription. He had in fact seen the Forsa Ring in his native Orsa, Sweden, and as a schoolboy he had learned something about runes. He was a reader who had bound into a volume a series of newspaper articles on the history of his native land. He had owned since 1891 an encyclopedic work that included detailed information about runes. He knew Biblical lore. He knew something of ancient religions.

Winchell regarded Ohman as one of the "plain and simple farmers" and he praised his "honesty and candor." But it must not be forgotten that Winchell also wrote that, if there was fraud in the Kensington affair, it lay with one or all of the trio of Ohman, Fogelblad, and Andrew Anderson.

In any summary of the Ohman story a few special circumstances need to be mentioned. One is the finding of a worn whetstone near the place where the rune stone was discovered. Such a whetstone could not have been from the fourteenth century. The incident deserves notice because the story was told by Ohman to a neighbor. A whetstone is of course a very common tool, and the episode may be without significance. But why did Ohman speak of it in a rune-stone context? Was its mention a mild effort by a fundamentally honest man to suggest the idea of a hoax?

To have in the background not only this reference by Olof Ohman to a whetstone but also a documented report of the purchase in Alexandria of a chisel for cutting the Kensington inscription must put some strain on the credulity of defenders of the stone. When one adds that its finder was born and spent his youth in a country noted for its runic inscriptions, the strain is increased. When, then, it is remembered that Ohman wanted to devise some-

[2] Flom, who met Ohman, reported that the latter returned to Sweden from 1884 to 1886 and that he thereafter spent six months in Portland, Ore. Flom, in Illinois State Historical Society, *Transactions*, 1910, p. 122.

thing to crack or "Bother the Brains of the Learned" and that he owned a book containing an exposition of runes, real doubt must creep in. When it is still further added that Ohman's friend Sven Fogelblad was believed to be well versed in runes — and that both he and Ohman were of nonconforming intellectual views — the strain on credulity must become nearly unendurable. If on top of these considerations it is recalled that runic scholars declare the Kensington inscription cannot possibly be from the fourteenth century, even the most robust "will to believe" must be shaken.

A strange problem in relation to the Kensington riddle is that of the date when the stone was discovered. This has already been discussed in relation to near-contemporary reports which strongly support November, 1898; the affidavits, which allege August, 1898; and Wahlgren's hypothesis of a "reincarnation."

Little more need be said. Although there has been almost endless discussion of the supposed age of the tree, not a great deal of attention has been devoted to the flattening and bending of its roots. In connection with a document of challenged authenticity, all circumstances are *suspect,* and as early as 1910 Upham wondered if the roots were a part of the deception. Yet their condition is more consistently attested than is the age of the tree, and the testimony goes back to 1899.

As early as May 16, 1899, Olaus Olson, who saw the tree stump, wrote, "Two large roots, one on each side of the stone, had grown down into the earth and shaped themselves along its sides, so that the stone was bound in between them." Ohman, in his affidavit of 1909, said, "One of the roots penetrated directly downward and was flat on the side next to the stone. The other root extended almost horizontally across the stone and made at its edge a right angled turn downward. At this turn the root was flattened on the side toward the stone. This root was about three inches in diameter."

O. G. Landsverk in *The Discovery of the Kensington Runestone: A Reappraisal* gave some attention to the roots, quoted from the affidavits, and included a statement made by Arthur Ohman, a son of the finder. Arthur recalled (in 1961) a question raised by Nils Flaten as to how, if the stone had been inserted underneath the tree, the roots could have grasped it so firmly that when the tree was pulled over by means of a winch the stone was hoisted in the roots. Arthur Ohman also contributed a sketch showing how he remembered the stone to have been clasped. Neither this sketch nor drawings used by Holand or by the museum committee took into account the slanting position which Olof Ohman said the stone occupied, with a corner "almost protruding" from the ground. The sketches picture the stone as lying, not on a slant, but just about horizontally, several inches below the surface. The point is worth some notice when one recalls Turner's suggestion that the "stone could have been *placed under* the tree so that the roots could in a few years have clasped" the stone. Ohman spoke of the stunted appearance of the tree. One wonders what made it stunted.

I have consulted foresters and botanists and have learned that the roots could not have been flattened and bent from August to November, 1898 — the period assumed in the Wahlgren theory of the "reincarnation" of the stone.[3] The longest time one could allocate for that assumed period would be from August 1 to November 8, 1898, that is, three months and ten days. Since no one knows what day in August was meant, it might be nearer the truth to say from about August 15 to November 8 — that is, a little less than three months.

The theory of a late substitution postulates a search for a tree with roots already suitably shaped by contact with some similar stone, and then the planting of an inscribed stone. Such a procedure certainly cannot be ruled out. It may have been followed. When considering the possibility of a substitution of stones, it is of interest to recall that Winchell in 1909 reported finding samples of rocks comparable with the Kensington slab at the edge of the slough below the hill where Ohman found the rune stone, at

[3] Frank H. Kaufert, director of the University of Minnesota's School of Forestry, to the author, February 13, 1967, Kensington file, Blegen Papers, reporting on a discussion of the question with a number of his staff members. The length of time needed, according to Professor Kaufert, would depend upon the "degree of flattening, location of the stone and roots, etc." One staff member commented that the "roots may have been flattened by contact with another stone or stones that were removed when the rune stone was planted." Mr. Kaufert suggested that whoever prepared the stone might have spent considerable time digging for "suitable rocks" to replace with a "plant."

nearby fence lines, and "along the road between Kensington & Ohmans." Five slabs in a hundred, Winchell noted, "may be compared" with the engraved stone. He found some that, he said, "resemble it," but only one that was "exactly like it." That Winchell found, somewhere near the site of the Kensington stone, a slab "exactly like it" is the overwhelming evidence that the inscribed stone was of local origin. The finding of such a slab also lends plausibility to the theory of a substitution of one stone for another. It does not confirm that theory, however, or shed light on the question of when such a substitution could have been made, if in fact it was made.

Such a "plant," if it had been done less than three months before the rune stone was unearthed, in all probability would have left conspicuous marks in the ground. The testimony of Nils Flaten, as recorded in his signed affidavit, must be used with caution. He said that he had visited the place of the discovery earlier on the same day and had been there "many times previously," but he "had never seen anything suspicious there." The spot, he said, had been "covered by a very heavy growth of underbrush." Obviously, if Flaten was a party to the imposture, his testimony was deceptive, but the mention of the underbrush has the sound of truth. When Edward Ohman was interviewed in 1949, he was asked if the "earth where the stone was found" had "ever been farmed or plowed or disturbed in any way." His answer was "Never."[4]

One must always be wary in dealing with a possible hoax, for the ingenuity of hoaxers has been demonstrated often in European and American history. Yet the story of the entwining roots seems to make the theory of a quick "reincarnation" doubtful. A substitution at the last moment, after the tree had been pulled over, is perhaps implied by Wahlgren's assertion that there is no record of anyone having seen the stone in place except Ohman himself. But Ohman's son Edward, in the affidavit he signed on July 20, 1909, is quoted as follows: "I saw the stone in the ground, and the roots in their undisturbed position on the side and on the surface of the stone." Edward was a little past twenty when he signed the affidavit, ten when the stone was uncovered. Granting

[4] Edward Ohman interview, December 28, 1949.

that the affidavits are proper matters for careful scrutiny, I do not find any plausible reason for believing that Edward would have lent his name to a lie.

On the assumption that the inscription is a hoax, it seems probable that it was engraved and placed under the poplar before 1898. Several indications point to the collaboration in one way or another of two persons, probably three, in the hoax. If the concept and wording of the inscription were the work of Fogelblad, the date might be in the 1880s. Laurence M. Larson, a careful scholar, suggested the early 1880s, with 1884 as the latest possible date since a house was built nearby in that year.[5] If Ohman played a part in the framing of the inscription, it is logical to assume that he did so after he acquired (presumably on March 2, 1891) the encyclopedic work that contains what linguists regard as a highly revealing section on runes.

Somewhere between 1890 or 1891 and 1895 might be a plausible time to assume for the working out of the hoax. This would allow from three to seven years for the flattening of the roots of the tree under which the slab of stone could have been inserted at an angle, face down. It might mean that there had been a secret depositing of the stone (or even the connivance of the near neighbor).

The interval would be one when Fogelblad was frequently in the neighborhood, and perhaps it was during one of those years that he was a guest for a week at Ohman's house. Certainly, within the period there must have been opportunity and time for the two men to talk matters over and to work together (as well as with Anderson). In the light of what is now known about Fogelblad, he could himself have devised and cut the inscription. Since the task of placing the slab under a tree certainly would have been laborious, it is more tenable to assume co-operation with Ohman, perhaps both in the writing of the runes and in the cutting and burying of the stone. Collaboration in the chiseling of the incisions is a possibility not to be disregarded, for John K. Daniels, a modern sculptor who was interviewed in 1955, suggested that the inscription must have been cut either by two men, or by one man

---

[5] Larson, in *Minnesota History*, 17:37. Holand wrote an answer to Larson, "Concerning the Kensington Rune Stone," in *Minnesota History*, 17:166–188 (June, 1936).

who was ambidexterous (judged by the evidence of both right- and left-hand strokes).[6]

All too little is known about Andrew Anderson, although his name appears repeatedly in the Kensington story. Certainly he was well acquainted with Ohman and Fogelblad. It was in his home that Fogelblad died in 1897. Some of Fogelblad's books were left there. One may assume that Anderson, as Ohman's neighbor, had access to such books as he owned, including the encyclopedic work.

Winchell's field book yields a little more substance about the enigmatic Anderson than has hitherto been available. Winchell learned about him from a conversation with Samuel Olson of Kensington. He wrote that Anderson was "a political agitator of the third party type, or socialist, or people's party."[7] The characterization offers no specific details, but it suggests someone who did not go along with the majority views of his time. Thus between Fogelblad, Ohman, and Anderson the bond of iconoclasm seems to have been a triple one.

Ohman once referred to Anderson as a man who could recite Swedish poetry when he was drunk; Ohman denied a report that Anderson had studied at Uppsala or that he knew Greek or Latin. It is not easy, however, to dismiss the image of Anderson as an agitator in politics and as one who (given sufficient stimulation) could recite Swedish poetry. Nor can one readily dismiss as negligible a man who could meet and talk with the formidable Rasmus B. Anderson and leave him "in the small hours of the morning as the best of friends." In departing Anderson gave the noted visitor "some significant winks." Why?

In a letter of June 3, 1910, to Winchell, Andrew Anderson added a postscript: "I do believe the stone to be genuine."[8] Dr. Asgaut

[6] Jay Edgerton interview with Daniels, a Minneapolis sculptor, in the *Minneapolis Star*, July 1, 1955, p. 10. The carving had been done with "sure deft strokes," according to Daniels, and the job may have "taken about two hours." Holand quoted a part of the interview in *Explorations in America Before Columbus*, 175.

[7] Winchell Field Book, March 18, 1910, Appendix 8, below. It is amusing to note that Winchell recorded Anderson's nickname as "Speer Anders which means slim Andrew." Probably the Swedish neighbors said "Spir," meaning a spire.

[8] Andrew Anderson to Winchell, June 3, 1910, reported in *Norwegian-*

Steinnes, a distinguished Norwegian scholar, commented in private correspondence in 1956 that of course the *stone* was genuine just as a stone was reported to be genuine in the joke inscription Dickens described in *The Pickwick Papers.*[9]

Assuming a hoax, the question is whether Anderson played more than a casual part in it. Dr. Steinnes went so far as to suggest that possibly the Ohman-Hedberg supposed copy or draft of the inscription was in fact a copy made by Ohman from a draft by Andrew Anderson. If this seems difficult to believe, it is scarcely less so than the idea that Ohman knowingly put into J. P. Hedberg's hands a draft that he, Ohman, knew was different in many respects from the inscription. The character of Andrew Anderson is that of a person who might have delighted in a hoax and might have played more than a casual role in the Kensington affair.[10]

Were others, beyond the three mentioned, involved? Professor Wahlgren suggested that there may have been "discussants"— persons who "may have had a hand in preliminary stages of the

American, June 10, 1910, p. 1. Anderson also wrote a letter in Swedish dated May 1, 1910, to *Svenska Amerikanska Posten*, which appeared in that paper on June 7, 1910, p. 13. It did not include the postscript of the English letter, and in fact it was quite different from the one sent to Winchell. Much of the Swedish letter was a defense of Fogelblad, who Anderson said had not been defrocked in Sweden but withdrew because he no longer accepted the tenets of the Swedish church.

[9] Dr. Steinnes to the late Birger Osland of Chicago, July 20, September 10, 21, 1956. Dr. Steinnes was then the *riksarkivar* (National Archivist) of Norway, an authority on the Norwegian language and culture of the fourteenth century. He has given me permission to refer to his correspondence with Osland which was, in effect, a sustained criticism of Holand's scholarship and of the Kensington inscription. The correspondence, including two letters by Holand, is in Kensington file, Blegen Papers.

[10] A tantalizing story told by Andrew's son, John Anderson, was reported by Otto Zeck of Detroit Lakes, Minn., a friend of John's. An interview with Mr. Zeck was recorded on tape by Mrs. Wallace of the Carnegie Museum on November 4, 1964, and she permitted me to hear the recording. The Anderson family, so the story goes, had moved to a farm near Detroit Lakes. One day (the date is not mentioned) Andrew Anderson received a letter from Olof Ohman that made him angry. He wrote a reply and asked his son to take it into the post office immediately. John recalled that his father said that he would "settle this thing once and for all times." He added that the "gates of Stillwater are fast closing on old Ohman." By "Stillwater" he meant the Minnesota State Prison. Mr. Zeck says that a later search of the former Anderson house revealed no letters.

hoax." As noted, he placed the execution of the plan in the second half of 1898. Thus he named Fogelblad, since he died in 1897, as a possible discussant, suggested that the neighbor Nils Flaten "cannot be ruled out," and thought that J. P. Hedberg "knew a great deal more about the inscription than he was willing to acknowledge." But Wahlgren declared that the circumstances pointed to Olof Ohman as "the prime mover in this affair." He did not include the banker, Samuel Siverts, who was reported to have made an early translation of the inscription, was a skilled penman, and probably sketched the inscription for Professor Breda.[11]

The mention of Hedberg invites comment. Turner in 1910 asked which one of those who knew Ohman took the "most interest in the stone—to have it looked up—to urge its authenticity, etc." It was Hedberg who first wrote of the stone to someone outside Kensington in his letter of January 1, 1899. With the Hedberg letter, it will be remembered, was the version of the inscription which Holvik and Wahlgren believe to have been a draft, not a copy. The precise origin of the document is not clear, but it definitely bears some relationship to whatever it was that Hedberg sent with his letter, if it is not the original document enclosed by Hedberg. In addition, Hedberg's comment that the inscription appeared "to be old Greek letters" is a suspicious phrase. He made no reference to runic writing, and yet one can scarcely doubt that Olof Ohman, who persuaded Hedberg to look at the stone, knew that the inscription was runic. If Hedberg did know, his allusion to Greek was a piece of deception.

Some findings, not necessarily pertinent to the question of authenticity, are nevertheless interesting from the point of view of historical method in relation to the rune stone and the controversies, including the reading of the date inscribed on the stone. Professor Wahlgren has disproved Holand's claim that he was the first person to give the correct date of 1362, pointing out that Curme had done so in 1899. Nearly all other writers who discussed the stone in 1899 also gave the date as 1362, including the Minnesota laymen who made nearly perfect translations of the

[11] Wahlgren, *Kensington Stone*, 174, 175.

inscription. Those who excavated the site in the spring of that year also thought the date on the stone was 1362.

The point would not be worth emphasis except for the fact that Holand built not a little of his structure of theory on a false foundation. This was that the rune stone was rejected in 1899 because it did not fit in with the sagas of the Viking voyages three and a half centuries before the middle of the fourteenth century.

Since the question of the affidavits has been considered in detail, only a few summarizing comments need to be added. The originals have vanished; only copies are known; and Professor Wahlgren was so skeptical that he even questioned whether or not any originals ever existed. The present writer believes that Hoegh and Holand did procure affidavits. Late in the Kensington discussions Holand implied that the originals were destroyed when his house burned in 1934, but he did not state this explicitly. The writer's theory is that Dr. Hoegh retained the affidavits and Holand had only copies.

The important question is the historical value of the affidavits as copied. They are in formal, legalized language, certainly not that of the signers. At one stage they were read aloud to the signers and Ohman stated that he did not understand the language as read. This is made evident in Winchell's field book, in Fossum's account of the bill of sale in 1911, and by Ohman's own emphatic assertion that he never intended "to sign the stone" to Holand. I do not wholly reject the affidavits as source materials, but I feel that they must be used with caution. The comments on the roots of the poplar seem to me to be based on direct observation, though I bear in mind the fact that a decade had passed. In the case of the roots, however, there is not a little confirmation from 1899.

It is of related interest to note once more that in all probability Hjalmar Rued Holand did not merely "chance upon" the Kensington stone in 1907. Evidence is reasonably convincing that he knew about it from 1899 on and visited Kensington in 1907 for the purpose of seeing the stone.

Did Ohman give the rune stone to Holand? In 1910 and 1911 Holand offered more than once to sell the rune stone to the Minnesota Historical Society. Holand's own stories of how he "procured" the stone vary. He paid nothing. He paid $25. He "persuaded" the owner. He offered $5. But according to Winchell's field book, Ohman did not give or sell the stone to Holand as his personal property. He turned it over to be placed by Holand with what Ohman called the "Norwegian Historical Society," that is, the Norwegian Society of Minneapolis, which had sponsored Holand's settlement studies. Ohman flatly denied that he gave the stone to Holand, and his sons confirmed his understanding that it was a transfer. The episode of the bill of sale of the rune stone to the Minnesota Historical Society in 1911 confirms the evidence in Winchell's field book. Ohman, wrote Fossum, "denied explicitly and emphatically that he had sold the stone" or that he had given it to Holand. He did indeed sign two papers, one an affidavit, the other a handwritten paper for Holand. But he did not know enough English to understand what he signed. He never "intended or wanted to sign the stone to Mr. Holand." If he "signed away the stone, he says he must have done so unknowingly." The Fossum letters suggest that in 1911 when Ohman said "the Society" he meant the Minnesota Historical Society rather than the Norwegian Society of Minneapolis.

The four photographs of the Kensington stone reproduced in this volume were sent by John F. Steward of Chicago on October 15, 1899, to L. F. A. Wimmer, the Danish runologist. The photographs date from some time after March 1, 1899. Apart from their intrinsic interest, they have another value. In some Kensington discussions, it has been asked whether the stone at present preserved in Alexandria is in fact the same stone taken from the ground in November, 1898, and sent to Curme in late February, 1899. This question can be answered definitely. At my suggestion Mrs. Wallace made a detailed comparison of the photographs with the stone now at Alexandria. Beyond all question they show the same stone that she studied in Alexandria. This removes any possible suspicion that there has been a substitution in the period since the stone was examined by Curme in 1899.

The central question is whether the historical circumstances sustain or nullify the conclusions of runologists with respect to the Kensington inscription. These specialists are as convinced that the inscription is not authentic as they would be if they had in hand an unimpeachable confession. In fact, the inscription, to them, is tantamount to a genuine but anonymous admission of fraud. They find its anachronisms and other internal evidences proof that it is modern.

It is in a "problem context" — and not in any combative spirit — that I have written these chapters. From the outset to the present, I have been conscious of no emotional concern as to whether my findings would or would not confirm those of the runologists. To me the matter was simply a puzzle on which, following the evidence as carefully as I could, I hoped to be able to throw a little light.

I read widely in the "Kensington literature," and as my studies went forward I was impressed by the fact that the most authoritative runologists in the world found it impossible to equate the language of the inscription with that of the date it bore. This increased my interest in the circumstances attending the discovery of the stone and in the people involved in that discovery. Patently if the inscription was a fake, one or more persons perpetrated it, and the deed in all probability took place in the next-to-last or last decade of the nineteenth century.

It matters little what one individual's opinion is on the question of authenticity. What matters is the sum total of historical, runological, and archaeological evidence. The total on the runological and historical side is, in my judgment, conclusive. The inscription is a fake. The evidence points to a hoax, with Olof Ohman as the principal originator. My conclusion sustains the chief conclusion offered by Wahlgren. On the other hand, I do not accept his hypothesis of an 1898 "reincarnation" of the stone. The hoax was committed, I believe, several years earlier, quite probably in the early 1890s, and there is reason to assign to Fogelblad a major role in it.[12] Nor do I find cogent reasons for omitting Andrew An-

[12] I am indebted to Professor Einar Haugen of Harvard University for the suggestion that Fogelblad, as a native of the parish of Fåglum in Västergötland, Sweden, may be the explanation of the priority given in the Kensington inscription to "8 göter." Fogelblad was a graduate of Skara in Västergötland and a member of the student club or fraternity at Uppsala known as "Västgöta Nation." Some defenders of the stone have wondered why the Kensington inscription begins with 8 Goths instead of with 22 Norwegians, and it has been suggested that a Goth wrote the inscription. Here Professor Hau-

derson from the inner circle. Until and unless additional evidence turns up, it seems hazardous to name others beyond these three as the hoaxers, although I would include Hedberg among possible "suspects."

I have omitted from the foregoing discussion any consideration of alleged mooring stones as well as axes, swords, fire steels, and other artifacts that have been drawn into the Kensington story by Holand and others. Such evidence as I have examined makes me dubious of the claims advanced for them as medieval in origin, but I await with interest the fruits of the researches in this field undertaken by Mrs. Wallace.

As information about Kensington backgrounds has increased, not a few of the actors in the drama have emerged from the shadows into a clearer light. This process will continue, I am confident, as new information is found. Meanwhile, in future discussions of the stone I hope there will be a turning away from the temper of debaters eager to score "points" against opponents. In the place of such a spirit we need sincere efforts to uncover further evidence.[13] All too many "leads" in my own studies took me into blind alleys. New sources, as yet unused, will turn up; there will be further discoveries. I write these lines with confidence, for I am aware of tape recordings of interviews with two persons qualified to throw new light on the origin of the Kensington inscription as modern and local. These are in private safekeeping and are not available. I have not heard them and do not know their contents. I do know that ultimately they will be placed in the Minnesota His-

gen agrees with the defenders except that his Goth is of a somewhat later vintage than 1362 — in fact, a native of Västergötland in the nineteenth century. He also suggests that the two words öh and man — "crucial linguistic weaknesses" in the inscription — are a reference to Ohman, the two parts separated to avoid too obvious a ploy. Haugen to the writer, March 7, 1968, Kensington file, Blegen Papers.

[13] More than a half century ago Flom and Hagen denounced the ignorance and dishonesty of those who based support of the authenticity of the rune stone on nationality. Professor Wahlgren, reporting on letters received after he pronounced the inscription a hoax, makes it clear that the early condemnation needs to be repeated. One letter opened thus: "How one of your nationality can . . ." I wish to put myself on record by saying that pride of nationality as a basis or motive for endorsing the rune stone is false, ignorant, and offensive to intellectual honesty. See Wahlgren, "Reflections around a Rune Stone," in *Swedish Pioneer Historical Quarterly,* 19:37 (January, 1968).

torical Society. I mention them here, not to bolster the evidence I have presented, but as an example of pertinent information yet to come on the genesis of the rune stone. The present book, I trust, will stimulate further searches for the papers of Breda, Curme, Hagen, Hedberg, Hoegh, Siverts, Steward, Turnblad, and others whose records might prove important.

Appendixes

Appendixes

1. *MINNEAPOLIS JOURNAL* REPORT OF THE KENSINGTON STONE

The main heading of the *Minneapolis Journal* article is "DONE IN RUNES," and there are the following subheads: "Stone With Puzzling Inscription Dug Up in Minn.; TALE OF EARLY NORSEMEN; Professor Breda Inclined to Think It a Fake. SOME MODERN WORDS EMPLOYED While the Balance of the Inscription Is a Swedish-Norwegian Jumble." The illustration of the Kensington inscription and the map showing where the stone was found (reproduced on p. 31) appeared with the article. It is of interest that the newspaper speaks of "copies" of the inscription, and it adds that one copy had been sent to Professor Curme of Northwestern University.

[*Minneapolis Journal*, February 22, 1899]

A stone bearing inscriptions in runic characters, found three miles northeast of Kensington, in Douglas county, Minnesota, has created something of a sensation among students of early Norse discoveries in this country, and is now in the hands of Professor C. [*George*] O. Curme of the Northwestern university at Evanston, Ill., who is making a careful examination of the inscriptions.

The stone was found last November by Ole [*Olof*] Ohman, a farmer in the southwest corner of Douglas county, while grubbing under a tree of thirty or forty years' growth, and its position under the roots of the tree, as well as its tombstone shape and the peculiar characters, at once attracted attention.

One who has seen the stone describes it as about thirty inches long, fifteen inches wide and six inches thick, the inscriptions being on the side and face in characters about an inch in length. It weighs about 215 [*202*] pounds. An investigation led to the belief that it was of ancient origin. The inscriptions impressed some of those who saw them

129

as Greek and copies were forwarded to the department of Greek at the University of Minnesota, where it was discovered that the characters were runic, and the copies were turned over to Professor O. J. Breda, who has charge of the department of Scandinavian languages. After a careful examination of the inscriptions, which he discovered to be only partially in runic characters, he decided that the whole thing was a hoax, or the result of an effort on the part of some one in part familiar with runic inscriptions to amuse himself. He, therefore, made no effort to secure the stone. Professor Curme of Evanston was furnished with a copy of the inscriptions and later the stone itself was shipped to him, and now is in his hands.

Professor Breda, when seen to-day, stated that on first blush, when the inscriptions were submitted to him as being from a possible runic stone found in the western part of Minnesota, he was disposed to laugh. No runic stones had ever been found in Minnesota and not only that but none had ever been found in America. How a runic stone of six, seven or eight centuries ago could ever have gotten within fifty or sixty miles of the western border of Minnesota, was, therefore, a question which floored him. On its face the proposition struck him as preposterous. Nevertheless, he took the inscription, picked out the characters, which were true runes, gave values to the characters which were evidently not runes, and of which he was in doubt, and made up the following translation of the inscriptions, dashes indicating the location of words or characters which he could not make out, not being correct runes:

> — Swedes and — Norsemen on a journey of discovery, from Vinland west — We camped — one day's journey north from this stone. We fished one day. After we came home we found — man red with blood and dead. AVM save from — Have — men at the ocean to look after our ships — days journey from this island. Year —

This corresponds exactly almost with a translation made shortly after the discovery of the stone and submitted by S. A. Siverts of Kensington, and is not far different from the translation made by Professor Curme of Evanston, which is as follows, the numerals having been supplied for the dashes in Professor Breda's translation:

> A company of Norsemen are out on expedition of discovery from the Vinland of the West. We had a camp along with two boats one day's journey north from this stone. We go out daily and fish. One day after we came home we found a man red with blood and dead. Ave (good-bye). Rescue from fire. Has one ever had a comrade such as we have had. We are on our way to look after our ship, fourteen days' journey from this island.

It will be noticed that Professor Breda omits the expression, "along with two boats," and changes "Has any one ever had a comrade such as we have had" to "Have men at the ocean to look after our ships."

He also does not attempt to translate the "AVM," which Professor Curme makes "Good bye."

Aside from the fact that no runic stones have been found in this country, and that the position in which this was found made it most improbable that this was genuine, Professor Breda states that there are internal evidences in the inscription that it is not authentic. The chief of these, he says, is the fact that the inscriptions seem to be a jumble of Swedish and Norwegian in late grammatical forms with here and there an English word, but all spelled in runic characters. They are not old Norse, he says. As an example of the mixture of Norwegian and Swedish, he cites almost the first word, which, spelled in English letters, is "apthogelsefart" [sic]. On the other hand, the word "from" is the plain English word in runic characters. Again, the word "sten" or stone is strictly modern in form, while the word "apter," the professor says, looks as though the writer had tried to make the word appear old fashioned.

Since receiving the first copy of the inscriptions the professor has received a letter stating that the stone is a soft slate or soapstone such as would easily be cut by an ordinary penknife, making it entirely possible that the work was that of some one who sought to amuse himself by carving the characters with which he was partially familiar for the purpose of exciting the interest of the public at some later date. The fact that a somewhat similar stone was found a few years ago in Wisconsin bearing cuneiform inscriptions, telling a story not unlike that of the recent discovery though not of Norsemen, but which seems to have been a fake, would apparently bear the professor out in his theory as to this.

Nevertheless, Professor Curme seems to regard the stone as possibly genuine. His theory is that at the time the stone was deposited at the place found it was on the shore of Lake Superior, which then — 500 years ago — was several hundred feet above its present level, making it entirely possible that the piece of ground at the place was an island. From the inscription he infers that the explorers left one of their number to guard the camp while they went away to fish, and that when they came back they found him dead, slain; possibly, by Pottawatomies.

After a thorough investigation, photographs will be made of the stone, and sent to the authorities on such matters. Professor Breda suggests as the ablest authorities on runic inscriptions, L. V. [F.] A. Wimmer of Copenhagen, and Sophus Bugge, also a Scandinavian, and thinks they would have no trouble in determining without delay whether the inscriptions were genuine.

2. NORTHWESTERN REPORT OF THE KENSINGTON STONE

Since the following account from *Northwestern* has not previously been noted in books and articles about the Kensington controversy, its full text is offered here. Although the newspaper said that the University of Minnesota's *Ariel* had introduced the stone to the college world "nearly three months ago," it was less than two months since the *Ariel*, on January 14, 1899, published its story. Note that the translation does not give the number of the men who were found "red with blood and dead," but that it does include the year 1362.

[*Northwestern* (Evanston, Illinois), March 9, 1899]

THE RUNIC STONE.

Last week the Runic stone, much heralded by the Chicago papers, came into the hands of Professor Curme of the German department. The *Ærial* [sic] of the University of Minnesota introduced the stone to the college world nearly three [sic] months ago.

The Runic stone was found last November near Kensington, Minn. It is a trap stone, 32 inches long, 18 inches wide, and 6 inches thick, and bears the date 1362. In runic characters on one side and one edge of the tablet is the following inscription:

Eight Goths (from Sweden) and twenty-two Norwegians on an expedition of discovery from the Vinland of the west. We had a camp with two boats a day's journey from this stone. We went out fishing one day. After we came home we found a man red with blood and dead. Good-by, rescue from evil. We have men at the ocean to look after our ships fourteen days' journey from this island. Year 1362.

Professor Curme is well versed in the Runic tongue, but to make sure of the authenticity of the tablet he has sent a copy of the inscription to Adolph Nor[e]en of Up[p]sala University, Sweden, the greatest living authority on the Runic language. Runic stones are very common in Norway and Sweden, but this is the first one ever found in America. The first thought is to consider it a hoax and to treat it accordingly, yet if proved authentic, this stone will change the whole history of America. Therefore, Professor Curme is justified, as a seeker of truth, to disregard the smiles of the uninitiated and to use every power at a scholar's command to prove the sincerity of the Runic stone.

3. F. NOSANDER'S TRANSLATION OF THE KENSINGTON INSCRIPTION

In a letter to the Minneapolis Swedish newspaper, *Svenska Amerikanska Posten*, dated March 1, 1899, at Taylors Falls, Minnesota, F. Nosander offered a translation of the Kensington inscription based on a sketch which had been printed in the same newspaper on February 28, 1899.

Nosander wrote in Swedish. He produced the best translation made by anyone in 1899 — one that bears comparison with the authoritative versions by eminent scholars in later years. The chief point at which there is any marked difference is in the phrase "We had camp by 2 lakes." The approved translation is "2 rocky islets" or "skerries." Apart from this, the Nosander text is almost without a flaw, though it does include in parentheses the word "fire" as an alternative to "evil" in the phrase "save from evil." Nosander thus made it clear that he preferred the word "evil." A few very small errors may possibly be a result of faulty newspaper proofreading.

No information has been found about F. Nosander — what books he had studied, how he had come by his knowledge of runes, or how he earned his living. A curiosity, presumably coincidental, is the similarity of the name of Nosander to that of Rosander, the compiler of the book entitled *Den kunskapsrike skolmästaren,* a copy of which was owned by Olof Ohman.

In view of these facts it seems appropriate to reproduce, first, the Swedish version as offered by Nosander in *Svenska Amerikanska Posten,* March 14, 1899, and thereafter an English translation made by the present writer.

8 göter ok 22 norr men po opdagelsefärd fro Vinland of vest. Wi hade läger wid 2 sjöar en dags rise fro dena sten. Wi var ock fiskt en dagh, äpter vi kom hem fann 10, man röde af blod og döde. AVM. frailse fro ill (eld) har 10 mans ve havet at se äptir wore skip 14 dagh rist from deno öh. Åhr 1362.

8 Goths and 22 Norwegians on a journey of exploration from Vinland of the west. We had camp by 2 lakes a day's journey from this stone. We were and fished one day, after we came home found ten men red with blood and dead. AVM save from evil (fire) have 10 men by the sea to look after our ships 14 days' journey from this island. Year 1362.

4. J. K. NORDWALL'S TRANSLATION OF THE KENSINGTON INSCRIPTION

The following translation of the Kensington inscription was sent to *Svenska Amerikanska Posten* by J. K. Nordwall of Sebeka, Minnesota, in a letter dated March 7, 1899. The Swedish text is printed below as it appeared in that newspaper on March 28, 1899; the English translation which follows was made by the present writer.

8 göter ok 22 norrmän po opdagelsefärd fro vinland af vest vi hade läger wid 2 skiär en dags rise norr fro dene sten vi var ock fiske en dagk äptir vi kam ohem [*sic*] fan man (aller män) röde af blod og ded AVM fräilse af illu har mäns ve havet at se äptir vore skip 14 dagk rise fram deno öh år 1362.

8 goths and 22 Norwegians on a journey of discovery from Vinland of west we had camp by 2 skerries a day's trip north from this stone we went and fished one day after we came home found man (or men) red with blood and dead AVM save from evil have men at the sea to look after our ships 14 days' journey from this island year 1362.

Nordwall, after offering his translation, explained that he omitted the number of men red with blood and the number of men left at the sea to look after the ships (in both instances ten) because he did not understand the numerals. He added that perhaps there was a mistake in the transcription and that the rune might stand for a 5 or a 10. Thus, like Nosander, he came close to making an accurate translation.

5. OLAUS OLSON'S ACCOUNT OF THE EXCAVATION IN 1899

This is a translation of a letter written in Swedish to *Svenska Amerikanska Posten* by Olaus Olson, a member of the party of twelve men who excavated the site of the Kensington stone in the spring of 1899. In making the following English translation, I have had the benefit of assistance from Mrs. Lilly Lorénzen, an expert in Swedish and a retired member of the faculty of the Scandinavian department in the University of Minnesota.

[*Svenska Amerikanska Posten,* May 23, 1899]

THE RUNESTONE IN MINNESOTA

Holmes City, May 16, 1899

The Editor of *Svenska Amerikanska Posten.*

Some time ago a facsimile of the so-called Kensington runestone appeared in your honored newspaper *Svenska Amerikanska Posten* [*February 28, 1899*]. Other Swedish-American newspapers have given meager reports concerning the same. Professor Breda's report that the runes were not genuine (Norwegian), but a mixture, has given some Norwegians the idea that a big Swede had carved the runes. A Norwegian in this neighborhood has become so sure about the matter that, in the presence of several persons, he took oath that the discoverer of the stone had himself made the runes.

A few, whom one might call little Swedes, have also allowed themselves to be misled into believing the same thing.

That the runes were not carved by a Norwegian, but by the hand of a Swedish master, may readily be granted. That Mr. Öman [Ohman] or any other Swede now living did this is most emphatically denied, however.

The undersigned has himself been at the place and observed not only the stone, but also the spot where it lay at its discovery. An aspen tree ten inches in diameter at its root stood just above the stone. Two large roots, one on each side of the stone, had grown down into the earth and shaped themselves along its sides, so that the stone was bound in between them. The tree is at least 25 if not 30 years old, and Mr. Öman has been on the land 8 years. When Mr. Öman grubbed the tree, the stone, which appeared very large, was discovered, but not the runes. When the father left, one of his boys happened to poke with a wooden stick along the stone, discovered the characters on its side, and called his father to come and see that there was writing on the stone. Mr. Öman, together with a Norwegian [Nils Flaten] who had helped him in the work, came and pulled up the stone and thus discovered the runes on the flat side, which had been turned downward. The stone is blue gray and in its formation is similar to slate but might contain a good deal of copper ore or other metal; for if you strike it with a hammer it gives a good ring, like the rock ledges at Taylors Falls.

Mr. Öman is an honest man who feels that it is a matter for scorn that he should be looked upon as a humbugmaker. We know, from what has taken place and much else, that he cannot have been the author of the runes.

The runes are no doubt genuine and were composed at the time indicated, the year 1362, by one who for his time was a soundly learned Swedish West Goth. For this reason some prominent Swedish American should send an accurate transcription to the Vatican in Rome so that they may be read and judged; they may be of historic importance. One could turn to Bishop [John] Ireland for help in expediting this. The stone was discovered under such circumstances as my letter describes. Fourteen days ago the superintendent of schools from Alexandria [Cleve W. Van Dyke], with eleven men, came together to undertake an investigation by means of an excavation. About four feet deep they found, on the north side of the excavation, some fragments 4 to 5 inches in length which resembled limestone but were thought to have a great likeness to moldered bones. It is believable that the ten men who, according to the stone, were killed, are buried at the spot where the stone was found, and a careful search might reveal strong evidence for the genuineness of the stone.[1] The place where it was

[1] In 1964 the Minnesota Historical Society undertook an exploratory excavation at the supposed site of the finding of the rune stone. Actually two

found lies about 4 miles north of Kensington. And in the Chippewa River, near Evansville, the travelers may have kept their boats, since the stone refers to a day's journey north from here.   OLAUS OLSON

6. THE STEWARD LETTER OF 1899

The name of J. F. Steward printed at the head of his letter is followed by a printed address which has been crossed out: "2850 Kenmore Av. Station Y. N. Edgewater." Underneath, in Steward's handwriting, is his Chicago address "1889 Sheridan Road." Steward misstated the weight of the stone as 100 pounds. Wahlgren suggested that Steward may have meant kilograms, but he called attention to the figure of 100 pounds as given in the *Chicago Daily Inter Ocean* for March 1, 1899, and also in an article in the *Saturday Evening Post* as late as August 21, 1948.[1] The established weight of the stone is about 202 pounds.

[John F. Steward to Professor L. F. A. Wimmer, October 15, 1899, in "Collectio Runologica Wimmeriana," item no. 556, Royal Library, Copenhagen, Denmark; photo copy in Kensington file, Blegen Papers, Minnesota Historical Society]

PROF LUDWIG F. A. WIMMER
COPENHAGEN DEN.
Dear Sir.

I send you photographs I made of a stone recently discovered in the state of Minnesota, U.S.A. near the headwaters of the Mississippi River. It may interest you whether the stone is genuine or a fraud. It is genuine in that it was an honest discovery of a stone found in the recently settled lake and swamp regions of the state, by a farmer some distance below the surface when clearing a knoll in a swamp of its trees. The stone is a Trap boulder, split by natural causes, such as are plentiful in those regions. The glacial marks can be seen on the surface of the boulder. The inscriptions are on the two cleavage surfaces of the stone, which have received no dressing. They are cut as with a "diamond-pointed" tool. The grooves show no more newness than the natural surfaces of the rock; on the contrary all show age. The stone

sites were investigated — one based on an undated photograph that included Olof Ohman, the other remembered as the finding place by Ohman's son Arthur. More than 300 linear feet of trenches were dug down to sterile subsoil. Nothing of significance was found. The archaeologist in charge, Mr. Loren C. Johnson, concluded in view of the uncertainty as to the precise identification of the site, a large-scale excavation would be needed in order to be certain that the exact spot was included. Photographs, a map of the excavation, and a summary report on the 1964 archaeological field season are in the files of the MHS archaeologist.

[1] Wahlgren, *Kensington Stone*, 193.

may have been cut by some smart Scandinavian traveler, as one connected with the Fur Companies, early in this century, in an effort to establish the claims of the Norsemen to have been first to explore this country[.] It is possible, of course that, as early as the date found on the stone, the Norsemen did make efforts in the direction of voyages of discovery

ᛏᛒᚦᚷ ᚤ ᛏᚱ ᚦᛏ ᛆ ᚷ ᚱᚦ

The stone was found precisely where most of the efforts to discover a way from the Great lakes to the sea of the west were made.

The size of the stone is about 75 x 20 x 36 c.m. and weighs about 100 [202] pounds. I am getting together all possible facts connected with the matter with a view to sifting it to the bottom. If it is a fraud the fact must be known so that future historians shall not be deceived. If it proves to be a genuine record it is important. The record as found on the stone is likely to remain the only evidence of fraud as the circumstances connected with its finding are all favorable to age and genuineness. The runes differ from those found in Stephens "Runic Monuments,"[2] but no more than those there found differ from each other. You will have no difficulty in reading the inscriptions and I kindly ask you to favor me with your versions of them if you find it of sufficient interest.

In return I will give you whatever facts are at my disposal[.]

Very Respectfully JOHN F. STEWARD

P.S. I am sending this and photograph to several scholars.[3]

7. THE AFFIDAVITS, 1909

Not a little attention in the text of this book has been necessarily given to the four Kensington affidavits of July 20, 1909, signed by Olof Ohman; his son Edward Ohman; a neighbor, Nils Flaten; and (jointly) by two friends, Roald Bentson and Samuel Olson.

The affidavits have been published previously, but it seems desirable for handy reference to reproduce their texts once more. The originals have not been found, and the texts therefore are available only in copies. As given below, the first affidavit, by Olof Ohman, is from Holand, "First Authoritative Investigation of 'Oldest Native Document in America,'" in *Journal of American History*, 4:178 (1910). Though

---

[2] George Stephens, *The Old-Northern Runic Monuments of Scandinavia and England* (4 vols., London, Copenhagen, 1866–84).

[3] The photographs are reproduced on p. 44 and 45, above.

typewritten copies of the other three affidavits, supplied in 1909 by Holand, are available in the Minnesota Historical Society's manuscripts collection, they were carelessly made, with omissions of the notarial statements and with an error in the name of S. Olson, who appears as "L. Olson." It seems better, therefore, to use the texts as Holand printed them in his book on the *Kensington Stone*, 34–37, 292–295.

[OLOF OHMAN AFFIDAVIT]

I, Olof Ohman, of the town of Solem, Douglas County, State of Minnesota, being duly sworn, makes [*sic*] the following statement:

I am fifty-four years of age, and was born in Helsingeland, Sweden, from where I emigrated to America in the year 1881, and settled upon my farm in Section Fourteen, Township of Solem, in 1891. In the month of August, 1898, while accompanied by my son, Edward, I was engaged in grubbing upon a timbered elevation, surrounded by marshes, in the southeast corner of my land, about 500 feet west of my neighbor, Nils Flaten's house, and in full sight thereof. Upon moving an asp, measuring about 10 inches in diameter at its base, I discovered a flat stone inscribed with characters, to me unintelligible. The stone laid [*sic*] just beneath the surface of the ground in a slightly slanting position, with one corner almost protruding. The two largest roots of the tree clasped the stone in such a manner that the stone must have been there at least as long as the tree. One of the roots penetrated directly downward and was flat on the side next to the stone. The other root extended almost horizontally across the stone and made at its edge a right angled turn downward. At this turn the root was flattened on the side toward the stone. This root was about three inches in diameter. Upon washing off the surface dirt, the inscription presented a weathered appearance, which to me appeared just as old as the untouched parts of the stone. I immediately called my neighbor, Nils Flaten's attention to the discovery, and he came over the same afternoon and inspected the stone and the stump under which it was found.

I kept the stone in my possession for a few days; and then left it in the Bank of Kensington, where it remained for inspection for several months. During this interval, it was sent to Chicago for inspection and soon returned in the same state in which it was sent. Since then I kept it at my farm until August, 1907, when I presented the stone to H. R. Holand. The stone, as I remember, was about 30 inches long, 16 inches wide, and 7 inches thick, and I recognize the illustration on page 16 of H. R. Holand's History of the Norwegian Settlements of America (Ephraim, Wisconsin, 1908), as being a photographic reproduction of the stone's inscription.

[*Signed*] OLOF OHMAN.

Witness: R. J. Rasmusson. George H. Merhes.
State of Minnesota, County of Douglas

On this 20th day of July, 1909, personally came before me, a Notary Public, in and for Douglas County and State of Minnesota, Mr. Olof Ohman, to me known to be the person described in the foregoing document, and acknowledged that he executed the same as his free act and deed.

R. J. Rasmusson. Notary Public, Douglas County, Minnesota. [SEAL] My Commission expires November 17, 1915.[1]

[Nils Flaten Affidavit]

I, Nils Flaten, of the town of Solem, Douglas County, Minn., being duly sworn, make the following statement:

I am sixty-five years of age, and was born in Tinn, Telemarken, Norway, and settled at my present home in the town of Solem in 1884. One day in August, 1898, my neighbor, Olof Ohman, who was engaged in grubbing timber about 500 feet west of my house, and in full view of same, came to me and told me he had discovered a stone inscribed with ancient characters. I accompanied him to the alleged place of discovery and saw a stone about 30 inches long, 16 inches wide and 6 inches thick, which was covered with strange characters upon two sides and for more than half their length. The inscription presented a very ancient and weathered appearance. Mr. Ohman showed me an asp tree about 8 inches to 10 inches in diameter at its base, beneath which he alleged the stone was found. The two largest roots of the asp were flattened on their inner surface and bent by nature in such a way as to exactly conform to the outlines of the stone. I inspected this hole and can testify to the fact that the stone had been there prior to the growth of the tree, as the spot was in close proximity to my house. I had visited the same spot earlier in the day before Mr. Ohman had cut down the tree and also many times previously — but I had never seen anything suspicious there. Besides the asp, the roots of which embraced the stone, the spot was also covered by a very heavy growth of underbrush.

I recognize the illustration on page 16 of H. R. Holand's History of the Norwegian Settlements as being a photographic reproduction of the inscription on the face of the stone.

[Signed] Nils Flaten.

[Edward Ohman Affidavit]

I, Edward Ohman, of the town of Solem, Douglas County, Minn., being duly sworn, make the following statement:

I am twenty years of age and was born in the town of Oscar Lake, Douglas County, Minn.; in August, 1898, when about ten years of age, I was helping my father, Olof Ohman, in grubbing on the southeast corner of his land, about 500 feet west of Nils Flaten's house, and in

---

[1] The names of the same two witnesses and the same attestation by the notary appeared on each of the other three affidavits which follow.

full view of same; in removing an asp, a stone was found imbedded in the ground and embraced by two roots of said asp, one root going downward on one side of the stone and so close to it that its surface was flattened from contact; the other root pursuing a nearly horizontal course across the surface of the stone, where it bent down into the ground, forming a right-angle. The stump of the asp was about ten inches in diameter at the base, the horizontal root about three inches in diameter. I saw the stone in the ground, and the roots in their undisturbed position on the side and on the surface of the stone. After my father had got the stone out of the ground, and we had rolled it to one side, I noticed that some characters were inscribed on the stone and called my father's attention to it. The stone was taken to my father's house and from there sent to the Bank at Kensington, from which it was returned. It remained in my father's possession until he gave it to H. R. Holand, in the year 1907. The stone was about thirty inches long, sixteen inches wide and seven inches thick.

I recognize the illustration on page sixteen of H. R. Holand's History of the Norwegian Settlements as being a photographic reproduction of the inscription on the face of the stone.

[*Signed*] EDWARD OHMAN.

[ROALD BENTSON AND SAMUEL OLSON AFFIDAVIT]

We, the undersigned, residents of Kensington, Minn., and vicinity, hereby testify to the fact that we have seen a stone with an inscription in characters to us unintelligible, of which it was alleged and which we truthfully believe, was discovered and dug out of the ground in August, 1898, about four miles N. E. of Kensington, Minn., on the S. E. corner of the S. W. ¼ of the N. E. ¼ of Section 14, Town 127, Range 40 W., by one Olof Ohman, and his son, Edward Ohman. We further testify that we saw the hole in the ground in which it was stated that the stone had been imbedded. The inscription as seen by us presented an ancient and weathered appearance, similar to the uninscribed parts of the stone. We saw the root of an asp that was from eight inches to ten inches in diameter at the bottom of the trunk, of which it was alleged that it had grown on one side of the stone, and in close contact with same. We saw the stump of this tree, and are convinced that it had been in close contact with the stone because of its peculiar shape. One of the roots that had pursued a perpendicular course downward was flattened on one side, as we think because of its contact with the stone.

We saw another root of the same stump about three inches in diameter which had taken an almost horizontal course from the body of the stump. About eighteen inches from its junction with the first mentioned root, this second root made a right-angled bend and continued downward. It was flattened and expanded on its interior bend. We are convinced that the two roots above described exactly conformed to the configuration of the stone. The stone was about thirty inches long, sixteen inches wide, and seven inches thick. We recognize the illustration on page 16 of H. R. Holand's History of the Norwegian Settlements as being a photographic reproduction of the inscription on the face of the stone.

[Signed] ROALD BENTSON
S. OLSON

8. NEWTON H. WINCHELL FIELD BOOK

On three trips to Kensington — November 29–December 2, 1909, March 3–5, 17–19, 1910 — Winchell wrote penciled notes in the pages of a small field book. He used this contemporary record of his findings when he drafted the report of the Minnesota Historical Society's museum committee, which was published in 1910 and again in 1915. Students of the Kensington stone have long known that such a record was kept, but they have not hitherto been able to use the field book because it could not be located. An intensive and systematic search of the University of Minnesota archives and the manuscripts collection of the Minnesota Historical Society by Miss Lucile M. Kane and me resulted in the location of the field book tucked away at the society among the archaeological materials left by Winchell.

That the record had not been located in earlier years is understandable. Winchell's notes of his Kensington trips were written toward the center of a thick pocket-sized book which bore the date 1906 on its flyleaf and was crammed with items about his many other interests. Even the Kensington pages are interrupted at one point by entries that have nothing to do with the stone.

Readers of this volume do not need to be reminded that I have made extensive use of the Winchell field book, which contains many details that for one reason or another the geologist did not choose to include in his published report. On one critical point, however, the book surprisingly yields nothing new, namely the exact date of the stone's discovery. Winchell noted only "It seems to have been found in Nov.," leaving us in the dark as to precisely how he arrived at the date November 8, 1898, which he used in the published report of the committee.

The book is a travel-worn, smudged document, its pages filled with crowded lines. The notes were hastily scribbled, and the drawings are not as clear as one might wish. In the text which follows, the sketches are placed as Winchell shows them in the original. Plate numbers have been added for convenience in referring to them. In addition, Winchell did not speak or understand Swedish. Thus the name of Sven Fogelblad appears frequently as "Flugelblad," and there are other errors which Winchell corrected in the published report. It is worth noting, however, that Holand did not accompany Winchell on his trips to Kensington. What one finds in the field book, therefore, is authentic Winchell, not a Holand-guided Winchell, as was the case with much of the committee's published report.

[Rune-Stone Notes, N. H. Winchell Field Book, November 29, 1909–March 19, 1910, vol. 59, Winchell Papers, Minnesota Historical Society]

To Kensington.
1909.

Nov	29		Car far[e] (and ret.)	10	
"	29.		Ticket to Kensington	2.79	
"	30.		Hotel, Kensington	85	
"	30	"	Noon, Ohmans	1.05	
Dec.	1.		Eredahl [*Erdahl*] (hotel)		2.00
"	1	"	Dinner & feed	1.00	
"	2	"	Night for 2 & team	2.00	
"	2	"	Livery 2½ days	8.75	
"	2	"	Lunch	.25	
"	2	"	Fare to Minneapolis	2.79	
				21.58	

Archological — Nov 30, '09

The Rune Stone was found S E cor of sec 14, in Solum [*sic*] township in Douglas county, by Olaf [*sic*] Öhman, on his farm, about three miles north of Kensington station.

Under a poplar about 5 or 6 in[.]

Not found on a hill, but on the south slope of hill.

The engraved stone was at first brought to the house & then to Kensington & was exhibited in a window by Hedberg or Johnson. Hedberg sent it to Minneapolis, where it seems to have been examined by Prof Breda — and perhaps to Chicago.[1] It was brought back and lay some years in the shed at Öhmans Then Mr. Holand took it up[.]

No. 1 Samples of rock somewhat like the engraved slab, taken along the road between Kensington & Ohmans[.]

No. 2 Taken near the place of finding the slab, but SW from the exact spot perhaps 20 rods at the edge of the slough[.]

No. 3 Taken at, or very near the place of the slab, from piles along fence lines and at the edge of the Slough.

I have not found a stone exactly like the engraved slab but apparently some that resemble it[.]

About 75 in a hundred of the boulders are of granite, about 5 in a hundred are of limestone, about 5 in a hundred are of gabbro or gab-

[1] The stone was sent to Evanston, Ill., but apparently not to Minneapolis.

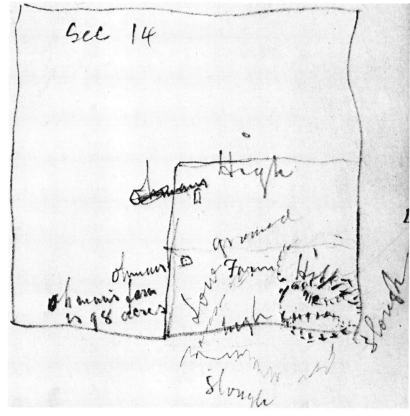

[PLATE 1]

broid rocks, about 5 in a hundred are of Kewatin [sic] greenstone including Ogishke conglomerate, about 5 in a hundred are of dark non-descript rock, sometimes quartzose, and the other 5 in a hundred may be compared with the rock of the engraved slab, but only one is exactly like it.[2] I got 5 which are of graywacke.

There are also some rocks that belong in the iron ore series of the Mesabi, and probably other varieties that should be adjusted in the foregoing rough estimates.

The till is yellowish-gray, at the surface, and is quite clayey. Some of the knolls of the morainic area are very stony about their summits, and the stones have sometimes been gathered together by the farmers in great heaps, rendering it easy to make estimates of the proportions of the various kinds. The till is in general so free from large boulders that

[2] Winchell here contradicts what he wrote a few lines earlier.

there is a suggestion that the till is of later date then [*sic*] the stony knobs and has left the knobs comparatively thinly covered by the till. Yet I have not examined far enough to warrant such an opinion. At least it is plain that the till is not a normal stony till. It approaches rather a "pebbly clay."

The inscription on the stone refers to "this island," as the place of its erection. There is a striking topographic feature which may have given rise to that expression. There is an island of high morainic land rising 30 to 50 feet above the slough which surrounds it on all sides. The island is approximately round, and somewhat less than a quarter of a mile in diameter, divided into two more elevated parts by a low stretch that runs east and west across it[.]

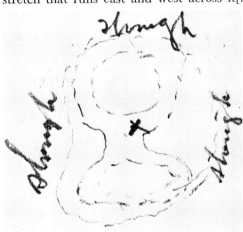

[PLATE 2]
*Island in its approximate
shape, showing by the mark
x the place of the stone.*
[Winchell's caption.]

It is quite likely that formerly the slough was more wet than now, and that the high land was actually an island in the midst.

Mr Öhman's sons told me that they let Mr. Holand have the stone with the condition that it would be deposited by him in some public museum, & that there are two witnesses to the agreement.

With Öhman when the stone was found was his neighbor Mr. Flotten [*Nils Flaten*].

stayed at Eredahl [*Erdahl hotel*]

DEC 1, 1909

No 4. Collected at various places, between Öhmans and Eredahl. Arriving at Nate Johnsons we find the lake [*Pelican Lake*] covered, in part, with ice too thin to travel on. The projecting point is terminated by two great boulders, one of red porphyritic granite cut by a coarse red dike 3 in wide, 6 ft by 3½ by 4 ft, with rounded contours, the other of gray gneiss banded with light red laminas, 6 ft x 4½ x 4 ft, showing some bracciation and a pegmatyte vein about an inch wide, shape is somewhat irregularly angular. Numerous other smaller boulders lie about and form the immediate water barrier, but the basis of the point is sand which probably lies on morainic accumulations. These also no doubt extend under the lake eastward, forming the 12 apostles and one or two other islands further east.

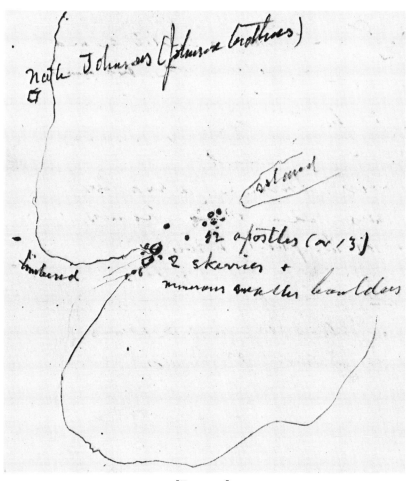

[PLATE 3]

In case these large boulders are the skerries referred to the explorers must have had an ideal camping spot, as the point is low and widens out gradually toward the west. There is a recently formed beach of boulders and sand spreading from the skerries and between them at about 20 ft from the skerries rises another elevation the level of which is maintained or raised a foot or two toward the west, and which was formerly the beach between the two portions of the lake. At that time these two boulders must have been surrounded by water. It is certain that the present water level is very low, and also that the present sandy land immediately west of the skerries is and always was subject to change and that the sand and small boulders have been shifted by the ice perhaps annually.

[PLATE 4]

Rev Mr. [O. A.] Normann of Ashby was here with Mr Holand.

Ole Stenberg was witness to the terms of agreement between Öhman and Holand.

Stopped at Hakenson's also Sam Olesson [*Olson*] of Kensington[.]

DEC. 2. Start at 6:45[.] Stone was given to the Norwegian Historical Society to keep till found to be genuine.

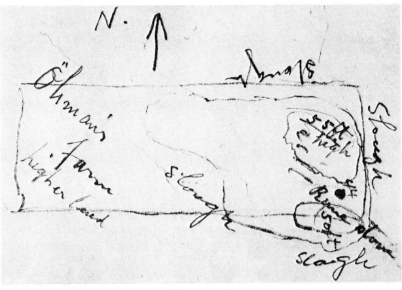

[PLATE 5]

Stone was sent to Prof Curme at Evanston who wrote several interesting letters to Sam Oleson of Kensington, now in possession of Holand, who wants them returned.[3] Curme suggested that the stone may have been made by some employés of the Hudson Bay Co, who put the wrong date on it. He found that long ago a Dane was employed by that company, but he seems not to have formed a definite conclusion.[4]

History of Norwegian Settlements. Sketch of Immigration & the building up of Norwegian Northwest, from the discovery of America, to the Indian War of the Northwest, by Hjalmar R Holand Ephraim, Wis, 1909 [1908].

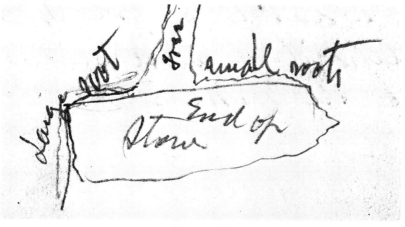

[PLATE 6]

Laborer really uncovered & discovered the stone, but did not notice at first the engraving. He was Ohman's Son [Edward] & was working for Ohman with neighbor Flotten[.]

Mr. Sam Oleson confirms the statement of Ohman, that the stone was not given to Holand for his personal property, but was intended to go to the museum of the Norwegian Historical Society. Mr Ohman was paid nothing for it.

Mr. Ohman emphatically repeated that the stone is not Holands and told me to not to let it go from St. Paul, not even on loan to Holand to take to Chicago, but to keep it. He said that he had no use for it,

[3] It is not known whether or not Holand returned the letters to Samuel Olson. If he did not, they probably were lost when Holand's house was destroyed by fire in 1934.

[4] Curme may possibly have had in mind Willard F. Wentzel, a Norwegian fur trader employed by the North West Company in the early years of the nineteenth century. See Hjalmar R. Holand, "An Early Norwegian Fur Trader of the Canadian Northwest," in *Norwegian-American Studies and Records*, 5:1–13 (1930).

and seemed only to want to see it preserved and deposited at a suitable place in Minnesota.

Julius Hotvet [sic] says: in "Noerrena"—Tongue of the North, by R. B. Anderson editor, Vol xvi, is an account of a runestone found on west coast of Greenland, Lat. 72 deg. north.[5]

Notes on the rune stone[6]

Evgen [Evjen] (John O.) Augsburg Seminary, Minneapolis, Feb. 18, says: "Holand's copy (i.e. translation) in his book is faulty, and could have been better if he had exercised more care. I have called attention to a few of his mistakes. They are really trifles, but bear on the philological phase of the monument, at the same time that they indicate that Mr. Holand is a novice in palaography [sic] and epigraphy, auxiliary subjects that every philologist and historian has to be acquainted with." This seems to exclude Holand from any probability of guilt in fabricating the engraving as a fraud or otherwise.

"What is said a[d]versely on our side of the water is an echo of the opinion held in Norway,—by how many I do not know."

"My doubts lay in the linguistic phase of the matter." Urges that the stone be sent to European experts.

The inscription was made apparently by a Swede, and Swedish language at that time was in a transitional stage, was more simple in its inflections. Regards Mr. Holand as honest and as having used his best "scientific conscience," but as incompetent.

1[.] What side was down (inscribed side) 2. Another affidavit as to Ohman's character   Preacher's name is T. A. Saettre [Sattre] Evansville Minn   Get Ohman's Claim   See Roald Bentson 1 m. from Ohman's One of the old settlers

MAR 3, 1910. Evansville[.] I called on Rev T. A. Saettre but found him absent ("at the cities"). I learned from Mrs Saettre that Öhman is not a church member, but, as she thinks, some of his children have been confirmed by Saettre in a small Lutheran church situated near Öhman's, a branch of the Evansville church.

Mrs Saettre said that the young people of the vicinity are stirred up about hunting about the lakes in the region for relics of the Scandinavians supposed to have been killed by the Indians. She under-

[5] On the Kingigtorssuaq or Kingiktorsooak inscription in Greenland, see chapter 5, note 25.

[6] Succeeding paragraphs as far as the entry for March 3, 1910, are pasted into the field book at this point, following an entry of February 2, 1910, which does not concern the rune stone. John O. Evjen, mentioned below, professor of theology and church history at Augsburg Seminary, was a prolific author; see Norlie, ed., *Norsk lutherske prester i Amerika, 1843–1913*, 402. For Evjen's later views on the rune stone, see "Er vi færdig med Kensington-Stenen?" in *Reform* (Eau Claire, Wis.), August 18, p. 2, August 25, p. 2, September 1, p. 2—all in 1927.

stands that the skerries and the camp were found by Prof [Andrew A.] Fossum at Lake Christina.

John Nornberg, Evansville
J J. Jacobson
These might know something about it—both absent[.] Jacobson has met Holand, says Holand never lectured here. Has no relatives about here, so far as he knows.

I have inquired of several about the stone & about Holand. Most of the people know little or nothing of either. A banker (not at the Evansville state bank) said that it appeared to him strange that such a party, having lost ten by the Indians, should take the time necessary to make so long an inscription. It is a good point against the stone.

See Fergus Falls Journal Issue 2 '10 for an article by A. B. Pedersen of Eau Claire, Wis, defending the stone and rebuking Anderson.[7]

Editor of the Free Press, Fergus Falls. (Odland) (Martin W. Odlund)

Free Press of Fergus Falls, of Mar 2, 1910, has an article—the same as that written by Anderson in reply to Upham.

Rev O. A. Norman[n], Ashby, was with Holand—& it was he that called Holand's attention to the 12 apostles, both of them ignoring the true skerries.

I had a long & satisfactory conversation with him at his house. He is very positive the runestone is genuine. He said Holand was never in the region till about two or three years ago—at the time when he got the stone of Ohman. Holand has no relatives, or other inducement to visit this region. He was getting data for vol II, of his history and came into knowledge of the stone at Ohman's.[8] His first vol pertains to Wisconsin and Iowa—though as frontispiece he has the rune stone. Holand, as stated by Norman, was wandering about the lakes in this region. He said Fossum & himself, after considerable search, had not satisfactorily located the camp, and asked him if he knew of stones that might be considered the skerries referred to. When Norman described the rocks standing in the water between the point and and the little island Holand said he must go and see them. Norman volunteered to accompany him. The result was that, though on account of the storm then prevailing it was impossible to go out to them. Mr Holand accepted them as the skerries referred to. It was those rocks also that Holand described to me as the skerries. Mr Nate Johnson stated the same. Yet later, when I gave the reasons for considering the two boulders on the point as the skerries Holand fell in with my view. This seems to indicate that Holand was honestly endeavoring to

[7] A brief editorial appears in the *Fergus Falls Daily Journal* of March 2, 1910, p. [2], but the Pedersen letter was printed February 25, 1910, p. [2].
[8] There was no volume 2 of Holand's *De norske settlementers historie.*

find the truth, and knew nothing about any fraud in connection with the stone, for he would at once have gone to the large boulders on the point as confirmation of the record.

Mr. Norman said that according to his understanding of the Norsk word for skerry, it might apply to a series of rocks in water, as well as to a single rock, & that there are two lines, or series, of stones standing out of the water, at that place, not parallel exactly but running at different angles toward the main reef. Such can not be discovered, however, according to my observation, by viewing them from the point. They seem to be a single group, and I called them the *Twelve apostles* — though I think I counted thirteen.

Mr. Norman related the fact of discovery of a large iron Key, like the old European Keys used in door locks. It was found a few feet below the surface, & was brought home by his son who was working with the men who were sinking a well by drilling in the clay. He thinks it can still be found, as it was at the house for some time after the discovery. It was found not far from Ashby, 4 or 5 ms. out from Brandon towards Elbow lake. [*See Plate 8.*]

He also mentioned the fact that in an old Norsk song of the 14th Century the refrain was a repetition of the line, "AVM, save us from the evil," and was in common use in connection with the burials of those who died of the black plague at that time. He said he would write out for me the facts about that line.

Note. Was the article "the" which must have been used in a definite sense (the evil, i.e. the black plague) also on the rune stone? It would indicate, if so used, a literal transcription of a line then in common use at the burials of the black plague victims. It is my impression that it has been sometimes translated "the evil." (See Telesoga, by Torkel Oftelie Fergus Falls, 1909.)[9]

The title of the little poem is *Fornesbronen.* The bay horse from the farm called Fornes.

The gist of the whole song is the description of the ravages of the Black Death, especially in the district called Mostrand. The refrain of the verses is quite similar to the expression "A.V.M. Deliver us from the evil," but varying somewhat from verse to verse.

I received from Mr. Norman his copy of the little pamphlet, for the Hist. Soc.

KENSINGTON MAR 4, '10

The tree was about 4 or 5 inches in diameter at about 15 inches above the stone, and about ten inches in diameter at six inches or 8 inches above the stone.

The root which spread over the surface of the stone was flattened on

[9] The ballad referred to appeared in *Telesoga*, March, 1909, p. 62, a quarterly published by Telelag, an organization of natives of Telemark, Norway.

the lower side. Those that went down across the edge of the stone were also flattened, and spread somewhat from each other.

Mr Oleson made a drawing (attached) intended to show the probable position of the stone and the tree, as described above [*See Plate 7.*]

About in the spring (May) of (1890?) [*1899*] Mr Sam Olson and a party visited the place and made some excavation where the stone was found.[10] He saw, and all his party saw, the stump of the tree that grew on the stone. This was in the spring after the Summer when it was found. (It seems to have been found in Nov.) The members of this party were the following, besides Mr Olson.

Cleve Van Dyke (sec. to Gov Johnson [*Samuel R. Van Sant*]) Then Supt. Schools of Douglas Co

J. P. Hedberg, now at Warroad

John M. Olson, (now at Alexandria, who furnished a team)

Albert Larson, (now in Canada.)

John E. Johnson (of Kensington)

Emil Johnson (now at Warroad)

Gulick Landsvark, (2 ms. E. of Kensington)

Lars Coldberg (Bowbells N. Dak)

Mr. Olson and Mr Johnson (John E.) are positive that the tree must have been at least ten years old, & was more likely 20 or 30 years old   Mr. Johnson thinks it was an ash, but is not certain[.] Signed John E. Johnson   Sam Olson

Mar 4 1910

Ohman came on to the farm about 1896 [*1891.*]

So far as I can see the agency of Holand in the making of the inscription is wholly excluded by the circumstances that are well established.

Ohman called the tree an "asp", i.e. aspen, or trembling poplar of the region, very common in the state.

Mar 5, Kensington.

Anon Hotvedt is his brother[.]

Joseph Hotvedt, whose wife runs the boarding house at Kensington has a farm adjoining Ohman's, & was there before Ohman came. He is of the opinion that Ohman may have made the inscription. He said Ohman had some old books, telling about runes and is "quite a mechanic when he wants to be." He says Ohman talked about runes & showed his books. On the other hand Holand declared that he saw Ohman's books & that the only rune characters he ever found there were in a school book which gave the alphabet which Ohman brought from the old country.

It was reprinted with editorial comment by O. E. Hagen, in *Samband*, October, 1911, p. 363–369.
[10] On the excavation of the site, see Appendixes 5 and 13.

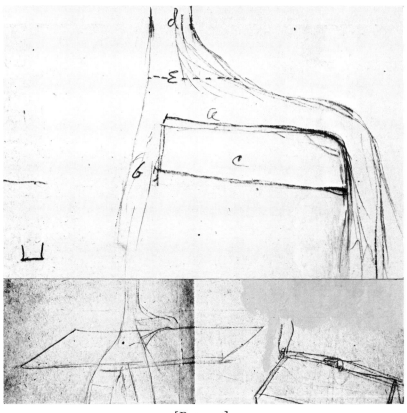

[PLATE 7]
Drawing by S. Olson [11]
a the largest root
b smaller roots that went down perpendicular
c end of the stone
d tree 4 or 5 in. in diam
e tree ten inches in diameter
Ohman & his boy told me that the main root went down the side instead of over the top[.] [Winchell's caption.]

Mr Hotvedt saw the roots & verifies the description of their flatness, "such as would be caused by lying against a stone." He is the only man I have found who doubts the authenticity of the stone.

Mar 5 Mr. Ohman declares that the tree was asp (poplar), & had two main roots & the larger one was that which ran down vertical, & the rune inscribed side was down; Of that Mr O. is very positive. His boy says the same, was about 10 years old.

[11] Olson's sketch is pasted into the field book at this point.

Mr. O. says he never gave the stone to Holand, & if he signed such a statement he did not know it. He did not read it all, & never gave the stone to Holand. Ole Stenberg will corroborate Ohman's statement as to Holand's not getting the stone for himself. He heard the agreement, made with Holand.

A Kansas man says that on an old church window in Norway the inscription has the word *from*. It is in the 14th century. (Ohman) Ohman's education 6 terms of 6 weeks each, in Sweden, rotating school. Borrowed the alphabetic runic book for the purpose of reading the stone, but found a lot of characters not in the book. Had no other rune book, could make nothing of it.

Mr. Ole Stenberg says that while Mr. Holand said he was a poor fellow and received the stone for the Norwegian Hist. Soc, & could give only a copy of his book, Mr. Ohman let the stone go for the book. "If Ohman got the book, why, the stone belongs to Holand."

Mr. Sam Olson says that the stone belongs either to the Nor. Hist. Soc, or to Mr. Ohman, as Mr. Holand got it of Ohman for the Society.

Mr. Holand called first on Mr Olson, inquiring about the stone and the owner, & was directed to Mr. Ohman by him[.]

Mrs Ohman told my livery man that Ohman borrowed the school book after the stone was found, for the purpose of deciphering the inscription.

Mr. Ohman said the main root of the tree was at the edge & went down nearly perpendicular, in that respect differing from Mr. Olson & his sketch.

I had a long talk with Mr. Ohman, and am impressed with the evident candor and truthfulness of all his statements, and also I find he is a more intellectual man than I had supposed.

He gave me more of the details of the history of the stone than I had learned. He had never heard of Holand till he called on him at Kensington. Holand has no relatives in the neighborhood, and as far as I can find out is a stranger except since he took up the rune stone.

Mounds in Douglas Co. Mr. Olof Ohman told me that about his farm in several places, in the woods, are "mounds" in groups, the largest so far as he has noticed being about six feet high, with smaller ones round about. This is in Sec. 14, Solem township in Douglas Co[.]

My livery man made light of the statements of Mr. Hotvedt as to Mr. Öhman's making the rune record. "You cant go much on what he says. He is always off, and contrary."

It will be noted that he (Hotvedt) confirms the aspect of the roots — which is fatal to his idea that Ohman made the inscription, since by all opinions the tree was older than the residence of Öhman on the farm.

MAR 17, 1910 ELBOW LAKE.

Rev. M. B Juul, 4 ms. S of Brandon, may assist in this matter of the rune stone.

Gunnar (Gunder) Johnson knows a man who made rune characters on walks. He is 1 m. E. of M. B. Juul. This information is obtained of Rev O. G. Juul of Elbow Lake.

Rev. Statstad [*Anders I. Stadstad*],[12] Brandon Minn, lost cast & went to N. Dak, not living, but he is not the man whom rumor connects with runes.

Evansville Mar 17.

Ohman is a Swede. Must have come to that locality since Mr Saettre's coming, and *did* to his knowledge. Mr. S. has been here 25 yrs. He is confident that Mr Ohman whom he has known ever since he came here is utterly incapable of making the inscription. He has never heard that Ohman traveled about and made runes on sidewalks and granaries in idle hours, nor has he ever heard of a clergyman in this country who did so, as is claimed by a rumor that is vogue in Grant & Douglas counties.

Mr Saettre's opinion of Mr. Jos Hotvedt's reliability agrees with the opinion of Mr. Peterson (my livery man) of Kensington, & that his brother Anon Hotvedt is a different kind of a man, whose word and judgment can be relied on.

Ashby. Mr Norman says he remembers a preacher who was a queer character. He lost cast before he came to this country. He was a drunkard & was in jail often in Fergus [Falls], does not know what became of him, was 10 or 15 years senior of Mr Norman who is now 66. This man was round here in 1872–1875, but had disappeared in 1879, when Mr. Norman came back here. Never knew of his making any rune char-

This key was found about (8 ft?) below the surface in sinking a well between Brandon and Elbow Lake, & is owned by Ferdinand Normann of Spooner, son of Rev. O. A. Norman. [Winchell's caption.]

[12] Stadstad was a minister in Douglas County from 1876 to 1886. See Norlie, *Norsk lutherske prester i Amerika, 1843–1913,* 161. Hegge, mentioned below, has not been identified.

acters. He was a Norwegian, a good scholar, & flouted his learning. Seems to have been Fogelblad.

The preacher who is rumored to have made runes was named Hegge as remembered by Mr Normann. He was not at all inclined to perpetrate jokes of that kind. All he wanted was to take it easy & have as many drinks as possible. This was in 1872–1875. (O A Normann's statement)

According to Mr. O. G. Juul of Elbow Lake, the only man on earth who could make Mr Ohman tell the facts of the finding of the stone is Mr. O. F. Olson, of Brandon.

BRANDON, MAR 18

Mr O. F. Olson has known Mr. Ohman for 26 or 27 years. He used to live at Brandon. He used to make rune characters about Brandon. He built Mr Ingemon's store & others, and was known as a "queer genius," talked but little, thought much. He is (now) reported to have been practicing in making runes when working here, but Mr Olson says he did not himself see characters made by him. Never knew of a preacher living with Ohman who has been married since he left. At Brandon he lived with Dr. Snar, a distant relative of his. He knows the bible from one side to the other. Would not say that Ohman made or could not make the stone, but always had an impression that he may have made it. Dr. Snar is not living. They were from northern Sweden — Helsingerland.

Rev M B. Juul lives at Moe, 4 ms S. from Brandon[.]

Mr. Gunder Johnson says his little testimony is not worth anything one way or the other. He knew Mr. Ohman who built his house where he lives, about 26 or 27 years ago. Mr O. & he were talking about old Norsk one day, & Ohman said there were old letters which were called runes, & that Mr. O took a pencil and made some on a board saying they were runes. Mr. Johnson never knew of his making runes at any other time, nor of any preacher living with Ohman who made runes nor any living in this country who could make them nor anyone passing through here who could make them.

Mr. M. B. Juul knows nothing more of Mr. Ohman that [sic] what has emanated from Mr. Gunder Johnson or from Mr. Olson of Brandon. He says Mr. Holand came direct from Mr Ohman's when he first saw the stone, and was then convinced that the stone was genuine. Mr. Juul sent him to Mr. Gunder Johnson, and he visited Mr. Johnson. After the interview with Mr. Johnson Mr Holand returned to Mr Juual's [sic] and his opinion of the stone was not changed[.] He thought Mr. Johnson was very skeptical, & that his opinion was not worth much.

Mr. Holand told Mr Juul that the stone had been given to him by Mr Ohman[.]

WAYNESBURG COLLEGE LIBRARY
WAYNESBURG, PA.

["]Stockholm["] "Sv. Fogelblad" is written in the (1868), book owned by him.[13]

Flugelblad, is said to be the name of a man who stayed with Ohman. This was told to Mr Carl Nelson, neighbor of Roald Bentson, by a man at Hoffman. Nelson does not know his name[.] He was simply driving with him[.] Nelson's father was living when the stone was found. He did not express an opinion as to who made the stone, but did not believe that Ohman had anything to do with it.

Bentson is in Minneapolis. Christ Ashby is son in law of Bentson. He is a large saloon keeper in Minneapolis.

"Most of the people about here do not think that Ohman had any thing to do with the stone" and "that the stone is all right." Ohman has not been known to be a stone mason. H[e] is a carpenter. Mr. Carl Nelson knows nothing of Mr. Ohman's making runes. Mr Carl Nelson says that Mr. Ohman gave the stone to Holand in consideration of his getting Mr. Holand's book, but that up to last summer he had not received the book. He may have it by this time.

Kensington

Mr. S. Olson says that Mr. Flugelblad was dead before he came to Kensington as stated by Mr. Ohman, that he and Anderson & Ohman all queer characters, lived (chummed) together.

Andrew Anderson (or Speer Anders which means slim Andrew) lives now in Hoffman[.] He could tell about Flugelblad. He is a political agitator of the third party type, or socialist, or people's party. Mr S. Olson came to Kensington 15 years ago.

These three (Ohman, Flugelblad and Anderson) are all Swedes, and if there be any fraud in it it lies with one or all of them.

19 MAR, ÖHMANS

Sv. Flugelblad was preacher in Sweden (not here) went among the farmers to get a living, sometimes taught the children, but did not work, was pretty near 70 years old, was dead before I got the stone, was intemperate, drinking when ever he had any money, was always poor — like a gentleman in manners but he was too fond of "booze." When Flugelblad died he died at Anderson's who then had a farm between Kensington & Hoffman. He left his books with Anderson. When Mr Ohman found the stone Mr. Anderson (whose wife is cousin of Mrs Ohman said that Mr Ohman should take Mr Flugelblad's little book so as to read the stone, & it has been with Mr Ohman since. Flugelblad died about 14 or 15 years ago. (Mrs Ohman thinks so, but is not positive as to the year).

Mr Ohman says he can not remember talking with Mr Gunder Johnson, nor of making runes for him, 26 or 27 years ago (Ohman came

[13] This entry occurs in two lines in the original. The order has here been reversed for readability.

to America in 1879). He says it was about 1883 when he worked for Mr. Johnson, & that at any time if he said anything about runes it was because he had learned it in school in Sweden. Every school boy, and every Norwegian knows something about runes, but not so as to use them.

I prevailed on Mr Ohman to let me take the rune book which has caused the widespread talk about his knowledge of runes. He would not sell it but I left 50c saying it must go with the stone. I told him I wanted to keep it, but he was reluctant to give it up because it has much about old Swedish language and he could not get any such book again. I replied that he would never want such a book again, & it is important that the characters in it be compared with those on the stone. "All right" he said, "you can take it." I think he will be reconciled to let it remain with the stone, in the custody of the Historical Society permanently.[14]

I found Mr Gunder Johnson a very talkative man. I recall it now and record it for its bearing on the existence and spread of the idea that Ohman knew runes long ago and had a number of books on runes & made runic characters on the walks, the window casings and the granary doors about the country. I have traced up, under the direction of those who believed and repeated this story, all the promising lines of evidence, and I have found the report especially prevalent and detailed about Brandon where Mr. Ohman lived 26 or 27 years ago. I have asked, not for the story, but for positive statements as to whether the parties affirming the story actually knew of Mr. Ohman's making runes. They all said they had not except Mr. Gunder Johnson. His account has been given a few pages back. It seems that when at work for Mr. Johnson a conversation arose about the old Norsk language or languages when Mr. Ohman stated that there were formerly runic characters in which the ancient Scandinavians wrote, and with a pencil made, or attempted to make, several on a board. I judge that this incident was dormant until Prof Breda and Prof Curme pronounced the stone a fraud, and the stone had been returned to Ohman's farm. Then all the people began to speculate as to how the stone was inscribed, and naturally all minds turned to Ohman and all began to suspect he was the deceiver. Here the knowledge of Mr Gunder Johnson about Ohman's making some runes on a board at the building of his house sprang into importance, and through Mr. Johnson, I have no doubt, the idea was (very naturally) given broad cast. There was no other possible explanation of a fraudulent rune stone found on Mr. Ohman's farm and kept by Mr. Ohman, however indifferently. Mr. Ohman is a rather taciturn man, and he took no pains to counteract the report that he

[14] The allusion is to Almquist's *Svensk språklära*, which is in the MHS library.

was the impostor. His neighbors made sport of him for having, or even having made, a fake inscription. Mr. Gunder Johnson's knowledge was amplified by rumor, and some intimated that as Fogelblad was a scholar he was the man who traced out the runes for Mr. Ohman to cut on the stone. More lately as it became known that Mr. Ohman had "rune books," the story was credited by many who had no personal acquaintance with Ohman, and during the last few years it seems to have been accepted by many (all) who took any interest in the stone.

When the recent renewal of inquiry about the stone became known by the people of this region of course all the rumors, however increased in detail, were revived also, and there is no doubt that some have innocently spread the story, for they thought that what was common report must be true. In the exaggerated form it was sent in a letter to Mr. Upham by Mr (Rev.) Otto G. Juul, of Elbow Lake, and it was his letter that prompted this thorough examination.[15]

I had a long talk this morning with Mr. Ohman. I thought I had some queries to make of him which would stagger him.

1. Who was the broken-down preacher?

2. Did you make runes for Gunder Johnson?

The first question he answered consistently, and the second he answered in the negative, but he added that he could not recall any conversation with Johnson, nor had any recollection of making runes for him.

As I can find no one, except Johnson, who affirms that he has seen Ohman make runes, and as the rumor is most definite and common about Brandon, where Mr. Johnson lives, and as Mr. Johnson said he never knew of Ohman making runes at any other time than at the conversation 26 or 27 years ago, I became convinced that the rumor is due to Mr. Johnson, and is based only on that occurrence 26 or 27 years ago.

Fogelblad turned over (or Anderson did) some of the books to Rev. M. A. Nordstroem, 1120, Orange, Riverside Cal. (J. A. Holvik, U. C.[?] Seminary, St Anthony Park, Pierce St) wrote to Mr. Nordstrom. He replied that Fogelblad had no book by Fryxell, & could not have made the inscription. Nordstrom got two books on philosophy.

Mans (man) is found in legal documents, meaning servants, or hired men. The last word is not on the stone.

9. THE OHMAN LETTER OF 1909

As I have explained in chapter 4, the following letter written in Swedish by Olof Ohman to Warren Upham was a response to an invitation to attend the meeting of the executive council of the Minnesota Historical

Society on December 13, 1909. With his letter of invitation (dated
December 6, 1909), Upham sent Ohman a printed circular announcing
the meeting, and Ohman in his reply wrote on the backs of the pages
of the circular.

It seems desirable to present this letter both in its original Swedish
and in an English translation. The original has been translated for this
book by Professor Erik Wahlgren of the University of California at
Los Angeles, who also helped me in making a copy of the Swedish
text. Since the drawing is an integral part of the letter, it is reproduced
as an illustration on page 161.

The text of the Swedish original was first published by Sven B. F.
Jansson, the Swedish runologist, in his incisive and memorable article
entitled " 'Runstenen' från Kensington i Minnesota," in *Nordisk Tidskrift*, 25:398n (1949). Jansson had found a copy of the letter among the
papers of Otto von Friesen, the noted Swedish linguist, in the manuscript collections of the University of Uppsala. The copy, Jansson wrote,
had been certified by Joseph E. Osborn, a clerk in the office of the Minnesota state auditor in St. Paul. Osborn presumably understood Swedish and made the copy himself, for he was the son of a well-known
Swedish church leader, Lars P. Esbjörn. Jansson does not give the
date of the transcript.

Warren Upham had written to Von Friesen on March 10, 1910, asking for the linguist's opinion of the Kensington rune stone. Von Friesen
replied in Swedish on an undated postal card; an attached translation
in Upham's handwriting bears the date April 4, 1910. Von Friesen
wrote that the Kensington inscription was a modern fabrication *"by
a man who was partly acquainted with runes but where this partial
knowledge failed, he created himself new characters."* [1] Von Friesen
added that he had commenced a "detailed study" of the inscription,
and he requested from Upham "a detailed account" of the discovery as
well as information about the nationality and personality of the finder.
Upham answered in a letter of May 10, 1910, in which, he said, he
enclosed a copy of Olof Ohman's letter of December 9, 1909. Thus we
have an explanation of how a copy of the Ohman letter came to be
reposing in the library of the University of Uppsala. [2]

[1] The italics are Von Friesen's.
[2] Von Friesen's card and the translation are in MHS Archives. See also
Upham to Von Friesen, March 10, May 10, 1910, in MHS Letter Press Books.
On Osborn, see Minnesota *Legislative Manual*, 1909, p. 331; obituary in
Minneapolis Journal, September 8, 1932, p. 17. It should be added that Wahlgren, *Kensington Stone*, 55, published an extract from the Ohman letter, derived from Jansson. Wahlgren commented that the letter "is written in

The original Swedish letter is not the work of an educated man, for it has many errors in spelling and grammar. It blends Swedish and English forms, as in the word "kottade," which is the English word for "cut" given the Swedish past tense. The letter is unquestionably in Ohman's own hand, and it is entirely intelligible and very much to the point.

[Olof Ohman to Warren Upham, December 9, 1909, in Minnesota Historical Society Archives]

KENSINGTON DEN 9 DEC. 1909
MR WARREN UPHAM ST. PAUL

Eder skrifvelse är mig tillhanda, och får upplysa, att mina tillgångar i ekonomisk hänseende icke tillåter mig att infina vid eders Societys meeting, och ej heller jag kan inse att min närvaro är nödvändig. på eder fråga öfver Runstennens finnande får jag upplysa att nämda sten är funnen under en asprot

Af neddan teknade utseende, af roten stennen var inbäddat mellan dessa rötter med runorna vänd nedåt samt runorna på sidan vänd emot järtroten, som vi kallar på farmarspråket, Jag kottade af den ytre roten som vi ser på tekningen och äfven järtroten på samma plats som det visas på tekningen Seden fall trädet och stenen var blåtat [3]

Jag såg att stenen var tun, jag helt enkelt satte grubhån under den och vände den undra sidan upp så att runorna kom upp i dagen, min pojk Edvar är fodd 1888 han var omkring 10 år han såg först att det var någonting ritat på stenen. pojkarne trodde att de har funnit en Inde allmanacka. Jag själf såg ochså att det var någonting skrivit. men att läsa hvar för mig et mysterie. Jag är svensk, född i Helsingland, men jag har alldrig sedt någon runsten förr Stenen låg 44 fot åfvan nu varande vaten läfvel. Aspträdet var omkring 8 tum i Diameter.

Aktningsfult OLOF OHMAN

KENSINGTON 9 DEC. 1909
MR. WARREN UPHAM ST. PAUL

Your letter is at hand, and I must inform that my assets financially speaking do not permit me to attend your Society's meeting, nor can I see that my presence is necessary. As to your question concerning the finding of the rune stone I can state that the stone in question was found under a poplar root.

From the appearance pictured below, of the root, the stone was im-

imperfect Swedish, with incorrect spellings and mixed Swedish-English expressions." It is a strange circumstance that the report of the MHS museum committee did not mention Von Friesen or make any allusion to his opinion of the Kensington inscription.

[3] Under the drawing, Ohman wrote "stenens ända" meaning "the stone's end."

A PAGE FROM *Olof Ohman's letter with his drawing of the tree roots*

bedded between these roots with the runes turned downward and the runes on the side turned toward the taproot, as we say in farmer language. I cut off the outer root as we see in the drawing and also the taproot in the same place as shown in the drawing. Then the tree fell and the stone was revealed.

I saw that the stone was thin. I simply put the grubbing hoe under it and turned the under side up so that the runes were exposed. My boy Edvar[d] was born in 1888. He was about 10 years old. He was the first to see that there was something inscribed on the stone. The boys believed that they had found an Indian almanac. I myself also saw that there was something written. But to read was a mystery to me. I am Swedish, born in Helsingland, but I have never seen any rune stone before. The stone lay 44 feet above the present water level. The poplar tree was about 8 inches in diameter.

Respectfully OLOF OHMAN

10. GEORGE O. CURME'S ADVICE IN 1910

George O. Curme figured prominently in the history of the Kensington controversy. As early as February, 1899, he produced a translation of the inscription, and in 1899 he studied the stone itself, which was sent to him from Kensington. He was the earliest linguist to examine the inscription at firsthand.

Curme kept the stone for a month or more and worked on it daily. He was inclined, at first, to favor the authenticity of the inscription, but as he continued his studies, he came to the conclusion that it was modern. Once satisfied, he did not waver in his judgment that the inscription was fraudulent.

In the light of Curme's relationship to the controversy in its earliest stages, the following three letters, written in 1910, are of interest because they record what he said about the rune stone eleven years after he had first examined it. The three handwritten letters were composed at Evanston, Illinois, in reply to inquiries requesting Curme's opinion on the inscription from Warren Upham, dated February 19, 25, 1910. In a letter of March 8, 1910, Upham sent his thanks to Curme and mentioned that Winchell had also written to the linguist. Copies of Upham's letters may be found in Minnesota Historical Society Letter Books in the society's archives.

[Curme to Warren Upham, February 21, 1910, in Minnesota Historical Society Archives]

MR. WARREN UPHAM:

I have just received your letter. I think your question is a very serious one, but I think there is only one way of settling this question. The stone or a photograph must be sent to the first Scandinavian scholars of Scandinavia. I suggest you send a photographic reproduction of the stone and the inscription to Professor Adolf Noreen, Up[p]sala, Sweden. Professor Noreen is the most distinguished linguist of Scandinavia and will be able to tell you in a few minutes whether the stone is genuine or not. This question lies off my territory, but I have studied it very carefully and find the inscription ungenuine. However, I am no authority in this field, but Professor Noreen is. I urge you to do this at once and set to rest all doubt. You might also send it to Mr. Axel Louis Elmquist of our university who is a pupil of Professor Noreen. Mr. Elmquist's address is Northwestern University, Evanston, Ill.

I beg that you inform me of Professor Noreen's decision.

Yours truly GEORGE O. CURME

[Curme to Warren Upham, February 28, 1910, in Minnesota Historical Society Archives]

MR. WARREN UPHAM,
Dear Sir:

In reply to your second letter would say that I do not know Mr. Holand. I became well acquainted with Mr. Olof Ohman as far as one can get together by letter. I have not the slightest lack of confidence in him. To me there is no doubt that he found the stone under the roots of a tree about forty or fifty years old. I do not know anything more about the stone. He sent it to me and I kept it a long while for a month or even longer. I worked on it daily. It was easy for me to read the inscription, but it was much more difficult for me to come to a conclusion as to the genuineness of the inscription. I am not an expert Scandinavian scholar and my opinion would not be final. My field of work lies in old German. I am acquainted with runes and old Germanic and Scandinavian somewhat and it was a pleasure to me to work on the question. I came to the conclusion there were features in the language much more modern than was in accord with the date on the stone. The umlauts for instance are modern. I sent a photograph to several scholars in Christiania and they agreed with me and I lost all interest in the stone.

Now be patient and await the decision of Professor Noreen and his advisors. He is a great scholar and you will get the facts from an authoritative source.

Yours truly GEORGE O. CURME

[Curme to Newton H. Winchell, March 9, 1910, in Archaeological Records, Minnesota Historical Society Archives]

MR. N. H. WINCHELL,
Dear Sir:

In reply to your letter concerning the old stone I would say that the solution of the questions lies entirely in the hands of linguists. The genuineness can be disproved or established beyond a doubt. The question is solely a linguistic one. Anyone could tell that Shakespeare's works were not written in the present century. Now as so much depends upon the linguist here I think that this question ought to be settled by the most distinguished Scandinavian scholars. My opinion ought not to have much weight. My power lies in Old German where I am perfectly at home. I am used to working in language and I tried my power on your runic stone. It seemed to me ungenuine. Now it would be a pity to stop with me. It would be a great document if it were genuine. I believe you will get the facts when the answer reaches you from Sweden.

You wanted more reasons than my remark that the umlauts were modern. I answer that would be absolutely decisive in and of itself. There are other points, however, which I would rather leave to the Scandinavian scholars as their views will be decisive and authoritative. I myself would have complete confidence in their decision. Such matters are very easily settled in linguistic questions as there are in a document so long enough *facts* to place the matter beyond doubt.[1]

I do not give you a detailed answer to your request for more proofs because I desire to be unkind, but because I am prompted by my feeling that the Scandinavian scholars ought to decide this question. They know more about it and are more prepared to pass judgment. I should not have *absolute* confidence in my opinion as I am not thoroughly at home in this field. I would greatly rejoice if the Scandinavian scholars would find the inscription genuine. It would be a tremendously big document, one of the greatest in history. My linguistic training, however, leads me to doubt it very strongly. I urge you to await patiently the answer from Sweden. I think you owe it to me to communicate to me the final answer. I have worked hard on the old stone.

Yours truly GEORGE O. CURME

11. O. J. BREDA'S LATER VIEWS

Olaus J. Breda worked out the first known translation of the Kensington inscription in January, 1899. Anything he wrote about the subject, therefore, is necessarily of interest in relation to the Kensington controversy.

It has not hitherto been generally known that on March 7, 1910, Breda sent to Upham from Christiania a handwritten, eleven-page letter in English. It was a reply to a request from Upham (February 19, 1910) for Breda's opinion as to the genuineness or fraudulency of the Kensington inscription. On March 20, 1910, Upham thanked Breda for his

---

[1] The italics here and below are Curme's.

APPENDIX 11 165

"important discussion," and said that the society's museum committee was still at work on the Kensington problem and that Winchell had recently made a third trip to Kensington. Upham referred to the forthcoming *Symra* (6:65–80) article by Breda as one that would have "great weight," but no evidence has been found to show that either the article or Breda's letter of March 7, 1910, influenced the committee's report. Copies of Upham's letters are preserved in Minnesota Historical Society Letter Press Books in the society's archives.

[Breda to Upham, March 7, 1910, in Minnesota Historical Society Archives]

DEAR SIR:

Your favour of Feb 19th came to hand to-day. I suppose you were aware, when you posted that letter, *Feb 20th*, of the utter impossibility of my reply reaching you before *March 14*, the date you give for your report.[1] If my reply would be useless to you if arriving after that date, you certainly would not have put me to the trouble of stating at some length my opinion of the Kensington stone. I have recently written an exhaustive review of the matter which will appear some time in April in the next issue of the "*Symra*" Magazine published at *Decorah, Iowa* in the Norwegian language. If the matter is still before your society by that time, you might write to Mr. Johs. B. Wist, 106 Washington St. Decorah Iowa for a copy of that issue of the Symra and get some competent person to translate the article. Meanwhile I shall endeavour to give some of the points made in that article. But as my school work keeps me very busy, I have no time to reduce my remarks to a form suitable for publication. The intention is to give the substance of the matter in the briefest possible shape.

About New Year 1899 I was first informed of the existence of the alleged Runic inscription at Kensington. At my request Mr. Siverts of K. sent me a rough draft of the inscription which I deciphered and read substantially in the same way that it was afterwards read by Runic experts in Norway. I found several very suspicious features about it.

1) That an inscription which for 500 years had been exposed to the severe climate of Minnesota, should be in *such an excellent state of preservation* that a man absolutely ignorant of Runic characters should be able to make, off hand, a draft of it that could be easily read and deciphered by a man like myself, who has never made a special study of Runic inscriptions, was in itself suspicious. One of the commonest difficulties in reading genuine Runic inscriptions is that the action of the weather makes it very difficult to trace the characters and distinguish them from natural cracks in the stone and indentations produced by natural causes.

[1] The italics here and below are Breda's.

2) The *utter absurdity of the story* told by the inscr. In 1362, 40 Norwegians and Swedes landed somewhere on the American coast and in the incredibly short time of 14 days 30 of them have found their way to Douglas Co Minn. through trackless forests and over wild prairies, across wide rivers and lakes where boats had to be built to get across, surrounded by untold dangers, wild animals, savage Indians, obliged to find sustenance by hunting and fishing. After arriving in Douglas Co. they went a fishing, discovered a couple of extremely interesting "skerries" at Elbow Lake and on their return from the merry fishing party they found 10 of their comrades, ⅓ of the total strength of the expedition, brutally butchered by the Indians. And then, in the centre of a strange continent, thousands of miles away from home and succour of any kind, surrounded by howling blood-thirsty savages, these wonderful men calmly and deliberately sit down to carve in stone an elaborate account of the fishing trip, the remark-able Elbow Lake skerries and the massacre — an account so elaborate that the persons murdered are not simply described as "dead" but even "red with blood." The annals of discovery contain nothing like it unless it be Dr. [Frederick A.] Cook's famous expedition to the North Pole [*in 1909*].

3) *The language of the inscription* appeared to be a peculiar jumble of ancient forms, old-fashioned spellings and entirely modern Swedish words intermixed with occasional English forms — which could not possibly represent any genuine Northern language of the period indicated. The Runes also exhibited certain suspicious peculiarities but not being an expert in that field, I could not build much on that observation.

For these reasons I pronounced the inscription a *modern forgery and* declined to have anything further to do with the matter. (cf an interview in the Mpolis Journal Feb. 22. 1899. Also an article in the Mpolis Tribune April 16th 1899).

Meanwhile the matter has been referred to three great Runologists and Norse linguists at the University of Norway: Professors Sof[ph]us Bugge, Gustav Storm and Oluf Rygh and from them came a cablegram which according to the Mpolis Tribune of April 16. 99. was to the effect that the socalled Runic Stone *is a grand fraud, perpetrated by a Swede with a chisel and a slight knowledge of Runic characters and of English.* In an article in the 'Morgenbladet' of Christiania [*March 12, 1899*], *Professor Rygh* says that "the author of the inscription must have been some Swedish-American. The unusual Runic characters employed by him do not speak for but *against* the genuineness of the inscription." Thus the matter rested til Mr. Holand took it up again. Now it was referred to Prof *Magnus Olsen,* who has succeeded prof Bugge in the Univ. of Norway, an eminent Runologist and linguist. Prof Olsen did not see fit to meddle with the alleged Rune stone personally, but gave the matter over to one of his students as a proper theme for an exercise on Runic inscriptions. This student, Mr. *H[elge] Gjessing*, made it a special study and his exhaustive report was printed in the *Symra Magazine V. III. 1909* (Decorah. Iowa. J. B. Wist Editor). He goes thoroughly into the matter, examining the runic characters and the language of the inscription. His results may be summed up as follows. He finds "the form of language impossible, an extremely clumsy attempt at constructing an ancient form of language without possessing the requisite knowledge for doing so. For runological, linguistic and historical reasons the inscription cannot be genuine." If your society cares to go further into the matter you should send to Mr. J. B. Wist Decorah Iowa for the Symra Mag., 1909. nr. III and get some competent person to translate Mr Gjessings article.[2] I have not the time to go into detail but simply refer you to this exposition. Prof *Magnus Olsen* to me personally has repeatedly declared that he fully agrees with Mr. Gjessing that the inscr. is of comparatively recent date and cannot possibly be from the 14th century. Still another great authority in these matters, the great Runologist and linguist of Up[p]sala Univ. Sweden, professor *Adolf Noreen* has stated his views on the Kensington inscription in very emphatic language in "*Runic Inscriptions* from *Recent Times*,["] 1906.[3] After telling of famous Swedish forgeries in this line prof Noreen continues as follows: "The most recent phenomenon of this class is a runic stone from 1362 (!) which was discovered in 1899 [*sic*] near Kensington, Minn. and caused great exultation not merely among the American public but even among some 'scientific men,' although it must be evident, even *to the most unschooled*, that the whole thing is a jumble of Swedish, Danish and English, as follows:" (then comes the text of the inscr. whereupon prof Noreen proceeds as follows:). "Inasmuch as certain expressions indicate some Swedish dialect and certain Runic characters remind one of the Dale type of runes, one might be inclined to suspect that some emigrant from Dalarne (a district in Sweden) may have had a hand in it."

Thus *all the eminent specialists in* this *field in Norway and Sweden* have, thus far, *unanimously pronounced the Kensington inscription a fraud and a forgery of recent date*. I do not see that there is any higher tribunal to appeal the case to. Personally, of course, I feel highly gratified that all these eminent authorities have come to exactly the same conclusion that I did at the first perusal of the inscription.

It has been stated that the stone must have rested under the roots of the tree under which it was found, for 30–40 years. Very likely. There

[2] Helge Gjessing, "Runestenen fra Kensington," in *Symra*, 5:113–126 (1909). An English translation is included among the papers in Archaeological Records, MHS Archives.

[3] Breda quoted Noreen's article of 1906 in *Symra*, 6:74. See also chapter 2, note 42, above.

were white men in that county before it was settled in the early sixties. There was a chain of frontier forts: Fort Snelling, fort Ridgely, fort Ripley, fort Abercrombie, and detachments of troops moving through the country about Kensington occasionally, besides hunters and trappers. Now suppose that among these soldiers of Uncle Sam there was a *young Swede* who had enjoyed a good school education in the old country. If he had not exactly *studied* the old language of his native country which I do not think he had (for in that case his work would have been better), he had at least become *familiar with specimens of the old language* in his school Readers, and also with *Runic characters*. He may have hailed from the province of *Dalarne*, as prof Noreen suggests, which would easily account for his knowledge of Runic characters. In Dalarne Runes have been in use till quite recently, and as late as 1905 old people have been found who could read runes. Well this soldier may have read Dickens' "Posthumous Papers of the Pickwick Club" with the entertaining account of the Pickwick Controversy about the famous stone with the *Bill Stumps his mark* inscription. He foresees that the County will soon be settled and largely by Scandinavians, who were crossing into the Western states. He makes up his mind to surprise them at some future date with evidence of an early visit of Norsemen to the Western country. He is in camp in the neighbourhood of Kensington and in his rambles he discovers a stone which seems to have been specially made for the purpose. He procures a chisel and a hammer in camp, makes up an inscription from the *scraps of school knowledge* not entirely forgotten, and cuts it, at his leisure, into the stone — and then *buries it* in the ground, quite near the surface. He does not want it to be found too soon. If buried in the ground, say for 30–40 years, the characters would *acquire* from the action of the soil and moisture an appearance of old age. He trusts that at some future date, when the county is settled up, some farmer will turn it up and some Pickwick will come along and make it famous.

By looking over the language of his inscription, he had sense enough to discover that it would not do for the time of the Vinland discoveries, about 1000, so he contented himself with *dating it back 500 years*. That might seem to indicate the year 1862 as the probable date of the forgery.[4] I am aware of the Indian troubles in the fall of that year, but there undoubtedly were soldiers about in that part of the country in the summer of 62. Or the man may have been connected with some Indian Agency or been a member of a hunting party. The main thing is *the Swede with the hammer and chisel* and *the requisite knowledge of Runic characters.*

[4] Breda developed the same ideas about 1862 in *Symra*, 6:79. See also Wahlgren, *Kensington Stone*, 162, suggesting that the date 1362 was "'cover language' for 1862," conceived by the carver of the runes as a piece of "playful humor."

I have never seen any reason to connect Mr. Ohman or any one else now living in the neighbourhood of Kensington, with the forgery in any way. The man who cut the inscription into the stone and buried it in the ground has probably not lived to enjoy the turmoil caused by the discovery of it.

Now this is one theory to account for the inscription. There may be other ways that may suggest themselves. But I am of [the] opinion now as I have always been that the inscription *cannot be genuine and that it should not be so recognized by any scientific body*.

I have thus roughly stated my views on the subject broached in your letter. I have not the time to put it in better form but trust that it will answer all practical purposes as it is.

Yours very respectfully, O. J. BREDA

12. J. P. HEDBERG'S LETTER OF 1910

In chapter 2 of this book I discussed the letter J. P. Hedberg wrote on January 1, 1899, to Swan J. Turnblad, telling of the finding of the Kensington rune stone. This is the earliest known reference in manuscript or print to the stone. In 1910, more than eleven years later, Hedberg wrote a second letter relating to the Kensington problem. It was written by hand on the stationery of the Warroad Land and Investment Co., of which Hedberg was president. This company owned the "Fairview Addition to Warroad" and described itself as "Dealers in Farm and Timber lands, and City Property" and also "Loans and Insurance." The letter was dated at Warroad, Minnesota, March 12, 1910, and was addressed to Mr. A. [*sic*] H. Winchell at St. Paul.

[Hedberg to Newton H. Winchell, March 12, 1910, Archaeological Records, Minnesota Historical Society Archives]

DEAR SIR!

Your letter of the 10th inst in regard to the Kensington rune Stone as it is called. In the first place the stone was brought in to my office in Kensington by the finder Olof Ohman. I took quite much interest in the same. I copied the same and sent copy to S. J. Turnblad, who sent it to the State University but Prof. Breda thought it was a fake.

In the Spring of 1890 [*1899*] I together with some others went out and did some digging where the stone had been found and will try and answer the following questions

1 Yes I saw the Stump and roots.

2 the big root was grown as a bend and I am quite sure if we have had the stone there it would have fitted in   it could not have grown on side of stone   3 as said large root run on top of stone   4 it is hard to say how old the tree was but it was quite large and must have been

many years old any way a great deal older than the settlement there. I had quite a talk with one Nels Flaaten [*Nils Flaten*] an old farmer that was along and helped Ohman to grub I considered him absolute reliable — he was along and grubbed the tree and gug [*dug*] out the stone and his statements confermed [*conformed or confirmed?*] absolutely with Ohmans. While I know very little about runes — I never considered the stone a fake.

Very truly yours, J. P. HEDBERG

13. CLEVE W. VAN DYKE'S ACCOUNT OF THE EXCAVATION IN 1899

About eleven years after Olaus Olson described the excavation of the site where the Kensington stone was uncovered (Appendix 5, above), the leader of the excavating expedition, Cleve W. Van Dyke, who in 1899 was superintendent of the Douglas County schools and lived at Alexandria, wrote to Winchell from Arizona, recalling the happenings of 1899. In the intervening years Van Dyke had served as executive clerk under Governor Samuel R. Van Sant in St. Paul and had then gone to Arizona, where he was president of the Miami Townsite Company on whose letterhead he wrote.

Van Dyke does not specifically identify the "Olson" whom he mentions as having been associated with him in the decision to excavate the site. It may have been Samuel Olson of Kensington rather than Olaus Olson of Holmes City.

The reference to Ohman as a "character who had traveled a great deal" is of no little interest. Van Dyke's statement that he thought Ohman had told him of visiting a museum in England, where he had seen some rune stones, is the only reference the writer has found to a trip by Ohman to England.

[Cleve W. Van Dyke to Newton H. Winchell, April 19, 1910, Archaeological Records, Minnesota Historical Society Archives]

MY DEAR SIR:

Ten busy years have passed since we dug out the runestone near Kensington, Minn. The subject interested me considerably at the time. I had recently attended a course of lectures on Norse archaeology by Prof. Breda, of the University of Minnesota. Naturally, when this stone was found in my home county I investigated the thing quite thoroughly. Mr. Olson and myself, together with a number of others, decided to dig under the point where the stone was said to have been found.

I lived some twenty miles away from there and arrived later than the rest of the party so that the work had begun when I arrived. However, they showed me the stump of the tree and how the stone had lain in same. The tree, as indicated by its roots, had undoubtedly grown over some flat stone; whether it was this stone I could not say as I had not seen it in place. As I remember it, we judged the tree to be about twelve years old. The smaller root seemed to have been bent away under it and the larger, or tap root, was slightly flattened. Of course, I could not determine whether or not the stone was there before the growth of the tree. I forget now how deep the hole was dug, but I remember finding some scattered pieces of whitish material which appeared something like lime. I thought possibly they might have been the remains of bones. I gathered a few of these pebbles, intending at the time to have them examined to determine if any bony tissue existed, but not having a microscope available, I never examined the pieces.

I did not go further into the matter at the time because the stone was repudiated by Prof. Breda, according to newspaper reports, and his judgment on this point had great influence with me. I remember showing these pebbles to my brother, who, at that time, was a student of medicine in Rush Medical College, Chicago, and he gave it as his opinion that there was nothing which indicated bony tissue.

Mr. Ohman was an interesting character who had traveled a great deal and who seemed to have more or less knowledge concerning runestones and other remains. I believe, at the time, he told me he had visited some museum in England where he had seen a number of runestones.

I was county superintendent of schools at that time and naturally inquired about him. The school teacher in his district showed me one day a number of written excuses in rhyme for his children, written by him. My opinion at the time was that Mr. Ohman was underestimated by his neighbors and that he had more literary knowledge than he was credited by his community as possessing. If Mr. Ohman is still living it would be wise to investigate him. I had great difficulty in talking to him because I could not speak his language sufficiently well to carry on an extended conversation with him.

Yours very truly, CLEVE W. VAN DYKE

14. THE VÉRENDRYE STONE

The Vérendrye stone remains a mystery. No copy or tracing of its inscription has come to light. The stone itself, sent from Quebec to France in the 1740s, is lost. Sporadic searches have been made for it, but without success.

The reported resemblance to Tataric writing of the markings on the Vérendrye stone led the executive council of the Minnesota Historical Society to start a search for it as early as 1909 and also caused Hjalmar R. Holand to suggest that the lost inscription was runic.[1] His claim lacked proof, for no one knows what the language of the inscription was.

We know of the Vérendrye stone only because the Swedish scientist and traveler, Peter Kalm, recorded its finding in his diary for August 7, 1749. The diary, in three volumes, was published in Stockholm, Sweden, from 1753 to 1761, and the pertinent entry was in the third volume (1761). Kalm was an economic botanist, a student of Karl Linnaeus, and a professor at the university in Åbo (now Turku), Finland. He was sent to America to make scientific observations and to collect plants for Linnaeus. While in North America he traveled in the English colonies and in New France, visited such men as Benjamin Franklin and John Bartram (the colonial botanist), spent some time in the Delaware Swedish community, and went to Canada as a guest of the government of New France.[2]

While in Quebec, Kalm dined with the acting governor of New France, the Marquis la Galissionère, and at the table with him was none other than Sieur de la Vérendrye, who told the story of the stone. Kalm recorded the tale in his diary on the same date as the dinner, August 7, 1749.[3]

At the dinner La Vérendrye, explorer of interior America, told of making a journey far into the West, as far as a party of explorers could go in view of the difficulties of travel — a journey "past many peoples" to large areas that were bare of woods. Somewhere, at places where "no Frenchmen or Europeans had ever been before," the travelers saw, in woods and on prairies, stone pillars which they thought had been erected by human hands, the stones sometimes piled "as if masoned." They were curious and looked for inscriptions. Finally they found a

[1] Holand, *Kensington Stone*, 186.

[2] An informing study of Kalm is Martti Kerkkonen, *Peter Kalm's North American Journey: Its Ideological Background and Results* (Helsinki, 1959), which lists many editions of Kalm's book, *En resa til Norra America*, as well as articles by Kalm and a series of student theses that he sponsored. The original of the Kalm diary is in the Helsinki University Library; Kalm letters are in the collections of the University of Uppsala, the National Archives and the Royal Library, both in Stockholm, and in various other Swedish institutions. A valuable article is Esther L. Larsen, "Peter Kalm, Preceptor," in *Pennsylvania Magazine of History and Biography*, 74:500–511 (October, 1950).

[3] *En resa til Norra America*, 3:339–345. A new translation of the passage telling of the finding of the inscribed stone is in Blegen, "An Unsolved Mystery: Where Is the Vérendrye Stone?" in *Minnesota History News*, April, 1962, p. [4–7].

small stone "which on both sides was inscribed with unknown characters." This had been set into a larger stone that resembled a pillar. The Frenchmen broke the little stone loose and later "carried it back to Canada, whence it was sent to the State Secretary in France, Count Maurepas." No one knew what had become of it since, but it was believed to be in the count's collection (his *cabinette*).

The Frenchmen of the western expedition asked the Indians many questions about the people who had lived in the area where the inscribed stone had been found. Who erected the pillars? "What traditions and beliefs" did the natives have about them? "Who had written the characters? What did they mean? What kind of characters were they? And what was the language?" The only answer to their questions the French were able to get was "that these stones had stood where they were since time immemorial."

Where and when was the inscribed stone found? Kalm wrote that the "places where the pillars under discussion stood were reckoned to be 900 French miles from Montreal." Holand believed that the stone was found in 1738, when the elder Vérendrye visited the Mandan country, identifying the place of discovery as "along the banks of the Missouri" in what is now central North Dakota. This location coincided with his theory that some of the supposed Kensington Norsemen merged their lives with the Mandan Indians. It also fitted his assumption that the stone was located by La Vérendrye himself, though the latter, as reported by Kalm, did not specifically say that he found it.[4]

A sounder hypothesis has been offered by Father Ant. Champagne of St. Boniface, Manitoba, a student of the journeys of La Vérendrye and his sons. Kalm's diary account mistakenly stated that the Vérendrye group set out on its journey from Montreal "by horseback." The journey must have begun in canoes, but to Father Champagne the very mention of "horseback" eliminates 1738 as a date that can be given serious consideration, for the Mandans had no horses when La Vérendrye visited them in that year. Father Champagne favored, instead, the 1742–43 expedition of La Vérendrye's sons, the Chevalier de la Vérendrye and his brother François. The 1738 expedition did not go beyond the Missouri, but that of 1742–43 went to the Great Plains — how far west is uncertain. On its return to Fort La Reine it brought with it the first horses ever seen in the future province of Manitoba.[5]

[4] Holand, *Kensington Stone*, chapter 11; *Westward from Vinland*, chapter 20; *Explorations in America Before Columbus*, 261 (quote).
[5] Father Ant. Champagne to Robert C. Wheeler, MHS, June 30, 1962; a copy is in the Kensington file, Blegen Papers.

The distance from Montreal mentioned by Kalm — 900 French miles — points to a somewhat remote region. The French estimated 300 *lieues* (French miles) from Montreal to Michilimackinac and about 250 or 300 from that spot to Grand Portage on Lake Superior. The balance of the 900 miles must therefore have been from Grand Portage to the west. Father Champagne suggested northeastern Wyoming, east of the Big Horn Mountains, perhaps not very far from the present Pierre, South Dakota, as the site of the inscribed stone. It will be recalled that when the explorers returned to the Missouri from the west, they buried an inscribed plaque that was found in 1913 by a school child on a hill above Pierre, South Dakota. Father Champagne cogently suggested that the stone was taken east in 1744, after La Vérendrye had resigned from his position, and not in 1743, as Holand believed. It is known that in 1744 La Vérendrye also took with him some china beads that his sons had gathered. The beads were to be sent to Maurepas, presumably via the governor general.[6]

What was the exact size of the Vérendrye stone? Kalm referred to its length as about a French foot (*"en Fransk fot"*). This means a *pied*, or 12 *pouces*, each *pouce* equal to 1.066 inches. In a word, the length was close to 13 inches (12.79). The early English translation by John R. Forster gave the breadth of the stone as between four and five inches.[7] This probably was nearly correct, though the Swedish original did not mention inches. It used the phrase *"inemot af en hands bred,"* that is, about the breadth of a hand. We lack a scientific measurement of the stone, but one thing is certain: it was small, and this helps to explain the readiness of the Vérendryes to carry it back with them on the journey to Quebec.

The statement of the Jesuits in Quebec that they had found "rather many" of the markings on the Vérendrye stone "completely identical" with Tatarian symbols was based upon comparisons with illustrations in books which they had seen on Tataria.[8] These Jesuits undoubtedly

[6] Father Champagne to Wheeler, June 30, 1962. Father Champagne calls attention to the description of Prince Maximilian of Wied of places in the vicinity of White Clay Butte that resembled the area mentioned by Kalm. This was about two days' journey from Fort Pierre and near present-day Murdo, South Dakota, an area that the Vérendrye expedition passed through. See H. Evans Lloyd, trans., *Travels in the Interior of North America*, chapter 30 (London, 1843). On the plaque, see Bertha L. Heilbron, *The Thirty-Second State: A Pictorial History of Minnesota*, 9 (St. Paul, 1958).

[7] John R. Forster, trans., *Travels into North America* (London, 1771).

[8] Holand suggested that the Jesuits may have used a book by Philipp Johann von Strahlenberg, *Das Nord-und Östliche Theil von Europa und Asia*, pub-

were members of the faculty of a college or university maintained in Quebec, an institution where sciences such as mathematics, astronomy, hydrography, and medicine were taught. One of La Vérendrye's own sons, the Chevalier Louis-Joseph, had in fact been a student of mathematics and cartography there in 1734–35, just before he joined his father and brothers in the West.

That Kalm was genuinely interested in the Vérendrye stone is clear not only from his published book, but also from certain entries in his manuscript diary, only one volume of which has as yet appeared in print. They were supplied to the present writer by the distinguished Finnish scholar, Dr. Martti Kerkkonen of Helsinki, who is preparing a new edition of the diary. Thus on September 5, 1749, Kalm wrote that the Father Superior of the Jesuits had given him "a catalogue of the most common words in the numerous languages of the natives." This was supplied to him so that he could see whether or not there was any resemblance between Tataric and the Indian languages. Earlier (August 20, 1749) he spoke of the readiness of the Jesuits "to talk about the stone with its curious figures which had been found far to the west of Canada." One of the Jesuits who had been with Kalm on August 20, 1749, told of the stone having been removed from a larger stone which, it was believed, had been raised as a pillar. This priest said that he did not "know of any monuments which might indicate that Europeans had been here in earlier times." There was no mention in these additional diary entries of any tracing or copy of the inscriptions, and Kalm did not suggest any possible relationship of the "curious figures" to runic.[9]

Holand, eager to have the Vérendrye stone regarded as a runic inscription, wrote that its marks could not have been Indian pictographs. He rejected Tataric symbols because of the improbability that Tatars visited the American West. The Jesuits probably would not have confused marks of weathering with genuine incisions made by tools. And so Holand concluded that the writing must have been runic. But there are other possible hypotheses that he did not mention. It is known, for instance, that some stones with runelike markings actually carry traces

lished in German in Stockholm, 1730, with English translations in 1736 and 1738. The book included illustrations of Tataric, and Holand reproduced one in *Westward from Vinland*, 249.

[9] Kerkkonen to Blegen, September 12, 1964, Kensington file, Blegen Papers. The first volume of Kalm's diary, edited by Kerkkonen, was published in 1966 under the title, *Pehr Kalm: Resejournal över Resan till Norra Amerika* (*Skrifter utgivna av Svenska Litteratursäelskapet i Finland*–Helsingfors).

left by small prehistoric creatures. In some instances such markings, to a layman's eye, have seemed to resemble runic letters, though they do not mislead professional runologists. And there may be other languages that should not be ruled out in conjectures about the Vérendrye stone. In such an amorphous field, it is perilous to limit oneself, as Holand did, to a single hypothesis. In Holand's final book on the Kensington story he headed a chapter on the Vérendrye stone with the title "Another Runic Inscription." But he did not know that it was runic. Nor did anyone else.[10]

Did the stone reach France? There were hazards for sailing vessels in the eighteenth century, but most of the ships crossing from New France in peacetime did reach France. It is a tenable surmise that the Vérendrye stone got there, and the surmise is in fact the more tenable, as Father Champagne suggested, since Kalm was told that it probably was in the Maurepas *cabinette*.[11] Moreover, no recorded wreck is known to be related to the shipment from the governor general.

It is puzzling that nothing about the inscribed stone seems to have been recorded by La Vérendrye in his letters or reports, but it may have seemed to him a minor matter, a curiosity, not worth official notice at the very end of his service as a trader and officer. Although archival silence is disconcerting, there can be no doubt that Kalm was told about the stone by La Vérendrye and by the Jesuits, that the episode was recorded contemporaneously, and that there was such a stone.

It is surprising to learn that as early as 1858 Edward D. Neill, a pioneer Minnesota historian, commented on the Vérendrye stone, which he thought probably was an Indian pictograph, though he took note of the point that the inscription was thought to be "Tartarean." Neill's mention of the stone was known to members of the Minnesota Historical Society's executive council when, in 1909, they began to interest themselves in the Kensington inscription. The council initiated a search in France for the lost stone by formulating a resolution, requesting the governor of Minnesota to enlist the aid of the American ambassador in a search of the French archives for the Vérendrye stone. Warren Upham wrote to Governor Adolph O. Eberhart late in 1909 and again in the summer of 1910, and the governor seems to have made some effort to reach Ambassador Robert Bacon. Nothing came of the move, however. In 1910 the society's museum committee, in its report on the Kensington inscription, spoke of the Vérendrye stone, of Peter Kalm,

[10] Holand, *Pre-Columbian Crusade*, 180–184.
[11] Father Champagne to Wheeler, June 30, 1962.

and even of the theory that the Mandan Indians had European blood, but it made no further allusion to a search for the stone.[12]

Possibly the committee's inaction related to the fact that in 1911 Holand took the Kensington stone to Rouen, France, where he appealed for French help in finding the Vérendrye stone — "another runestone," he was reported to have said. Holand, meanwhile, had turned to Senator Knute Nelson and to Jean J. Jusserand, the French ambassador to the United States, for aid, and as a consequence the French colonial minister assigned a secretary to guide Holand to various museums in Paris. After a week, he found himself "pretty well fed up with Paris," and he left for further travels in Germany and the Scandinavian countries.[13]

In 1935, when I was superintendent of the Minnesota Historical Society, I bought on behalf of the society a Swedish original of Kalm's three-volume *En resa til Norra America,* and earlier I had asked Waldo G. Leland, the archivist who was surveying American historical materials in Parisian archives, to look for correspondence about the Vérendrye stone. He found nothing, and there is no reference to the stone in his published *Guide to Materials for American History in the Archives and Libraries of Paris.* About the same time I wrote Jesuit scholars in Canada, hoping that their early predecessors had made copies of the Vérendrye inscription which, possibly, had been preserved. The hope was a forlorn one, for if the Jesuits had made a copy or copies, they very likely would have informed Kalm and he in turn no doubt would have recorded the fact in his diary. Before World War II, I engaged Arne O. Johnsen, a scholar from Oslo who had worked much in French records, to make a new hunt for the stone in French museums. He surveyed some thirteen institutions before World War II ended his quest. Again the results were negative. In the meantime Grace Lee Nute, widely known for her scholarly studies of French exploration, took an interest in the Vérendrye stone, searched for it in France, and sought to enlist others in the hunt.[14]

[12] Neill, *The History of Minnesota: From the Earliest French Explorations to the Present Time,* 187 (Philadelphia, 1858); MHS Executive Council Minutes, December 13, 1909; correspondence and letter books, Eberhart Papers, in Minnesota State Archives; Museum Committee, in *Minnesota Historical Collections,* 15:267, 283.

[13] Holand, *My First Eighty Years,* illustration opposite p. 200, 206. See also Holand, "The Kensington Rune Stone Abroad," in *Records of the Past,* 10:260–271 (September–October, 1911).

[14] The Leland *Guide* appeared in two volumes (Washington, 1932, 1946). I am indebted to Miss Nute for helpful suggestions in a letter of May 21, 1962, Blegen Papers.

During and after World War II, occasional rumors about the Vérendrye stone were heard. One came to me from an American officer who wrote that a friend, a Catholic priest, had heard a story about the stone. It had been removed (from where was not stated) to a French port town, exhibited in a museum, and during the war the place where it was kept was bombed. The priest said that his information was secondhand. Holand wrote me in a letter of May 24, 1962, a long and circumstantial account of a small inscribed stone that had been stored by a museum in an adjacent building that was destroyed by a bomb. His story placed the episode in Rouen.[15]

Such rumors, unconfirmed, led me to suggest to the Minnesota Historical Society in 1962 that a new search should be made, with a reward offered for information leading to the discovery of the stone. The society promptly responded by offering a reward of a thousand dollars and giving the proposal wide circulation in France. Thus far no one has claimed the reward. The chances of success may be slight, but a search should go on as long as there is no conclusive evidence that the stone has been destroyed or irretrievably lost.

[15] My correspondence, in 1953, was with Professor Rodney C. Loehr of the University of Minnesota and the Reverend John P. Dolan; see Blegen Papers. Holand's letter is in the Kensington file, Blegen Papers.

À Note on Manuscript Sources

Although the manuscripts used in this book are cited in detail in the preceding chapters and some are printed either in the text or in the appendix, readers may wish to have a general conspectus.

One of the sources used extensively is the archives of the Minnesota Historical Society — the society's own records. These are cataloged in the following distinct units.

1. The Kensington Rune Stone Collection (1919–65) consists of correspondence and newspaper clippings isolated as a separate group by the manuscripts department. In this group are a few letters relating to the story of the purchase of a chisel or chisels supposedly used in the cutting of the Kensington inscription. Two letters of special significance are from Mrs. Arthur Nelson of Seattle, Washington, July 14, 1955, to F. Sanford Cutler, curator of the society's museum, and from Mrs. W. W. Christopherson of Kenyon, Minnesota, to Mr. Cutler, November 17, 1955. Mrs. Nelson and Mrs. Christopherson were cousins, granddaughters of Moses D. Fredenberg of Alexandria, who, according to the story, sold the chisel or chisels to two Swedes from "out of town."

2. Archaeological Records. Much material relating to the Kensington rune stone is in box 10 (1906–13). It consists chiefly of papers collected by Newton H. Winchell for the period from 1908 to 1913 — letters from Gisle Bothne, George O. Curme, A. Louis Elmquist, George T. Flom, John P. Hedberg, Knut O. Hoegh, P. P. Iverslie, Henrik Nissen, M.A. Nordstrom, O. A. Normann, Warren Upham, Cleve W. Van Dyke, and others. There are numerous letters and extensive notes by Hjalmar R. Holand (with copies of some of Winchell's replies).

The papers also include a bill of sale of the Kensington stone by Olof Ohman to the Minnesota Historical Society, April 19, 1911; several English translations of articles written in Norwegian; a translation of an important letter from Norwegian runologist Magnus Olsen, dated March 28, 1910, in which he advised the society "not to expend too much time and energy" on an inscription "entirely worthless" from a philological standpoint; and a preliminary draft by Winchell of the

179

report of the society's museum committee. A twenty-four-page letter of March 19, 1910, by Chester N. Gould to Upham is really a carefully written essay on the Kensington inscription which the committee neither used nor published.

The minutes of the museum committee's meetings for February 15, July 23, and August 18, 1910, are in this file, as well as a letter from Upham to Winchell reporting resolutions adopted by the committee on April 21, 1910, and published in the committee's report. Also in this group of papers is a notebook (1897–1900) of Jacob V. Brower containing the minutes of the museum committee's meeting held on October 23, 1912.

Three items from this file are kept on reserve. They are Hedberg's letter of January 1, 1899, to Swan J. Turnblad of Minneapolis, Olaus J. Breda's English translation of the Kensington inscription, and a copy (or possibly a draft) of the inscription.

3. The society's Correspondence File is rich in Kensington materials, especially for the period from 1908 to 1913. For the most part the letters about the Kensington stone are addressed to Upham, secretary of the society and also of the museum committee. There are many letters from Holand, particularly in 1910 and 1911, some from Dr. Hoegh in 1909 and 1910, a few from Ole E. Hagen, and a handwritten card (received April 4, 1910) from the Swedish linguist, Otto von Friesen. Other names that figure in the correspondence are Bothne, Breda, Flom, Andrew A. Fossum, Gould, and Judge Andrew Grindeland, who wrote about the fraudulent fossil man. One of the most important letters is that of Olof Ohman to Upham, written on December 9, 1909, with Ohman's drawing of the tree and stone.

The names that occur in the society's incoming letters appear frequently also in another segment of the correspondence files — the voluminous letter press books kept by Upham. Volumes 15 and 16, covering the period from December 2, 1909, to November 19, 1911, are especially important in the Kensington record, for here are copies of the many letters that Upham wrote to persons abroad and in this country about the Kensington inscription. The books also contain copies of his replies. His notices of meetings of the museum committee and occasional minutes enable us, with the aid of other sources, to fill out the chronology of the committee's meetings on the Kensington problem.

4. The Warren Upham Papers, box 12, of the Minnesota Historical Society's Archives contain a folder (1909–11) of miscellaneous materials and many tightly written annual notebooks kept by him. Most important in reference to the Kensington stone is the notebook for 1910, in which Upham tells of interviews held on March 4, April 28, and 29 in Madison, Wisconsin, with Julius E. Olson. The folder includes the text of the address given by Winchell at the meeting of the executive council of the society on December 13, 1909; typewritten copies, supplied by Holand,

of three of the affidavits dated July 20, 1909 and a draft copy of a report by the museum committee to the society's executive council, February 14, 1910, which states that the committee had already held two meetings.

5. The minutes of at least eleven meetings of the museum committee are scattered about in several groups of papers in the society's archives. As has been noted, a report to the executive council, (Upham Papers, box 12), made on February 14, 1910, refers to two earlier meetings of the committee. Upham's letter press books show that the committee met on December 16, 1909, and on January 14, 1910 (a letter from Upham to Olin D. Wheeler of January 15 reviews the meeting and reports that Holand had made the "astonishing proposition" that the society should pay him $5,000 to acquire the stone). A meeting was called for February 8, 1910, but no minutes have been found. The committee met on February 14, 1910, as Upham reported to the chairman on the fifteenth, and the minutes of the meeting on February 15, 1910, are in the archaeological records. The meeting of April 21, 1910, is referred to in the Upham letter book of that date. Minutes for July 23, 1910, are in the archaeological records and also in letter press volume 15 (p. 744). Other minutes exist for meetings on August 18, 1910 (archaeological records); February 7, April 13, September 7, 1911 (letter press books). The latter contain no allusions to the Kensington stone, but those for October 23, 1912 (in the Jacob V. Brower notebook mentioned earlier) do refer to the subject.

6. The minutes of the executive council of the Minnesota Historical Society are preserved in the office of the director. Of greatest interest are those of a meeting held on May 9, 1910, at which "the Council and Society" reserved "their conclusion until more light may be received on this subject" — that is, on the Kensington rune stone. It was this action that was changed in the published report to read: "until more agreement of opinions for or against the runic inscription may be attained."

In addition to its own archives, the society's manuscripts department has several groups of papers bearing on the Kensington rune stone. Among them are the Newton H. Winchell Papers, which contain a field book (volume 59) kept by Winchell recording his trips to the Kensington area on November 29–December 2, 1909, and March 3–5, 17–19, 1910. The text of the field book is printed in Appendix 8.

Another valuable group consists of the papers of Johan A. Holvik (1880–1960) for many years a professor at Concordia College, Moorhead. Holvik took an early interest in the Kensington stone. In his later years the subject engrossed his attention. He was an indefatigable collector of clippings and typewritten (or handwritten) copies of newspaper reports (as far back as 1899), articles, and materials that related in any way to the Kensington story.

The Holvik correspondence is arranged chronologically from 1921 to

1960 and includes copies of not a few of his own letters for the period of his greatest activity from about 1948 to 1955. His correspondence was wide and vigorous, and he evidently preserved everything that had to do with the Kensington question. There are many letters from such Norwegian, Swedish, and Danish linguists as Anton M. Brøgger, Sven B. F. Jansson, and Erik Moltke. Other correspondents include Holand, Erik Wahlgren, Frederick J. Pohl, Paul Knaplund of the University of Wisconsin, Henry H. Hendrickson, Dr. S. C. Shipstead, and Olof Ohman and his son and daughter Edward and Manda.

In addition to the correspondence is a subject file (four boxes) which contains notes and drafts of articles by Holvik, material copied from the Fogelblad-Ohman scrapbook, and copies of parts of certain books belonging to Ohman, as well as a number of photographs.

The Fogelblad-Ohman scrapbook is preserved on microfilm as are pages from Ohman's books relating to runes. The society also has a tape recording of an interview with Edward Ohman conducted by Lucile M. Kane and others on December 28, 1949.

The society's collection of Gisle Bothne Papers contains one very interesting and important document — the original handwritten letter by Frederick Jackson Turner dated February 10, 1910. Since Bothne served as a member of the investigating committee of the Norwegian Society of Minneapolis in 1909 and visited Kensington in 1910 for the museum committee of the Minnesota Historical Society, one might have expected to find notebooks or other records relating to the Kensington stone. But the only Kensington item is the Turner letter.

The correspondence of Andrew A. Veblen for 1928 includes maps, notes, correspondence, and clippings on the Kensington stone. Of major interest is an interchange of letters between Veblen and Johan Schröder having to do with Sven Fogelblad, with whom Schröder was well acquainted in the early 1880s. There is also an interesting letter from A. Frithiof Malmquist of Chicago to Schröder and a folder of clippings. A letter from Veblen to Knud Wefald, April 12, 1929, is in the society's Knud Wefald Papers.

The Minnesota Manuscript Census Schedules, housed in the Minnesota State Archives, St. Paul, were consulted for the years from 1875 to 1905. They are of value for detail on Olof Ohman's family in 1895 and 1905, and for data on other persons involved in the story who lived in or near Kensington.

The materials collected by the author in the preparation of this book form a Kensington file in the Blegen Papers in the manuscripts division of the Minnesota Historical Society. The file includes correspondence with Professor O. Fritiof Ander of Augustana College who was in Sweden in 1966 and there conducted an extensive and very successful hunt for information on the Swedish background of Sven Fogelblad.

Mr. Ander's many letters, written mainly from Uppsala and Stockholm in April and May, 1966, made a large contribution to the revised interpretation of Fogelblad presented in this book. His letters provide citations to the Swedish sources for this information. The file also contains a copy provided by Mr. Ander of a previously unknown article by Fogelblad in *Upplysningens Tidehvarf*.

The Kensington file in the Blegen Papers includes several letters and other materials relating to Peter Kalm received from the noted Finnish archivist, Dr. Martti Kerkkonen of Helsinki; there is also a letter of June 30, 1962, with an accompanying map, from Father Ant. Champagne of St. Boniface, Manitoba, to Robert C. Wheeler, and a six-page handwritten letter from Holand to Blegen, May 24, 1962, on the Vérendrye stone.

Folders of material on Ole E. Hagen include letters, notes, and documents from Donald N. Meeks, a graduate student at the University of South Dakota, and from Professors Cedric Cummins and Herbert S. Schell of the same university, as well as copies of several letters by former students of Hagen. A series of letters from the Norwegian archivist Asgaut Steinnes to Birger Osland of Chicago in 1956 and 1957 is supplemented by two letters from Holand to Steinnes. Other manuscripts in the file include scattered letters from Holand to Blegen, and a facsimile of John F. Steward's letter of October 15, 1899, to the Danish runologist L. F. A. Wimmer. Copies of the four photographs of the rune stone that Steward sent to Wimmer are preserved in the society's picture collection. The originals are in the Royal Library in Copenhagen, Denmark.

The affidavit of Victor Setterlund of Elbow Lake, Minnesota, dated May 9, 1965, has to do with a cheerfully acknowledged runic hoax by Mr. Setterlund. With his affidavit are several letters from William M. Goetzinger, also of Elbow Lake, and a letter of December 22, 1961, from Holand to Mr. Goetzinger about the so-called Elbow Lake stone.

In the Kensington file are carbons of many letters written by the author in a long-continued search for the papers of Breda, Curme, Hagen, Hedberg, Hoegh, J. K. Nordwall, F. Nosander, Samuel A. Siverts, Steward, Turnblad, H. M. Wagner, and others. Three of these men are but names attached to newspaper letters; their personal identifications remain a mystery. Though the search for papers of Samuel Siverts proved unsuccessful, the file contains several letters from his son Ingvald T. Siverts of Morris, Minnesota, in 1964 and 1967. Professor Ingrid Semmingsen of the University of Oslo made a search in Norway for the papers of O. J. Breda. She succeeded in finding three very interesting letters written by him from Minneapolis in 1886 and 1887 and now preserved in the library of the University of Oslo. But she found none from the Kensington period, and the Breda papers as such, if they have survived, have not been located. In some instances — a scrapbook kept by Hedberg, a letter book of Siverts — success in the hunt seemed for a time to be near at hand, but the documents remain undiscovered. It is the writer's hope that his letters and the replies they elicited will prove helpful as clues for others who may take up the hunt in the future.

T.C.B.

Bibliography

PRINTED WORKS ON THE KENSINGTON STONE
AND ITS BACKGROUND

Compiled by Michael Brook

THIS BIBLIOGRAPHY aspires only to reasonable completeness on the Kensington stone. To have listed every printed reference to the topic would have produced great bulk and little usefulness. Thus the sections dealing with the linguistic background and the Scandinavian discovery of America are indicative only of the literature on these subjects and are included to offer a starting point for readers who wish to continue their explorations of these complex fields.

On the Kensington stone itself, efforts have been made to include major discussions both in English and in foreign-language publications. However, only a few book reviews of more than usual significance have been listed, and routine newspaper stories, mentions in textbooks and similar references do not find a place here. In attempting to deal with the voluminous newspaper coverage of the stone, emphasis has been given to stories, interviews, articles, and letters dealing with its finding and with early interpretations of its inscriptions. Only a sampling is offered of contributions to the later stages of the controversy, which has raged perhaps even more fiercely and at greater length in the Norwegian and Swedish immigrant newspapers than in the English-language press.

My thanks are due to Theodore C. Blegen, author of this book, and to June Drenning Holmquist, the society's managing editor, for guidance on the darkling plain of Kensington rune-stone bibliography, and to my colleagues in the library of the Minnesota Historical Society, especially James Taylor Dunn and Patricia C. Harpole, for enabling me to devote the necessary time to its compilation. For help with individual bibliographical problems I am grateful to the following librarians: Miss Marguerite Christensen, University of Wisconsin; Mrs. M. A. Gargotta,

Italian Cultural Institute; Miss Margaret Gleason, State Historical Society of Wisconsin; Mr. George F. Heise, H. W. Wilson Company; Mr. Andrew Y. Kuroda, Library of Congress; and Mrs. Caroline T. Spicer, Cornell University.

THE LINGUISTIC AND RUNIC BACKGROUND

Agrell, Sigurd. *Runornas talmystik och dess antika förebild.* ("Skrifter utgivna av Vetenskaps-Societeten i Lund," 6). Lund: C. W. K. Gleerup, 1927.
Almquist, Carl J. L. *Svensk språklära: Tredje upplagan, öfversedd och tillökad med samlingar öfver tio svenska landskapsdialekter.* Stockholm: Högbergska boktryckeriet, 1840. På M. Wirsells förlag. Sven Fogelblad's copy is in the MHS library.
Bæksted, Anders. *Målruner og troldruner: Runemagiske studier.* ("Nationalmuseets Skrifter, Arkæologisk-Historisk Række," IV). Copenhagen: Gyldendalske boghandel, Nordisk forlag, 1952.
Bugge, Sophus, ed. *Norges indskrifter med de ældre runer.* Christiania: A. W. Brøggers bogtrykkeri, 1891–1924. 4 vols.
"Chips from Scandinavian History. XXI. Runes," in *North* (Minneapolis), January 20, 1892, p. 5.
Friesen, Otto von, ed. *Runorna.* ("Nordisk Kultur," VI). Stockholm: Albert Bonniers förlag, 1933.
Gould, Chester N. "Gematria," in *Modern Language Notes,* 45:465–468 (November, 1930).
Gram, J. S. "Runes," in *Scandinavia* (Chicago), 2:267–271 (November, 1885).
Hægstad, Marius. *Gamalt Trøndermaal: Upplysningar um maalet i Trøndelag fyrr 1350 og ei utgreiding um vokalverket.* Christiania: I kommission hos Jacob Dybwad, 1899.
Jacobsen, Lis and Erik Moltke. *Danmarks runeindskrifter.* Copenhagen: E. Munksgaard, 1941–1942. 3 vols.
Jansson, Sven B. F. *The Runes of Sweden.* Stockholm: P. A. Norstedt & Söners förlag, 1962.
Kongelige bibliotek, Copenhagen. *Collectio runologica Wimmeriana: Fortegnelse over Ludv. F. A. Wimmers runologiske o. a. samlinger.* Copenhagen: H. H. Thieles bogtrykkeri, 1915.
Krause, Wolfgang. "Runen in Amerika," in *Germanien* (Leipzig), 8:231–236 (August, 1937).
Ljungström, Claes J. *Rúna-list eller Konsten att läsa runor, folkskolorna och menige man meddelad.* Lund: Tryckt uti Berlingska boktryckeriet, 1866. 2nd ed., 1875.

Rosander, Carl. *Den kunskapsrike skolmästaren, eller Hufvudgrund-erna uti de för ett borgerligt samfundslif nödigaste vetenskaper.* Ny, genomsedd upplaga. Stockholm: Albert Bonniers förlag, 1882. Olof Ohman's copy was of this edition. A third edition was published in Chicago by the Swedish American Printing Co., 1893.

Stephens, George. *The Old-Northern Runic Monuments of Scandinavia and England, Now First Collected and Deciphered,* London: John Russell Smith. Copenhagen: Michaelsen and Tillge, 1866–1901. 4 vols.

Wimmer, Ludvig F. A., ed. *De danske runemindesmærker.* Copenhagen: Gyldendalske boghandel, Nordisk forlag, 1893–1908. 4 vols. (in 6).

—— *Runeskriftens oprindelse og udvikling i Norden.* Copenhagen: V. Priors boghandel, 1874.

VINLAND AND THE SCANDINAVIAN DISCOVERY OF AMERICA—
Books and Pamphlets

Anderson, Rasmus B. *America Not Discovered by Columbus: A Historical Sketch of the Discovery of America by the Norsemen, in the Tenth Century.* Chicago: S. G. Griggs and Co. London: Trübner & Co., 1874.

Brøgger, Anton W. *Vinlandsferdene.* Oslo: Gyldendal norsk forlag, 1937.

De Costa, Benjamin F. *The Pre-Columbian Discovery of America by the Northmen, Illustrated by Translations from the Icelandic Sagas.* Albany, N.Y.: Joel Munsell, 1868. 2nd and 3rd editions, 1890 and 1901.

Enander, Johan A. *Nordmännen i Amerika, eller Amerikas upptäckt: Historisk afhandling med anledning af columbifesterna i Chicago, 1892–1893.* Rock Island, Ill.: Lutheran Augustana Book Concern, 1893.

Fossum, Andrew. *The Norse Discovery of America.* Minneapolis: Augsburg Publishing House, 1918.

Hagen, Ole E. *Nogle ord om Vinlandsforskningen.* Madison, Wis.: 1908. Reprinted from *Amerika,* June 26, 1908.

Haugen, Einar I., ed. and tr. *Voyages to Vinland: The First American Saga.* Chicago: Holiday Press, 1941. Reissued, somewhat rearranged, as *Voyages to Vinland: The First American Saga.* New York: Alfred A. Knopf, 1942.

Hovgaard, William. *The Voyages of the Norsemen to America.* New York: American-Scandinavian Foundation, 1914.

Ingstad, Helge. *Landet under leidarstjernen: En ferd til Grønlands norrøne bygder.* Oslo: Gyldendal norsk forlag, 1960. Translated as

Land under the Pole Star: A Voyage to the Norse Settlements of Greenland, and the Saga of the People that Vanished. New York: St. Martin's Press, 1966.

—— *Vesterveg til Vinland: Oppdagelsen av norrøne boplasser i Nord-Amerika.* Oslo: Gyldendal norsk forlag, 1965.

Jones, Gwyn. *The Norse Atlantic Saga: Being the Norse Voyages of Discovery and Settlement to Iceland, Greenland, America.* London: Oxford University Press, 1964.

Magnússon, Finnur and Carl C. Rafn, eds. *Grönlands historiske mindesmærker, udgivne af det Kongelige Nordiske Oldskrift-Selskab.* Copenhagen: Trykt i det Brünnichske bogtrykkeri, 1838–45. 3 vols.

Musmanno, Michael A. *Columbus WAS First.* New York: Fountainhead Publishers, 1966.

Oleson, Tryggvi J. *Early Voyages and Northern Approaches, 1000–1632.* ("Canadian Centenary Series"). London and New York: Oxford University Press, 1964.

Olson, Julius E., ed. *The Northmen: Columbus and Cabot, 985–1503.* ("Original Narratives of Early American History"). New York: Charles Scribner's Sons, 1906. "The Voyages of the Northmen," pp. 3–74.

—— *Leif Erikson og Amerikas opdagelse: Foredrag holdt ved "Sønner af Norge"s Leif Erikson fest paa Normanna Hall, Minneapolis, den 11te November 1906.* Madison, Wis.: 1906. Offprint from *Minneapolis Tidende,* November 16, 1906.

Rafn, Carl C. *Antiquitates Americanae, sive Scriptores septentrionales rerum ante-Columbianarum in America.* Copenhagen: Typis officinae schultzianae, 1837–1845. 2 vols., and *Supplement,* 1841.

Shipley, John B. and Marie A. (Brown) Shipley. *The English Rediscovery and Colonization of America.* London: Elliot Stock, [1891]. A collection of papers on the general theme of the pre-Columbian discovery of America.

Shipley, Marie A. (Brown). *The Icelandic Discoverers of America: Or, Honour to Whom Honour is Due.* London: The Author, 1887.

Skelton, Raleigh A., Thomas E. Marston, and George D. Painter. *The Vinland Map and the Tartar Relation.* New Haven, Conn.: Yale University Press, 1965.

Strandwold, Olaf. *Runic Rock Inscriptions Along the American Atlantic Seaboard.* [Prosser, Wash.: The Author?], 1939.

VINLAND AND THE SCANDINAVIAN DISCOVERY OF AMERICA—
Periodical and Newspaper Articles

Babcock, William H. "Recent History and Present Status of the Vinland Problem," in *Geographical Review,* 11:265–282 (April, 1921).

Breda, Olaus J. "Hurrah for the Vikings!" a letter in *North* (Minneapolis), November 13, 1889, p. 1.

Brøgger, Anton W. "Vinlandsferdene," in *Norsk Geografisk Tidsskrift* (Oslo), 6:65–85 (1936). Translated as "The Vinland Voyages: Lecture in the Norwegian Geographical Society," in *American-Scandinavian Review*, 24:[197]–215 (September, 1936).

Dieserud, Juul. "Norse Discoveries in America," in American Geographical Society of New York, *Bulletin*, 33:[1]–18 (1901).

Hagen, Ole E. "Nogle ord om Vinlands-forskningen," in *Amerika*, June 26, 1908, pp. 10–13. Reprinted as a pamphlet.

Hermansson, Halldór. "The Northmen in America (982–c. 1500): A Contribution to the Bibliography of the Subject," in *Islandica*, vol. 2 (1909).

[Holand,] Hjalmar Rued. "En Bauta for Leif," a letter in *Skandinaven* (semiweekly, Chicago), March 15, 1899, p. 9.

Ingstad, Helge. "Vinland Ruins Prove Vikings Found the New World," in *National Geographic*, 126:708–734 (November, 1964).

Lendin, Waldemar. "Vinlandsproblemet: En Översikt över nyare litteratur rörande källorna," in *Historisk Tidskrift* (Stockholm), 71:322–338 (1951).

Lowther, G. R. "The Vikings in North America," in *Listener* (London), 77:321–322 (March 9, 1967).

Oleson, T[ryggvi] J. "The Vikings in America," in Canadian Historical Association, *Report of the Annual Meeting . . . 1954*, pp. 52–60 [1954?]. In the table of contents this article is entitled "The Vikings in America: Some Problems and Recent Literature."

——— "The Vikings in America: A Critical Bibliography," in *Canadian Historical Review*, 36:166–173 (June, 1955).

Olson, Julius E. "Present Aspects of the Vinland Controversy," in Society for the Advancement of Scandinavian Study, *Proceedings*, 1:147–156 (1913).

Shipley, John B. "The Vinland Sagas and Their Critics," in *North* (Minneapolis), December 24, 1890, p. 3.

——— and Marie A. Shipley. "Proposed Historical Exhibit. To Become a Permanent Museum for the City of Chicago," in *North* (Minneapolis), January 28, 1891, p. 5. This page is erroneously dated 1889.

Storm, Gustav. "Studier over Vinlandsreiserne, Vinlands geografi og ethnografi," in *Aarbøger for Nordisk Oldkyndighed og Historie* (Copenhagen), second series 2:[293]–372 (1887).

Swanton, John R. *The Wineland Voyages*, "Smithsonian Miscellaneous Collections," vol. 107, no. 12 (December 15, 1947). 81 pp.

"A Viking Ship Model," in *North* (Minneapolis), November 13, 1889, p. 4. Editorial.

"The Viking Ship Model," in *North* (Minneapolis), November 26, 1890, p. 4. Editorial.

Wallace, William S. "The Literature Relating to the Norse Voyages to America," in *Canadian Historical Review*, 20:8–16 (March, 1939).

THE KENSINGTON RUNE STONE—*Books and Pamphlets*

Alexandria (Minnesota) Kiwanis Club, Runestone Replica Committee. *Souvenir Booklet of the Runestone Replica Dedication.* Alexandria: 1951.

Blegen, Theodore C. "O. E. Hagen, A Pioneer Norwegian-American Scholar," in J. Iverne Dowie and J. Thomas Tredway, eds., *The Immigration of Ideas: Studies in the North Atlantic Community.* Rock Island, Ill.: Augustana Historical Society, 1968, pp. 43–65.

Boland, Charles M. *They All Discovered America.* Garden City, N.Y.: Doubleday & Co., 1961. "Paul Knutson," pp. [301]–324.

Christensen, Thomas P. *The Discovery and Re-Discovery of America.* Cedar Rapids, Ia.: Laurance Press Co., 1934. "The Kensington Rune Stone," pp. 70–80.

Coatsworth, Elizabeth. *Door to the North: A Saga of Fourteenth Century America.* Philadelphia: John C. Winston Co., 1950. A novel.

Curran, James W. *Here Was Vinland: The Great Lakes Region of America.* Sault Ste. Marie, Ont.: *Sault Daily Star*, [1939]. "Did Knutson Use Albany River?" pp. 254–257. Reprinted from *Sault Daily Star*, October 22, 1938.

Flom, George T. *The Kensington Rune-Stone. An Address . . . Delivered before the Illinois State Historical Society at its Annual Meeting, May 5–6, 1910 at Springfield, Illinois.* [Springfield: Illinois State Historical Society, 1910]. Cover title: *The Kensington Rune-Stone: A Modern Inscription from Douglas County, Minnesota.*

——— "The Kensington Rune Stone: A Modern Inscription from Douglas County, Minnesota," in Illinois State Historical Society, *Transactions*, 1910. Springfield: vol. published 1912, pp. 105–125. The appendix contains a paragraph not present in the previous entry. This volume is also described as Publication No. 15 of the Illinois State Historical Library.

Hennig, Richard. *Terrae Incognitae: Eine Zusammenstellung und kritische Bewertung der wichtigsten vorcolumbischen Entdeckungsreisen an Hand der därüber vorliegenden Originalberichte.* Leiden, Neth.: E. J. Brill, 1938. "Eine Normannen-Expedition ins Innere Nordamerika und das Rätsel des Runensteins von Kensington," vol. 3, pp. 268–299; 1953 edition, vol. 3, pp. 324–373.

Henry, Thomas R. "The Riddle of the Kensington Stone," in John Gehlmann, ed., *The Challenge of Ideas: An Essay Reader.* New York: Odyssey Press, 1950, pp. 45–56.

Herrmann, Paul. *Sieben vorbei und Acht verweit*. Hamburg: Hoffmann und Campe Verlag, 1952. "Der Runenstein von Kensington und das Rätsel der Grönland-Wikinger," pp. 255–320.

—— *Conquest by Man: The Saga of Early Exploration and Discovery*. London: Hamish Hamilton, 1954. "The Rune Stone of Kensington and the Mystery of the Greenland Vikings," pp. 217–266. A translation of the previous entry.

Hjelmeseth, Eilert. *Vinlands gaaten: Historisk roman*. Chicago: Skandinaven, John Anderson Publishing Co., 1934. A novel.

Holand, Hjalmar R. *America, 1355–1364: A New Chapter in Pre-Columbian History*. New York: Duell, Sloan & Pearce, 1946.

—— *Explorations in America Before Columbus*. New York: Twayne Publishers, 1956.

—— *A Holy Mission to Minnesota 600 Years Ago*. Alexandria, Minn.: Park Region Publishing Co., 1959.

—— *The Kensington Stone: A Study in Pre-Columbian American History*. Ephraim, Wis.: Privately printed, 1932.

—— *My First Eighty Years*. New York: Twayne Publishers, 1957.

—— *De norske settlementers historie*. Ephraim, Wis.: Forfatterens forlag, 1908.

—— *A Pre-Columbian Crusade to America*. New York: Twayne Publishers, 1962.

—— "Stones that Speak," in Vincent A. Yzermans, ed., *Catholic Origins of Minnesota*. [St. Paul?]: Minnesota Fourth Degree Knights of Columbus, 1961, pp. [14–20].

—— *Westward from Vinland: An Account of Norse Discoveries and Explorations in America, 982–1362*. New York: Duell, Sloan & Pearce, 1940.

Holman, William P. *Kensington Runestone Roll of Honor*. Alexandria, Minn.: The Author, 1966.

Izui, Hisanosuke. "[Inscription Indicative of 14th Century (Pre-Columbian) Riverine Traffic in North America and of Contact With North America: The Kensington Runic Stone]" in [*Essays on Linguistics and Folklore in Honor of Dr. Kindaichi's 70th Birthday*]. Tokyo: Sanseidō, 1953, pp. 827–844. The article is in Japanese.

Jensen, Arne H. *Den dansk-amerikanske historie: En udførlig skildring af de danske udvandrere til Amerika fra tidligste tid til vore dage*. Copenhagen: Arthur Jensens forlag, 1937, pp. 13–14.

Landsverk, Ole G. *The Kensington Runestone: A Reappraisal of the Circumstances under which the Stone was Discovered*. Glendale, Calif.: Church Press, 1961. Cover title: *The Discovery of the Kensington Runestone: A Reappraisal*.

Larson, Constant. *History of Douglas and Grant Counties, Minnesota: Their People, Industries and Institutions*. Indianapolis: B. F.

Bowen & Co., 1916. "The Kensington Rune Stone: An Ancient Tragedy," vol. 1, pp. 72–122.
—— The Story of the Kensington Runestone. [Alexandria, Minn.: Alexandria Chamber of Commerce?, 1938].
Lechler, Jörg. Die Entdecker Amerikas vor Columbus. Leipzig: Curt Kabitzsch, 1939, pp. 51–56.
[Leuthner, Margaret]. Mystery of the Runestone. Alexandria, Minn.: Park Region Publishing Co., 1962. Cartoons.
MacDougall, Curtis D. Hoaxes. New York: Dover Publications, 1958, pp. 109–111.
Magidovich, I. P. Istoriiā otkrytiiā i issledovaniiā Severnoĭ Ameriki. Moscow: Gosudarstvennoe Izdatel'stvo Geograficheskoĭ Literatury, 1962. "Zagadka 'Kensingtonskogo runicheskogo kamiiā,'" pp. 39–46.
Mallery, Arlington H. Lost America: The Story of Iron-Age Civilization Prior to Columbus. Columbus, O. and Washington, D.C.: Overlook Co., [1951]. "The Kensington Rune Stone," pp. 176–181.
Merling, Bert. The Runestone Pageant Play. [Alexandria?, Minn., 1962?]. Duplicated typescript.
Minnesota Historical Society. "The Kensington Rune Stone: A Scrapbook of Clippings." St. Paul: 1910–1968, 2 vols. Abbreviated hereafter as MHS "Scrapbook."
—— Museum Committee. The Kensington Rune Stone: Preliminary Report. St. Paul: Volkszeitung Co., 1910.
—— Museum Committee. "The Kensington Rune Stone: Preliminary Report," in Minnesota Historical Collections. St. Paul: Minnesota Historical Society, 1915, vol. 15, pp. [221]–286. This version contains a brief "Note" not present in the previous entry.
—— Museum Committee. The Kensington Rune Stone: Preliminary Report. St. Paul: Volkszeitung Co., 1915. Offprint of previous entry.
Mongé, Alf and O[le] G. Landsverk. Norse Medieval Cryptography in Runic Carvings. Glendale, Calif.: Norseman Press, 1967.
Montelius, Oscar. Sveriges hednatid samt medeltid, förra skedet, från år 1060 till år 1350 (Sveriges historia från äldsta tid till våra dagar, vol. 1). Issued with Svenska Amerikanska Posten, November 16, 1897–February 15, 1898. First published by Hjalmar Linnströms förlag, Stockholm, 1877.
Noreen, Adolf. Spridda studier: Tredje samlingen: Populära uppsatser. Stockholm: Aktiebolaget Ljus, 1913. "Runinskrifter från nyare tid," pp. [48]–57. Previously appeared in Föreningen Heimdals Populärvetenskapliga Tidningsartiklar (Stockholm?), No. 6 (1906).
Noreen, Erik. Svensk stilparodi och andra litterära och språkliga uppsatser. Stockholm: Bokförlaget Natur och Kultur, 1944. "Amerikanska runor," pp. [75]–82.
Nykl, A. R. KRS: The Death of a Myth. Madison, Wis.: [Privately printed?], 1955.

Oleson, Tryggvi J. *The Norsemen in America*. ("Canadian Historical Association Booklet," No. 14). Ottawa: [The Association], 1963, pp. 17–18.

Peterson, Clarence S. *America's Rune Stone of A.D. 1362 Gains Favor*. New York: Hobson Book Press, 1946.

—— *The Kensington Runic Stone Gains Favor*. Baltimore: [The Author, 1945]. Duplicated typescript.

Pohl, Frederick J. *Atlantic Crossings Before Columbus*. New York: W. W. Norton & Co., 1961. "Kensington Runestone," pp. 208–226.

—— *The Lost Discovery: Uncovering the Track of the Vikings in America*. New York: W. W. Norton & Co., 1952, pp. 200–204.

—— *The Viking Explorers*. New York: Thomas Y. Crowell Co., 1966. "Runes and Artifacts in Minnesota," pp. 207–217.

Reardon, James M. *The Catholic Church in the Diocese of St. Paul, from Earliest Origin to Centennial Achievement: A Factual Narrative*. St. Paul: North Central Publishing Co., 1952. "The First White Men in Minnesota," pp. 3–11.

Robbins, Roland W. and Evan Jones. *Hidden America*. New York: Alfred A. Knopf, 1959, pp. 152–[155].

Roddis, Louis H. *The Norsemen in the New World*. Minneapolis: Augsburg Publishing House, 1923. "The Kensington Rune Stone," pp. [7]–20.

Salverson, Laura G. *Immortal Rock: The Saga of the Kensington Stone*. Toronto: Ryerson Press, 1954. A novel.

Sandbeck, Oscar P. *The Kensington Rune Stone*. [Moville, Ia.: The Author, ca. 1935]. Broadside supplementary to Sandbeck, *There Was A Flood* [Taopi, Minn.: Compass Publishers, 1935].

[Skog, Carl E.] *The Kensington Runestone: Illustrated*. Evansville, Minn.: Enterprise Printery, 1928. Published in the interests of the Kensington Runestone Foundation.

Strandwold, Olaf. *Norse Inscriptions on American Stones, Collected and Deciphered*. Weehauken [sic], N. J.: Magnus Björndal, 1948.

Stefansson, Vilhjálmur, ed. *Great Adventures and Explorations from the Earliest Times to the Present, as Told by the Explorers Themselves*. New York: Dial Press, 1947. "Northern Europe Discovers America," pp. 119–156.

Sulte, Benjamin. *Mélanges Historiques:Études éparses et inédites . . . compilées, annotées et publiées par Gérard Malchelosse*. Montreal: G. Ducharme, 1921. "Au Mississipi en 1362," vol. 7, pp. 7–12.

Thornton, Willis. *Fable, Fact and History*. New York: Greenberg, 1957. "The Kensington Stone," pp. 71–82.

Wahlgren, Erik. *The Kensington Stone: A Mystery Solved*. Madison: University of Wisconsin Press, 1958.

—— "The Runes of Kensington," in *Studies in Honor of Albert*

Morey Sturtevant. Lawrence: University of Kansas Press, 1952, pp. 57–70.

THE KENSINGTON RUNE STONE—*Periodical Articles*

Almagià, Roberto. "Cristoforo Colombo e i Viaggi Precolumbiani in America," in Accademia Nazionale dei Lincei (Rome), *Rendiconti delle Adunanze Solenni,* 5: [263]–279 (1951).

Andersen, Harry. "En omstridt runesten fra Amerika," in *Salmonsen Leksikon-Tidsskrift* (Copenhagen), 9: 315–319 (November, 1949).

Anderson, Rasmus B. "Another View of the Kensington Rune Stone," in *Wisconsin Magazine of History,* 3: 413–419 (June, 1920).

Andersson, Ingvar. "Kring Kensingtonstenen," in *Nordisk Tidskrift för Vetenskap* (Stockholm), new series 26: [132]–133 (1950).

Armstrong, John M. "The Numerals on the Kensington Rune Stone," in *Minnesota History,* 18: 185–188 (June, 1937).

Berge, Rikard. "Førnesbrunen," in *Samband* (Minneapolis), June, 1912, pp. 299–302.

Betten, Francis S. "The Kensington Stone," in St. Louis University *Historical Bulletin,* 12: 66, 72–73 (May, 1934).

Blegen, Theodore C. "Frederick J. Turner and the Kensington Puzzle," in *Minnesota History,* 39: 133–140 (Winter, 1964).

——— "The Kensington Rune Stone Discussion and Early Settlement in Western Minnesota," in *Minnesota History,* 6: 370–374 (December, 1925).

Breckenridge, R. W. "Norse Halberds," in *American Anthropologist,* 57: 129–131 (March, 1955).

Breda, Olaus J. "Rundt Kensington-stenen," in *Symra* (Decorah, Ia.), 6: [65]–80 (1910).

Brøndsted, Johannes. "Problemet om nordboer i Nordamerika før Columbus. . . . Med bidrag af Karl Martin Nielsen og Erik Moltke," in *Aarbøger før Nordisk Oldkyndighed og Historie* (Copenhagen), 1950: [1]–152, especially 64–90, [123]–152. Translated (in shortened form) as "Norsemen in North America Before Columbus," in Smithsonian Institution, *Annual Report, 1953,* 367–405 (1954).

Burt, Jesse C. "The Riddle of the Stone," in *American Mercury,* 83: 32–36 (November, 1956).

Christensen, Thomas P. "Study of the Kensington Stone," in *Annals of Iowa,* 32: 297–301 (April, 1954).

Davis, Emily. "New Chapters in American History: Studies Indicate that the Kensington Stone of Minnesota Is a Record Left by Goths and Norsemen in 1362," in *Science News Letter,* November 12, 1932, pp. 306–307.

"A Farmer's Fun," in *Time,* February 8, 1954, p. 69. In MHS "Scrapbook," 1: 73.

"Førnesbronen," in *Telesoga* (Fergus Falls, Minn.), 1: 62–63 (March, 1909).

Fogelblad, Sven. "Hvad är sanning." "Krig i Minnesota 1881." "Några ord om våra allmänna skolor" (in two parts). "Också ett ord i fråga om minnesfester." These four articles have been found only as clippings in the Fogelblad-Ohman Scrapbook (microfilm MHS). They may have been published in *Upplysningens Tidehvarf* (Hutchinson, Glencoe, Grove City, Minn.) published from 1877 at least until 1881, first as a weekly and then as a monthly.

—— "Presterna och religions-undervisningen," in *Upplysningens Tidehvarf* (Glencoe, Minn.), 1: [4]–[5] (December, 1877).

Gathorne-Hardy, G. M. "Alleged Norse Remains in America," in *Antiquity* (Gloucester, Eng.), 6: 420–433 (December, 1932).

—— "A Comment on the Kensington Rune Stone," in *American-Scandinavian Review*, 20: 382–383 (June–July, 1932).

Gjessing, Helge. "Runestenen fra Kensington," in *Symra* (Decorah, Ia.), 5: 113–126 (1909).

Godfrey, William S. "Vikings in America: Theories and Evidence," in *American Anthropologist*, 57: 35–43 (February, 1955).

Hagen, Ole E. "Førnesbronen: En mærkelig vise fra den sorte døds tid," in *Samband* (Minneapolis), October, 1911, pp. 363–369.

Hagen, Sivert N. "The Kensington Runic Inscription," in *Speculum: A Journal of Mediæval Studies*, 25: 321–356 (July, 1950).

Hartig, Hugo. "Mystery of the Kensington Runestone," in *Science Digest*, 24: 37–40 (July, 1948).

Hauge, Lars J. "Did the Norsemen Visit the Dakota Country?" in *South Dakota Historical Collections*. Sioux Falls, S.D.: South Dakota Historical Society, 1908, vol. 4, pp. 141–147.

Hennig, Richard. "Rassische Überreste mittelalterlicher Normannen bei eingeborenen Nordamerikas," in *Zeitschrift für Rassenkunde und die gesamte Forschung am Menschen* (Stuttgart), 6: 20–28 (July 9, 1937).

—— "Der Runenstein von Kensington: Eine rätselhafte skandinavische Expedition ins innere Nordamerikas 130 Jahre vor Kolumbus," in *Die Woche* (Berlin), 37: 30, 32–33 (August 14, 1935).

—— "Der Runenstein von Kensington: Eine vorkolumbische Kenntnis Amerikas in 14. Jahrhundert?" in *Vergangenheit und Gegenwart* (Leipzig and Berlin), 27: 36–44 (Heft 1, 1937).

—— "Zur Frage der Echtheit des Runensteins von Kensington," in *Petermanns Geographische Mitteilungen* (Gotha, Ger.), 84: 88–90 (March, 1938).

—— "Zur Normannischen Erstentdeckung Amerikas," in *Saeculum* (Freiburg, Ger.), 1: 306–317 (1950).

Henry, Thomas R. "The Riddle of the Kensington Stone," in *Saturday*

Evening Post, August 21, 1948, pp. 25, 109–110. Reprinted in John Gehlmann, ed., *The Challenge of Ideas.*

Hoegh, Knut O. "Kensington og Elbow Lake stenene," in *Symra,* 5:178–189 (1909).

Holand, Hjalmar R. "Are There English Words on the Kensington Runestone?" in *Records of the Past* (Washington, D.C.), 9:240–245 (September–October, 1910).

——— "The Climax Fire Steel," in *Minnesota History,* 18:188–190 (June, 1937).

——— "Concerning the Kensington Rune Stone," in *Minnesota History,* 17:166–188 (June, 1936).

——— "Da runestenen reiste utenlands," in *Jul i Vesterheimen* [for 1927] (Minneapolis), pp. [19]–[22] (1927).

——— "An English Scientist in America 130 Years before Columbus," in Wisconsin Academy of Sciences, Arts, and Letters, *Transactions* (Madison), 48:205–219 (1959).

——— "An Explorer's Stone Record Which Antedates Columbus: A Tragic Inscription Unearthed in Minnesota, Recording the Fate of a Band of Scandinavian Adventurers," *Harper's Weekly,* 53:15 (October 9, 1909).

——— "First Authoritative Investigation of 'Oldest Native Document in America,'" in *Journal of American History* (New Haven, Conn.), 4:165–184 (Second Quarter, 1910).

——— "Five Objections Against the Kensington Rune Stone," in *Scandinavian Studies and Notes,* 8:122–134 (November, 1923).

——— "A Fourteenth-Century Columbus," in *Harper's Weekly,* 54:25 (March 26, 1910).

——— "A Fourteenth Century Exploration in the Canadian Arctic," in *Minnesota Archaeologist* (Minneapolis), 21:1–11 (January, 1957).

——— "Further Discoveries Concerning the Kensington Rune Stone," in *Wisconsin Magazine of History,* 3:332–338 (March, 1920).

——— "The 'Goths' in the Kensington Inscription," in *Scandinavian Studies and Notes,* 6:159–175 (May, 1921).

——— "Hvad mener de lærde om Kensingtonstenen," in *Danske Studier* (Copenhagen), 46:[49]–58 (1951).

——— "Kensington-steinens mangfoldighet," in *Nordisk Tidskrift för Vetenskap* (Stockholm), new series 26:[121]–129 (1950).

——— "Kensington-stenens sprog og runer: Svar til hr. Helge Gjessing," in *Symra,* 5:209–213 (1909).

——— "The Kensington Rune Stone: A Reply to Criticism," in *Minnesota History,* 7:65–66 (March, 1926).

——— "The Kensington Rune Stone Abroad," in *Records of the Past* (Washington, D.C.), 10:260–271 (September–October, 1911).

——— "The Kensington Rune Stone: Is It the Oldest Native Document of American History?" in *Wisconsin Magazine of History*, 3:153–183 (December, 1919).

———— "The 'Myth' of the Kensington Stone," in *New England Quarterly*, 8:42–62 (March, 1935).

———— "The Newport Tower: Norse or English? The Measurements Give the Answer," in *American-Scandinavian Review*, 37:230–236 (September, 1949).

———— "Nicholas of Lynn: A Pre-Columbian Traveler in North America," in *American-Scandinavian Review*, 46:[19]–32 (March, 1958).

———— "Norske oldfund i Minnesota," in *Skandinavens Almanak og Kalender for 1927* (Chicago), pp. 52–59 [1926?].

———— "The Origin of the Kensington Inscription," in *Scandinavian Studies*, 23:23–30 (February, 1951).

———— "A Review of the Kensington Stone Research," in *Wisconsin Magazine of History*, 36:235–239, 273–276 (Summer, 1953).

———— "Skandinaviske minnesmerker i Amerika fra det fjortende aarhundre [*sic*]," in *Aarbøger før Nordisk Oldkyndighed og Historie* (Copenhagen), 1951:[227]–250; English summary, pp. 244–250.

———— "Stones that Speak: More Evidence on the Authenticity of the Kensington Inscription," in *Minnesota Archaeologist* (Minneapolis), 21:12–18 (January, 1957).

———— "The Truth about the Kensington Stone," in *Michigan History*, 31:417–430 (December, 1947).

———— "Was There a Swedish-Norwegian Expedition to America in the 1360's?" in *Swedish Pioneer Historical Quarterly*, 8:93–96 (July, 1957).

Huber, Raphael M. "Pre-Columbian Devotion to Mary in America: The Testimony of the Kensington Stone," in *American Ecclesiastical Review* (Washington, D.C.), 117:7–21 (July, 1947). Abbreviated as "Hail Mary: America, 1362 A.D.," in *Catholic Digest*, 11:67–72 (September, 1947).

Hvale, N. P. N. "Ogsaa lidt med hensyn til Kensington stenen," in *Kvartalskrift* (Eau Claire, Wis.), 15:25–28 (January, 1919).

Iverslie, P[eter] P. "Kensingtonstenen," in *Kvartalskrift*, 5:13–21 (July, 1909).

———— "Kensingtonstenen og Vinlands beliggenhed," in *Kvartalskrift*, 10:3–10 (January, 1914).

———— "Mere om Kensingtonstenen," in *Kvartalskrift*, 6:8–16 (January, 1910).

———— "Runestenen: Naegtet optagelse i *Mnpls. Tidende*," in *Kvartalskrift*, 7:6–11 (October, 1911).

———— "Stenen i Douglas County: Af en ikke aldeles ulaerd," in *Kvartalskrift*, 15:16–25 (January, 1919).

Jansson, Sven B. F. "'Runstenen' från Kensington i Minnesota," in *Nordisk Tidskrift för Vetenskap* (Stockholm) new series 25: [377]–405 (1949).

Janzén, Assar G. "Pre-Columbian Explorations and Scholarly Demonstration," in *Swedish Pioneer Historical Quarterly*, 9: 3–20 (January, 1958).

—— Review of Hjalmar R. Holand, *Explorations in America Before Columbus*, in *Swedish Pioneer Historical Quarterly*, 8: 25–31 (January, 1957).

Johnson, Amandus. "Kensington Stone a Fake," in *American Swedish Monthly* (New York), 47: 15, 18 (July, 1953).

Krogmann, Willy. "Der 'Runenstein' von Kensington, Minnesota," in *Jahrbuch für Amerikastudien* (Heidelberg), 3: 59–111 (1958).

LaFarge, John. "The Medieval Church in Minnesota," in *America* (New York), July 9, 1932, pp. 322–323.

Larsen, Erling. "The Superior Country," in *Carleton Miscellany* (Northfield, Minn.), 4: 3–32 (Summer, 1963).

Larson, Laurence M. "The Kensington Rune Stone," in *Minnesota History*, 17: 20–37 (March, 1936).

—— "The Kensington Rune Stone," in *Wisconsin Magazine of History*, 4: 382–387 (June, 1921). This article is followed by replies from H. R. Holand and R. B. Larson, pp. 387–391.

Liestøl, Aslak. "Cryptograms in Runic Carvings: A Critical Analysis," in *Minnesota History*, 41: 34–42 (Spring, 1968). A review-article on Mongé and Landsverk, *Norse Medieval Cryptography in Runic Carvings* (1967).

—— "The Runes of Bergen: Voices from the Middle Ages," in *Minnesota History*, 40: 49–59 (Summer, 1966). An appendix, "The Bergen Runes and the Kensington Inscription," is on p. 59.

Ljone, Oddmund. "Kensingtonstenen–i rette sammenheng," in *Nordmanns Forbundet* (Oslo), 49: 171–172 (August, 1956).

Loken, Hjalmar J. "Great Medicine," in *Classmate: A Paper for Young People* (Cincinnati), vol. 45, nos. 23–29 (June 4–July 16, 1938). Fiction.

"Message to Posterity," in *News from Home* (New York), 9: [6]–8 (Thanksgiving, 1948). Reprinted in adapted form, with same title, in *Gopher Historian* (St. Paul), 5: 12–14 (September, 1950).

Minnesota Historical Society, Museum Committee. "Preliminary Report to the Minnesota Historical Society on the Kensington Rune Stone," in *Records of the Past* (Washington, D.C.), 10: 33–40 (January–February, 1911). A summary of the report.

Moltke, Erik. "The Ghost of the Kensington Stone," in *Scandinavian Studies*, 25: 1–14 (February, 1953).

—— "Ist der Runenstein von Kensington echt?" in *Atlantis* (Zurich), 23: 263–264 (June, 1951).

—— "The Kensington Stone," translated by John R. B. Gosney, in *Antiquity* (Gloucester, Eng.), 25:87–93 (June, 1951). Reprinted in Massachusetts Archaeological Society, *Bulletin* (Attleboro), 13:33–37 (July, 1952).

—— and Harry Andersen. "Hvad de lærde mener om Kensington-stenen—og Hjalmar Holand," in *Danske Studier* (Copenhagen), 46:[59]–63 (1951).

—— "Kensington-stenen, Amerikas runesten," in *Danske Studier* (Copenhagen), 45:[37]–60 (1949–1950). "1. En alfabethistorisk undersøgelse," by Moltke; "2. En sproglig undersøgelse," by Andersen.

"New Evidence in Viking Exploration of America Found as Committee Launches Plans to Observe 600th Anniversary of Kensington Stone," in *Sons of Norway* (Minneapolis), 57:209, 213 (November, 1960).

Nordling, C. O. "The Kensington Stone—Fiction or Historical Truth," in *Norseman* (London), 15:19–22 (January–February, 1957).

Ogsaa 'En Ulaerd' (*pseud.*). "Omkring Kensington-stenen," in *Kvartal-skrift*, 15:29 (January, 1919).

"Olof Ohman's Runes," in *Time*, October 8, 1951, pp. 56, 59–60.

"Den omstridte steinen," in *Nordmanns-Forbundet* (Oslo), 42:96–97 (May, 1949).

Pastor, Eilert. "Der Runenstein von Kensington," in *Wacht im Osten* (Munich), 4:321–338 (May–June, 1937).

Petersen, Carl S. "Wimmer og Kensingtonstenen," in *Nordisk Tidskrift för Vetenskap* (Stockholm), new series 26:[130]–131 (1950).

Quaife, Milo M. "A Footnote on Fire Steels," in *Minnesota History*, 18:36–41 (March, 1937).

—— "The Kensington Myth Once More," in *Michigan History*, 31:129–161 (June, 1947).

—— "The Myth of the Kensington Rune Stone: The Norse Discovery of Minnesota, 1362," in *New England Quarterly*, 7:613–645 (December, 1934).

"Runestenen fra 1362," in *Kvartalskrift*, 12:49–51 (April, 1916).

"Runic Monument or 'Mare's Nest?'" in *Ariel* (Minneapolis), 22:208 (January 14, 1899).

Sandbeck, Oscar P. "The Vinland Expedition of 1362," in *The Compass (Of Interest To Those Who Explore)* (Moville, Ia.), January, 1938, pp. [1]–3. In MHS "Scrapbook," 1:23.

Saxe, Ludv. "Nordmenn i Minnesota i 1362?," in *Nordmanns-Forbundet* (Oslo), 34:97–98 (May, 1941).

Schaefer, Francis J. "The Kensington Rune Stone," in *Acta et Dicta* (St. Paul), 2:206–210 (July, 1910).

—— "The Kensington Rune Stone," in *Catholic Historical Review*, 6:330–334, 387–391 (October, 1920).

Skørdalsvold, Johannes J. "Kensingtonstenen og 'de lærde': Skrevet for 'Reform,'" in *Kvartalskrift*, 9:74–82 (July, 1913).

Steefel, Lawrence D. "The Kensington Rune Stone," in *Minnesota Archaeologist* (Minneapolis), 27:97–115 (1965).

Stomberg, Andrew A. "Kensingtonstenen i Minnesota: Är runristningen äkta eller ett falsarium?" in *Allsvensk Samling* (Gothenburg), 19:[1], 3–4 (August 30, 1932).

Struik, Dirk J. "The Kensington Stone Mystery," in *Mathematics Teacher* (Washington, D.C.), 57:166–168 (March, 1964).

Stoylen, Sigvald. "The Kensington Rune Stone," in *American Book Collector*, 16:6–9 (November, 1965).

Thalbitzer, William C. "Powell Knutssons Rejse," in *Grønlandske Selskabs Aarsskrift* (Copenhagen), 1948:54–60 [1948?]. In MHS, "Scrapbook," 1:41.

—— "To fjaerne runestene fra Grønland og Amerika" in *Danske Studier* (Copenhagen), 43:[1]–40 (1946–1947). Translated with added material as *Two Runic Stones, from Greenland and Minnesota*, "Smithsonian Miscellaneous Collections," vol. 116, no. 3. Washington, D.C.: Smithsonian Institution, 1951.

Ulærd, En (*pseud.*). "Den Sten paa vort hjerte," in *Kvartalskrift*, 14:8–14 (January, April, July, October, 1918).

Upham, Warren. "The Kensington Rune Stone, Its Discovery, Its Inscriptions and Opinions Concerning Them," in *Records of the Past* (Washington, D.C.), 9:3–7 (January–February, 1910).

—— "The Rune Stone of Kensington, Minnesota," in *Magazine of History* (New York), 13:67–73 (February, 1911).

Vanden Elsen, M. J. "130 jaar vóór Columbus! Een Europese Gemeenschap in het Hart van Amerika," in *Katholieke Illustratie* (Haarlem, Neth.), 82:305–307 (August 19, 1948).

Vickstrom, F. "America's First Ave Maria," in *Liguorian* (Oconomowoc, Wis.), 28:457–461 (August, 1940).

Vignaud, Henry. "Les Expéditions des Scandinaves en Amérique devant la Critique: Un Nouveau Faux Document," in *Société des Américanistes de Paris, Journal*, new series 7:[85]–116 (1910).

Wahlgren, Erik. "The Case of the Kensington Rune Stone," in *American Heritage*, April, 1959, pp. 34–35, 101–105.

—— "Reflections around a Rune Stone," in *Swedish Pioneer Historical Quarterly*, 19:37–49 (January, 1968).

Walsh, James J. "The First Prayer in America," in *Columbia* (New Haven, Conn.), 13:10, 20 (August, 1933).

[Washburn, Mabel T. R.] "Were There Fourteenth Century Christian Europeans in the Land That Became the United States?," in *Journal of American History* (Greenfield, Ind.), 26:121–145 (third quarter, 1932).

Willson, Charles C. "A Lawyer's View of the Kensington Rune Stone," in *Minnesota History Bulletin*, 2:13–19 (February, 1917).

Yzermans, Vincent A. "Our Lady of the Runestone," in *Marian Era* (Chicago), 5:73–75, 106–107 (1964).

THE KENSINGTON RUNE STONE—*Contributions to Newspapers*

"Alters Reading of the Runes. Professor Curme Confident the Relic Stone is in Existence—His Latest Translation," in *Chicago Tribune*, February 24, 1899, p. 3.

Anderson, Andrew. "Ett beriktigande," a letter in *Svenska Amerikanska Posten* (Minneapolis), June 7, 1910, p. 13.

Anderson, Rasmus B. Editorial in *Amerika* (Madison, Wis.), February 18, 1910, p. 8. A letter from Warren Upham dated February 9, 1910, is printed and Anderson comments on it.

——— "The Kensington Runestone Fake," in *Wisconsin State Journal* (Madison), February 7, 1910, p. 8. A revised version (in MHS "Scrapbook," 1:3) was published in *Amerika*, February 11, 1910, p. [1].

——— "The Kensington Rune Stone Once More," in *Amerika*, May 27, 1910, p. 1. Reprinted in *Minneapolis Journal*, June 2, 1910, p. 7, and in H. R. Holand, *Kensington Stone*, 280.

——— "The Minnesota Historical Society," in *Amerika*, February 25, 1910, p. 1.

——— "Two Ohmans? The Kensington Rune Stone Once More," in *Amerika*, March 11, 1910, p. 1. Unsigned.

——— "Thinks Rune Stone Fake," in *Minneapolis Journal*, June 2, 1910, p. 7. Reprinted in part from *Amerika*, May 27, 1910.

"Anxious to Test Runes. Arrival of Supposed Ancient Tablet at Evanston Delayed," in *Chicago Tribune* February 21, 1899, p. 7.

Breda, Olaus J. "Den amerikanske 'runesten,'" in *Verdens Gang* (Christiania), April 24, 1899.

——— "Runestone Hoax. How a Clever Swede, With a Chisel and a Knowledge of Runic Characters, Started a Story That Has Traveled Around the World," in *Minneapolis Tribune*, April 16, 1899, Section 3, p. 4. Interview with O. J. Breda.

Brøgger, A[nton] W. "Ble Kensington-steinen laget av en norsk Minnesota-farmer?" in *Dagbladet* (Oslo), April 2, 1949.

Conradi, P. W. "Kensington-stenen. Lidt om runeskrift i almindelighed og indskriften paa stenen. Er den ægte?" in *Skandinaven* (semiweekly, Chicago), March 10, 1899, p. 2.

Crane, Ed. "Professor Calls Runestone Fake, Says Swedish Pastor 'Carved It'," in *Minneapolis Sunday Tribune*, December 26, 1948,

Upper Midwest Section, p. 10. In MHS "Scrapbook," 1:42. The professor referred to was J. A. Holvik.

"Curme May Go to Minnesota," in *Chicago Tribune*, February 23, 1899, p. 7.

Dieserud, Juul. "Holand og Kensingtonspøgen," in *Skandinaven* (daily, Chicago), May 4, 1910, p. 2. Reprinted in *Amerika*, May 13, 1910, p. 8.

——— "Kensingtonstenens saarbareste Achilleshæl. Lidt om letfattelig filologi," in *Minneapolis Tidende*, December 8, 1927, p. 9.

——— "'Sidste kapitel'. Den eminente svenske sprogmand Elof Hell-quists kuusende dom over Kensington-indskriften," a letter in *Minneapolis Tidende*, December 22, 1927, p. 7.

"Done in Runes. Stone With Puzzling Inscription Dug Up in Minn. Tale of Early Norsemen. Professor Breda Inclined to Think It a Fake," in *Minneapolis Journal*, February 22, 1899, p. [1].

"Doubts Runic Stone's Origin. Professor Breda of Minnesota Gives Reasons for Thinking it of Modern Manufacture," in *Chicago Tribune*, February 23, 1899, p. 9.

"Draft of Rune Story Found, Skeptic Says," in *St. Paul Pioneer Press*, November 18, 1949, p. 24.

Edgerton, Jay. "Sculptor Argues for the Rune Stone. John Daniels Says Carving Evidence Favors Authenticity of Controversial Kensington Stone," in *Minneapolis Star*, July 1, 1955, p. 10.

Evjen, John O. "Er vi færdige med Kensington-stenen?," in *Reform* (Eau Claire, Wis.), August 18, 25, September 1, 1927, all p. 2.

"Find a Norse Tablet. Minnesota Farmers Unearth Ancient Stone Near Kensington. Bears Runic Record. Tells Story of Exploration America in 1362. Treasure Presented to Northwestern University—Inscription Translated by Prof. Curme," in *Chicago Daily Inter-Ocean*, February 21, 1899, p. 5.

Fossum, Andrew. "Hudson Bay Route to Solve Problem," in *Norwegian-American* (Northfield, Minn.) October 22, 1909, p. 1, 5.

——— "Study of Language on the Kensington Runestone Leads to Satisfactory Results," in *Norwegian-American*, February 24, 1911, p. 1, 3, 6.

Gimmestad, Lars M. "Prof. dr. O. E. Hagen: Rids af den afdøde videnskapsmands liv og virke," in *Skandinaven* (daily, Chicago), March 23, 1927, p. 3.

Hagen, Ole E. "Ad Utrumque Parati Simus," in *Amerika*, April 1, 1910, p. 1. In English.

——— "Kensington-Stenen. Lidt og [sic] ordet 'From' og andre sider af spørsmaalet," in *Skandinaven* (daily, Chicago), December 24, 1910, p. 3. Reprinted in *Amerika*, January 6, 1911, p. 9.

——— "Prof. O. E. Hagens hjem brændt," in *Reform* (Eau Claire, Wis.), April 29, 1926, p. 3.

Haugen, Einar I. "Haugen Doubts Kensington Runestone Is Real McCoy," in *Capital Times* (Madison, Wis.), June 4, 1955, Green Section, p. 15.
"Historic Stone's Enshrining Due," in *St. Paul Pioneer Press*, April 20, 1958, Third Section, p. 7.
Holand, Hjalmar R. "En ny runesten," a letter in *Skandinaven* (daily), January 28, 1908, p. 1.
———— "Fogelblad er ikke manden," in *Skandinaven* (daily), August 4, 1910, p. 5.
———— "Fogelblad Theory as to Runestone Is Attacked," in *Minneapolis Journal*, August 9, 1910, p. 4.
———— "Kensingtonstenen—Dieserud som sprogmand," in *Minneapolis Tidende*, December 29, 1927, p. 6.
———— "Kensingtonstenen. Ett sidste ord om runestenen," in *Decorah Posten* (Ia.), December 8, 1911, p. 6.
———— "Kensingtonstenen. Lad de døde hvile i fred. Fogelblad var ikke manden," in *Minneapolis Tidende*, March 29, 1928, p. 10.
———— "Olaf [*sic*] Ohman og Kensingtonstenen," in *Decorah Posten* (Ia.), April 22, 1954, p. 4.
———— "Runestenen fra Kensington," in *Skandinaven* (daily), January 11, 1908, p. 6.
"Holand Answers Holvik Runestone Charges," in *Clay Sunday Press* (Moorhead, Minn.), February 19, 1949, p. 1, 3. In MHS "Scrapbook," 1:44. This Sunday paper bears the previous day's date.
Holvik, Johan A. "Holvik Finds New Evidence Debunking Runestone," in *Concordian* (Moorhead, Minn.), November 18, 1949, p. [1].
———— "J. A. Holvik Presents Basis For Belief That Rune Stone Is Modern," in *Concordian*, December 10, 1948, p. 4. In MHS "Scrapbook," 1:38.
———— "Veteran of the Runestone War Repeats His Doubts," in *Minneapolis Sunday Tribune*, March 2, 1952, Editorial Section, p. 3. In MHS "Scrapbook," 1:68.
Ickler, Glenn. "Kensington Runestone Set for 'Boating' Trip," in *St. Paul Dispatch*, January 8, 1965, p. 1.
Ingvoldstad, Orlando. "'It Is False!' Says Hægstad," in *Norwegian-American* (Northfield, Minn.), August 4, 1911, p. 1, 4.
Jenstad, Forrest B. "Wisconsin Author Claims There Were Scandinavians in Minnesota 130 Years Before Columbus Discovered America." Five articles in *Minneapolis Star Journal*, January 5, 12, 19, 26, February 2, 1941—all in Sunday Magazine Section, p. 2. This is the title of the first article; the series did not have a general title.
Langland, Harold S. "Expert Findings Reviewed. Mooring Stones Cited to Prove Runes Genuine," in *Minneapolis Star*, May 20, 1955, p. 1, 23.

"Last Word Not Heard in Runestone Controversy," in *St. Paul Pioneer Press*, May 8, 1966, First Section, p. 16.

"Letters from Rune Suspects. State Archaeologist, Prof. N. H. Winchell, Receives Letters from Men Accused of Knowing Rune-Stone Secret," in *Norwegian-American* (Northfield, Minn.), June 10, 1910, p. 1, 8. Includes letters by Winchell, Andrew Anderson, and Olof Ohman in answer to R. B. Anderson, "The Kensington Rune Stone Once More."

Liestøl, Aslak. "Det trekker opp til rune-krig over Atlantaren," in *Verdens Gang* (Oslo), November 1, 1967. This review of Mongé and Landsverk, *Norse Medieval Cryptography in Runic Carvings*, started an exchange of articles in *Verdens Gang* between Landsverk (November 21, 22, 1967, February 9, March 26, 1968) and Liestøl (December 1, 1967, March 26, 1968).

Linder, O[liver] A. "Om 'Kensington-Stenen,'" in *Svenska Amerikanaren* (Chicago), November 3, 1910, p. 4. Revised and published in Swedish Historical Society of America, *Year-book*, 3: 49–54 (1910).

"Ett märkligt fornfynd i Minnesota," in *Svenska Amerikanska Posten* (Minneapolis), February 28, 1899, p. 6.

"More Anent Runes. H. M. Wagner Meets Some of Prof. Breda's Criticisms." A letter in *Minneapolis Journal*, February 24, 1899, p 11. Also includes Curme's translation.

Moster Emma [*pseud.*]. "Om Pastor Fogelberg [*sic*]," in *Svenska Amerikanska Posten* (Minneapolis), March 28, 1928, p. 9.

Narveson, Robert. "Pioneer Blasts Norse Mooring-Stone Theory," in *Concordian* (Moorhead, Minn.), December 10, 1948, p. [1].

Nordwall, J. K. "Runstenen i Minnesota," a letter in *Svenska Amerikanska Posten* (Minneapolis), March 28, 1899, p. 14.

Nosander, F. "Runstenen i Minnesota," a letter in *Svenska Amerikanska Posten* (Minneapolis), March 14, 1899, p. 6.

Olson, Julius E. "Runestenen. Hvem lavede Kensingtonindskriften?" in *Minneapolis Tidende*, August 24, 1911, p. 7. Interview with J. E. Olson.

Olson, Olaus. "Runstenen i Minnesota," a letter in *Svenska Amerikanska Posten* (Minneapolis), May 23, 1899, p. 7.

"Reads Runic Tablet. Professor Curme Receives Stone Found in Minnesota. Letters Clean Cut. Presence of Cement Throws Doubt Upon Authenticity. Three Theories Regarding the Discovery—Decision Will Be Given Today," in *Chicago Daily Inter-Ocean*, March 1, 1899, p. 4.

Rice, George. "Kensington Rune Stone—Hoax or History?" Six articles in *Minneapolis Star*, April 11–16, 1955—all p. 1.

"Runesten fra Kensington, Minn., omsattes med stigende interesse," in *Skandinaven* (semiweekly, Chicago), March 1, 1899, p. 1. Includes communications from E. E. Aarberg of Kensington and O. L. Kirkeberg of Chicago.

"Runestone Replica," in *Minneapolis Tribune*, August 12, 1951, Picture Roto Magazine, p. 10.

"Runestone Is Magnet at Fair," in *Minneapolis Star*, May 31, 1965, p. 1.

"Runic Stone Fails to Arrive," in *Chicago Tribune*, February 26, 1899, p. 11.

"Runic Stone is at Evanston. Arrives in the Afternoon and Professor Curme Makes a New Translation—Doubts its Antiquity," in *Chicago Tribune*, March 1, 1899, p. [3].

R[ygh], O[luf]. "Den amerikanske runeindskrift," in *Morgenbladet* (Christiania), March 12, 1899.

"Sandhed eller jux? En runesten beretter om Nordmaends reiser i Minnesota i 1362," in *Skandinaven* (semiweekly, Chicago), February 22, 1899, p. 4.

"Say Runestone is Authentic. Experts Declare Famous Stone Found Near Kensington is not a Fake," in *St. Paul Pioneer Press*, December 14, 1909, p. 1.

Schröder, Johan. "Historien om en Präst," in *Svenska Amerikanska Posten* (Minneapolis), January 25, 1928, p. 10.

———— 'Praesten Fågelblad. Erindringer om praesten som mistænktes for att ha lavet Kensington-runeindskriften,' in *Minneapolis Tidende*, March 8, 1928, p. 5.

"A Stone Bearing Runic Inscriptions," in *Alexandria Post News*, February 23, 1899, p. 1.

"Strange Tale on Tablet. Inscribed Stone May Shed New Light on America's History," in *Chicago Tribune*, February 20, 1899, p. [2].

"The Kensington Stone. With Facsimiles of the Inscriptions on Its Face and End, and a Diagram of the Place where It Was Found," in *Alexandria Post News*, March 2, 1899, p. 1. Illustration.

"The Runic Stone," in *Northwestern* (Evanston, Ill.), March 9, 1899, p. 12.

Thornton, R. S. and John Obert. "Claim of Hoax Attacked. Backers Defend Authenticity of Rune Stone," in *Minneapolis Star*, May 18, 1955, p. 1, 12.

———— "Was Ohman a Genius? Rune Forgery Held Impossible and Illogical," in *Minneapolis Star*, May 19, 1955, p. 1, 18.

Turner, Frederick J. "What Others Say. Prof. Turner on Runestones," in *Wisconsin State Journal* (Madison), February 10, 1910, p. 5. A letter refuting an inaccurate report of Turner's contribution to the discussion at H. R. Holand's lecture in Madison on February 8. Reprinted in *Minnesota History*, 39:140 (Winter, 1964).

Index

206

About the Author

THEODORE C. BLEGEN has rightfully been called "Mr. Minnesota History." Dean emeritus of the graduate school of the University of Minnesota and a former superintendent of the Minnesota Historical Society, he is now a research fellow of the society.

Born in 1891 in Minneapolis, he holds degrees from Augsburg College, Minneapolis, and the University of Minnesota. He has also been awarded several honorary degrees. Dr. Blegen taught history at Hamline University, St. Paul, from 1920 to 1927 and at the University of Minnesota beginning in 1927. He was dean of the university's graduate school from 1940 until his retirement in 1960. For many years he was the editor of *Minnesota History*, the quarterly magazine of the Minnesota Historical Society, and of the publications of the Norwegian-American Historical Association.

He is the author or editor of more than two dozen books, of which the best known are his two volumes on *Norwegian Migration to America* (1931, 1940) and *Minnesota: A History of the State* (1963). Other books which testify to his wide-ranging interests include: *Building Minnesota* (1938); *Grass Roots History* (1947); *The Land Lies Open* (1949); *The Crowded Box-Room: Sherlock Holmes as Poet* (1951); *Lincoln's Imagery* (1954); *Land of Their Choice* (1955); *Amerikabrev* (1958); *Abraham Lincoln and His Mailbag* (1964); *Lincoln's Secretary Goes West* (1965); and *The Voyageurs and Their Songs* (1966). He collaborated on four additional volumes entitled: *Norwegian Emigrant Songs and Ballads* (1936); *Iron Face* and *Frontier Mother* (1950); and *Sherlock Holmes, Master Detective* (1952). He and his wife Clara live in St. Paul.